DUBLIN

OFF-SEASON AND ON

Also by **Doris Lehman**

The Riviera Off-Season and On
London Off-Season and On with Robert Haru Fisher

DUBLIN
OFF-SEASON AND ON

A Guide to Special Pleasures,
Better Rates, and Shorter Lines

Doris Lehman

Illustrated by Amy Lehman

ST. MARTIN'S GRIFFIN ⚑ NEW YORK

www.stmartins.com

Maps by David Lindroth

Library of Congress Cataloging-in-Publication Data

Lehman, Doris.
    Dublin off-season and on : a guide to special pleasures, better rates, and shorter lines / Doris Lehman ; illustrated by Amy Lehman.—1st ed.
        p.   cm.
    Includes index.
    ISBN 0-312-28116-1
    1. Dublin (Ireland)—Guidebooks.   I. Title.

DA995.D8 L45 2001
914.18'3504824—dc21

                                                                              2001041615

First Edition: October 2001

10   9   8   7   6   5   4   3   2   1

*This book is dedicated to my granddaughters,
Carly and Lindsay Lehman. They already have
the love of travel, and I hope to take them to see
beautiful Ireland someday soon.*

Contents

Acknowledgments

I would like to thank the following people who helped to make this book a success.

To my editor, Julia Pastore, who worked diligently with me and whose enthusiasm and love for Ireland equals mine.

To my good friends Nuala Arnold and Tom Thunder from Ireland, who generously took me sightseeing, to the theater, lunch, dinner, the Kerrygold Horse Show at the RDS, the mountains, lakes, cities, golf clubs, and seasides. Tom also read the manuscript and made many valuable additions. I could not have done this book without them.

To Odile Murphy, who took me on my first walking tour of Dublin on my first trip and first morning there years ago. We walked for five hours in between the raindrops.

To John McGeehan, who took me sightseeing to the southside villages of Dublin, along the coast, and to the little villages for lunch.

To Robert Fisher, who helps me as an adviser and friend when writing these books. I don't know what I would do without him. He is a great travel writer and editor.

To Jennifer Elwood, who taught me everything I know about cutting and pasting, and everything else I needed to know about the computer.

To Greta Tedoff, who read the manuscript before anyone else and gave me her valuable advice.

To Amy Lehman, my daughter, travel companion, illustrator, and friend. To Amy's husband, Johnathan Anders, who accompanied Amy and me on a trip to Dublin. I got to see things through a younger person's eyes on that trip.

To Michael Lehman, my son, my lawyer, and a wonderful kid. To his wife, Heidi, who is always so enthusiastic, encouraging, and excited about my projects.

Special thanks to my husband, Mike, who loves my work as much as I do, loves to travel, drives me everyplace I need to go, stops when I need to look at something even if he doesn't find it interesting, and is just helpful all the time. Thanks everyone.

Ireland:
Republic of Ireland
and Northern Ireland

Introduction

Ireland's spectacular scenery and rich history have made it one of the most popular tourist destinations in Europe. It's comprised of the independent Republic of Ireland and Northern Ireland, which is part of the United Kingdom. The Emerald Isle is filled with ancient ruins, unspoiled villages, and some of the friendliest people you'll ever meet. Although Northern Ireland's troubles are far from over, the recent referendum is an encouraging sign of continued peace. Meanwhile, as a member of the European Community the Republic of Ireland has steadily built a strong tech-based economy and is enjoying a period of prosperity never before seen in its history.

As the Republic's capital and its most cosmopolitan city, Dublin is a wonderful introduction to the country. Filled with fine museums, hotels, restaurants, shops, theaters, and pubs, it is as beautiful and welcoming as you've always heard. The River Liffey bisects the city and many sights and attractions are described by their location either north or south of the river. Overall, Dublin is charmingly compact and easily navigable on foot.

I have sprinkled this book with Irish proverbs and blessings because they are so much a part of Ireland and its people, and also because they have a lot of wisdom and truth to them. Hopefully you will enjoy them as much as I do.

> *I am Ireland:*
> *I am older than the Old Woman of Beare.*
>
> *Great my glory:*
> *I that bore Cuchulainn the valiant.*
>
> ♣ PATRICK PEARSE, "I AM IRELAND" ♣

WHY OFF-SEASON?

Many travelers have discovered the joy of traveling during the off-season, and for good reason. Dublin especially has become a favorite off-season destination because of its mild year-round climate and easy accessibility. While the hordes flock to the island during the busiest tourist months of June through August, you will find that traveling during the rest of the year is just as enjoyable—more so since you will not have to fight the crowds for a table, hotel room, or tee time. Everything cultural is in full swing all year, so you'll be able to enjoy the theaters, golf courses, horse races, hiking trails, fishing, and anything else you have in mind no matter what the month.

Traveling off-season has many economic advantages. Rates for air and hotels are greatly reduced. Airlines usually offer off-season packages, though some agents don't always tell you about specials so you must ask.

Aer Lingus, Ireland's international airline, has some excellent off-season packages such as the Ireland for Two Package, round-trip air for two for $499 if purchased and used by a certain date. It fit perfectly into our travel plans and I was able to take advantage of it. The flight leaves JFK or Newark and arrives at Dublin, Shannon, Cork, or Belfast. It required a Saturday night stay. Dublin and Shannon are nonstop flights; Cork and Belfast require a stop, but not a change of plane. Other specials are Fly/Drive, Weekend Gems, and Irish Heritage. Packages change with the seasons and on occasion are changed or dropped, so call the airline for exact information. Aer Lingus: 800-IRISH-AIR or Web site: *www.aerlingus.ie*

Most hotels also offer excellent off-season rates. Just remember to always ask if tax, service, and breakfast are included in the rate you are quoted. Generally, they are. Ireland is wonderful because there are so many lodging options. From deluxe suites to youth hostels, to beautiful bed and breakfasts and castle hotels and everything in-between, you are sure to find something that fits your personality and your wallet.

Web Sites For Travel Information

Web sites are a great way to start planning a trip. Try these for tour information, hotel descriptions, and other useful advice:

www.paddy.net
www.dublins-fair-city.com

www.visit.ie/Dublin
www.iol.ie
www.irelandvacations.com

FUN IRISH WEB SITES

These are sure to pique your interest in everything Irish.

WWW.SHOPSHAMROCK.COM has just about anything you might be interested in that has to do with Ireland. It is a terrific source of information on genealogy, marriage records, gifts, posters, books, music, pottery, and much more. It also has a currency converter and links to other Irish Web sites.

WWW.IRELANDSEYE.COM is a fact- and fun-filled Web site with practical information such as B&B listings, weather, plus lots of fun links including instructions for knitting an Aran sweater and recipes for Limerick ham, Porter cake, boxty, Irish stew, and beef in Guinness. Also included are greeting cards that can be printed or e-mailed.

WWW.IRISHSHOP.COM is a great site in which to purchase all Irish products, from clothing to jewelry to art.

WWW.OSTLAN.NET has more than 250 restaurants and pubs in the Dublin area.

WWW.IRISHBOOK.COM Irish Books and Media, Inc. 1433 East Franklin Avenue, Minneapolis, MN, 55404-2135; phone: 612-871-3505 or toll free 800-229-3505; fax: 612-871-3358; e-mail: *irishbook@aol.com*. This is a wonderful bookshop with everything Irish from *Dublin Off-Season and On* to all other travel books, maps, CDs, videos, calendars, novels, and nonfiction. They will mail anywhere in the world and are very helpful on the phone.

WWW.ENTERTAINMENTIRELAND.IE is filled with information on everything connected to the entertainment field in Ireland including the music scene and theater, TV, and movie listings.

WWW.IRISH-RACING.COM is *the* Web site for horse and racing lovers. It has information on jockeys, betting, entries, reviews and statistics.

WWW.TOTALIRELAND.COM is called "Total Ireland" for a good reason: it includes information on business, finance, tourism, politics, accommodations, and lots of other links for more information.

WWW.SHAMROCK.ORG is a great source for brochures and information on traveling to Ireland. Call 800-SHAMROCK or visit their Web site for a free vacation trip and travel planner.

DUBLIN

OFF-SEASON AND ON

1. Practical Information

ENTRY REQUIREMENTS

Americans and Canadians need a **valid passport** to enter Ireland. British citizens coming from the UK do not need passports, but should carry them. Immigration officials are very strict since people now try to get into Ireland via Britain without passports. Also, it is always a good idea to have a passport for general identification, especially when renting a car or cashing traveler's checks. Citizens of other countries should check with their embassy for entry requirements. If you are not a citizen of the U.S. or European Union a visa may be necessary. If your passport is lost or stolen report it to your embassy and the local police.

The maximum stay in Ireland is six months unless you are a EU resident. Check with the tourist board if you plan an extended stay. Vaccinations are not required when coming from the U.S., Canada, or the EU.

PETS

All animals entering Ireland are quarantined for six months unless arriving from the UK, which has the same strict requirements as Ireland. Always check with the tourist board for policy changes, but unless you are planning a lengthy stay Fido and Fluffy should be left home.

TOURIST OFFICES

The Irish Tourist Board (ITB), also known as Bord Failte, maintains the following offices in North America:

NEW YORK 345 Park Avenue, New York, NY, 10154; phone: 212-418-0800, toll-free 800-223-6470; fax: 212-371-9052; Web site: *www.ireland.travel.ie*

BROCHURES AND INFORMATION 1-800-SHAMROCK, web site: *www.shamrock.org*

CANADA 160 Bloor Street East, Suite 1150, Toronto, Ont. M4W 1B9, Canada; phone: 416-929-2777; fax: 416-929-6783

THE UK 1 Regent Street, London, SWIY 4NS, UK, phone: 0207-518-0800

The Irish Tourist Office maintains the following offices in Dublin:

DUBLIN TOURISM Suffolk Street, Dublin 2; phone: 1-605-7799; fax: 1-605-7787 (see Telephone information on pages 10–11), twenty-four hour visitor information number: 1-550-112-233; Web site: *www.visit.ie/Dublin* for information and accommodation booking; e-mail: *reservations@dublintourism.ie.* Open July through September, Monday to Saturday 8:30 A.M.–6 P.M., Sunday 11 A.M.–5:30 P.M., October through June daily 9 A.M.–6 P.M. Closed December 25, 26, January 1.

Located in the converted Protestant St. Andrew's Church, which was built in 1866. In 1994 it opened as the major tourist center in Dublin. This office has brochures, leaflets, maps, and helpful people to assist not just on Dublin sights, but all of Ireland. You can get information on bus and rail tours. The tourist office also sells small Irish souvenirs such as crystal, Irish linen, postcards, and other gift items. There is a currency exchange desk, car rental desk, bookshop, and if you are hungry try the Belfry Café on the second floor. Dublin Tourism publishes a free newspaper guide filled with information on what to do and see, where to go, where to eat, and much more.

BORD FAILTE Irish Tourist Board, Baggot Street Bridge; phone: 01-602-4000; fax: 01-602-4100. Open weekdays 9:15 A.M.–5:15 P.M. (after hours there is a tape with information on various travel topics). Web site: *www.ireland.travel.ie*

Dublin Airport

Open daily from 8 A.M.–10 P.M. Closed December 25, 26, January 1.

Dun Laoghaire Ferry Terminal

Open daily from 8 A.M.–1 P.M. Closed December 25, 26, January 1.

DUBLIN AIRPORT

Open daily 8 A.M.–10 P.M.
Airport Information: 1-814-1111
Airport Police & Lost Property: 1-814-4481
Car Parks: 1-704-4328
Duty Free Inquiries: 1-800-747-747
Bus, Coach, and Rail Information: 9 A.M.–5 P.M., 1-677-1871

Flight Information:

AER LINGUS	1-886-6705
BA EXPRESS	1-814-4948
BRITISH MIDLAND	1-814-4259
CITYJET	1-844-5566
CONTINENTAL	1-407-3014
RYANAIR	1-550-920-200
SERVISAIR	1-814-4946

EMBASSIES

American

42 Elgin Road, Ballsbridge, Dublin 4; phone: 1-668-7122; fax: 1-668-9946

Consulate of Ireland, New York

345 Park Avenue, New York, NY, 10154; phone: 212-319-2555; fax: 212-980-9475

British

299 Merrion Road, Dublin 4; phone: 1-205-3700; fax: 1-205-3870

Canadian

65 St. Stephen's Green, Dublin 2; phone: 1-478-1988; fax: 1-478-1285

CLIMATE

The first rule on visiting Ireland: bring an umbrella. Ireland can be dry and sunny, but most likely you'll experience at least one "wet blessing" during your visit. Although Dublin is the dryest area of Ireland, with approximately thirty inches of rain per year, it pays to be prepared. The temperature is mild, ranging from a low of 34°F in January to a high of 77°F during the summer.

WHAT TO PACK

Ireland is a casual country and people do not overdress, even in hotels and restaurants. However, casual dress does not mean jeans or sneakers in certain places, and men do need jackets and ties in some restaurants. Just remember because of the unpredictable weather to bring a sweater, even in the summer, and always an umbrella.

CONVERSION TABLES

Average temperature in Dublin (To change Fahrenheit [F] to Celsius or Centigrade [C]: $F - 32 \times .555$. To change Celsius to Fahrenheit: $C \times 1.8 + 32$):

JANUARY	34–47°F	1–8°C
FEBRUARY	36–47°F	2–8°C
MARCH	38–50°F	3–10°C
APRIL	40–56°F	4–13°C
MAY	43–59°F	6–15°C
JUNE	49–65°F	9–18°C
JULY	52–68°F	11–20°C
AUGUST	52–67°F	11–20°C
SEPTEMBER	49–63°F	9–17°C
OCTOBER	43–58°F	6–14°C
NOVEMBER	40–50°F	4–10°C
DECEMBER	38–47°F	3–8°C

CUSTOMS

Customs Regulations and VAT: There is talk of abolishing the duty-free allowances. Right now the VAT, or value added tax, is still refundable for people living outside the Republic of Ireland.

If you want to know exactly what you can bring back home and the amount of money you can spend tax-free, the U.S. Customs Office publishes a brochure, "Know Before You Go." Write to U.S. Customs Service, P.O. Box 7407, Washington, DC 20044, phone: 202-927-6724.

VAT, If you are a visitor to Ireland who resides outside the European Union, you are entitled to a VAT (sales tax) refund paid on any purchases you bring home with you valued over a certain amount. Ask when you make any purchase if you are entitled to a refund. It's a good idea to shop where you see the Global Refund Tax Free shopping sign. The shopkeeper will give you all of the forms filled out and with a stamped envelope for your refund. When you get to the airport or point of departure from the EU get all forms stamped by customs and mail the envelope then and there. **Do not mail the envelopes from home; you will lose the refund.** They *must* be mailed in Europe. See the customs officer prior to checking in and sending your luggage through and it's important to have your purchases available for the customs officer to see, if requested. Keep them in a separate bag that is easily accessible—they do not take kindly to the excuse that those items are packed. If you plan to shop in Ireland you might want to send for the Global Refund brochure, which explains everything about getting the VAT returned to you.

GLOBAL REFUND, Spiddal Industrial Estate, Spiddal, Co. Galway, Ireland; phone from the U.S.: 011-353-91-553258; fax: 011-353-91-553403; e-mail: *cbgal@iol.ie*; 1Web site *www.globalrefund.ie*

DUBLIN AIRPORT OFFICE FOR VAT, phone: 1-844-5351

SHANNON AIRPORT OFFICE FOR VAT, phone: 61-472-454

In Ireland the inevitable never happens and the Unexpected constantly occurs.

♣ —SIR JOHN PENTLAND MAHAFFY ♣

CURRENCY

The Irish pound or punt (pronounced *poont*) is made up of 100 pence or pennies. Coins are 1p, 2p, 5p, 10p, 20p, 50p, and IR 1 (until 1/1/2002). Bills are IR 5, 10, 20, 50, and 100. Check with your bank for the exchange rate just before leaving home. Punts can be purchased at airports, banks, ATMs that accept Visa, MasterCard, PLUS, and CIRRUS debit cards. Irish banks are open Monday to Friday from 10 A.M.–4 P.M., and Thursdays from 10 A.M.–5 P.M., and usually give the best exchange rate. It is best to travel with credit cards or traveler's checks, not cash.

In Northern Ireland the British pound (sterling), Scottish notes, and Northern Ireland banknotes are the accepted units of currency, but currency from the Republic of Ireland isn't, so be sure to convert from one to the other when crossing the border. Northern Ireland banknotes are in the same denominations as English and Scottish notes and are identical in value. Although English and Scottish notes are accepted in Northern Ireland, Northern Ireland's notes are not accepted across the water. There is no limit to the amount of currency you can bring into the Republic of Ireland or Northern Ireland from the U.S.

ATM Locator, Web site: *www.visa.com.* Click on ATM Locator—this will take you to Europe, Ireland, Dublin, or whatever city you want to check.

Main Offices of Irish Banks in Dublin

Allied Irish Bank, Bank Center, Ballsbridge, Dublin 4, phone: 1-660-0311

Bank of Ireland, Lower Baggot Street, Dublin 2, phone: 1-661-5933

National Irish Bank, 7–8 Wilton Terrace, Dublin 2, phone: 1-678-5066

Ulster Bank, 33 College Green, Dublin 2, phone: 1-677-7623

Foreign Currency Delivered Overnight

Chase Manhattan Bank has an excellent new service for ordering currency so when you arrive in Ireland you'll be ready to start your trip without the hassle of hunting for a bank or ATM machine. They can be reached by phone at 1-888-CHASE84 or their Web site: *www. currency-to-go.com.*

The bank offers free home delivery for orders over $500, a small fee for smaller orders. The bank accepts Visa and MasterCard and their rates are competitive. For next-day delivery, telephone orders must be received by 5 P.M. EST and Internet orders must be received by 3 P.M. EST.

THOMAS COOK has a delivery service for ordering foreign currency online. Web site: *www.us.thomascook.com.*

There is a service fee of $5 when ordering up to $500, and one percent when ordering more than $500 worth. There is also a $10 minimum delivery charge for online orders.

EXCHANGE RATES, For the latest daily exchange rates visit *www. oanda.com*

May you live to be a hundred years
With one extra year to repent.
♣ —IRISH BLESSING ♣

EURO On January 1, 1999, the Euro became the official single currency in eleven European countries including the Republic of Ireland, but not the UK and Northern Ireland. Price tags will probably show both the local currency and Euro currency, but you will still only pay in local currency until the year 2002. Some credit card bills may show the price in Euros, but will be converted into U.S. dollars. American Express started issuing Euro-denominated travelers checks January 1, 1999. The Euro currency will have bills in 5, 10, 20, 50, 100, 200 and 500 Euros, and coins in 1, 2, 3, 10, 20, and 50 cents. Each Euro will be worth 100 cents. The Euro will be very helpful for travelers visiting more than one country; you will not have to change money at each border or pay a commission each time you change money. It will all be the same, at least in the eleven participating countries. Others may eventually join too. If you have a few Irish punts or coins left after your trip, save them. They will be a nice souvenir and who knows, perhaps in a few years they will be worth something. The countries currently participating in the Euro are Austria, Belgium, Finland, France, Germany, Ireland, Italy, Luxembourg, the Netherlands, Portugal, and Spain.

CREDIT CARDS Major credit cards are accepted in most hotels, restaurants, and shops. American Express, Visa, Barclaycard, Carte Bleue, Eurocard, MasterCard/Access, and Diners Club are the most often used cards in Ireland. It is always a good idea to pay for purchases with a credit card so if there is a problem you can deny payment or be reimbursed. Hold on to all receipts for customs and for the VAT refund on your credit card, and also be prepared to show your purchases to customs' agents.

Some banks charge a 2 percent fee for foreign exchange transactions, so it is advisable to check with the card company you plan to use.

WESTERN UNION, phone: in the U.S., 800-325-6000; in Canada, 800-235-0000. Web site: *www.westernunion.com.*

If you need money sent to Ireland from home it is only a phone call away. Western Union is open seven days a week, twenty-four hours a day. If you use a credit card the person in Ireland will receive the money as soon as Western Union receives an approval code from your credit card company.

> *Your feet will bring you to where your heart is.*
> ♣ —IRISH PROVERB ♣

LANGUAGE

English is spoken throughout Ireland, though Irish (called Gaeilge by its speakers) is the first official language of Ireland. Areas where Irish is the predominant language is called an An Ghaeltacht area. Irish is one of the oldest living languages in Europe. Conradh na Gaeilge, The Gaelic League, was founded in 1893 with the sole purpose of reviving the Irish language. There are classes held in all Irish towns, and many schools have started teaching the language again as a compulsory course. There is an Irish radio station, Irish newspapers, and Irish sections in English papers. Irish is spoken mainly on the west coast of Ireland.

A few phrases to please yourself and your Irish friends (if you can pronounce them!). Have fun.

Irish	Phonetic	English
Bord Failte	bord fall-cha	Irish Tourist Board
Dia duit	dee-a gwit	hello
Go raibh maith agat	guh rev mah a-gut	thank you
Slán	slawn	goodbye
Cad e mar ata tu?	Kajay mara ta too	how are you?
Ta go maith	taw gu mah	I'm fine
Oiche mhaith	ee hay vah	goodnight
Garda Siochana	gawda sheekawnah	police
Cad e an t-am?	Kajay un tam	what time is it?
Tabhairne	taw er nay	pub
Slainte	slawn tay	cheers
Te	cheh	hot
Fuar	fooar	cold
An maith leat tae?	Un mah lyat tay	do you like tea?
Fleadh	flah	traditional music event
Ta	taw	yes
Nil	neel	no
Más é do thoil é	mawshay duh hull eh	please
Fion dearg	feen jareg	red wine
Fion ban	feen bawn	white wine
Musaem	moosaym	museum
Galfchursa	galfkhoorsa	golf course
Rothar	ruhar	bicycle
Teimis amach ar shiuloid	tcheyimish amakh air hyooloij	Let's go for a walk
Baile Atha Cliath	blaa kleeu	Dublin
Craic	crack	fun, lively
Dail	doyle	Lower House of Irish Parliament

PUBLIC HOLIDAYS IN THE REPUBLIC

If you are in Dublin or anyplace in the Republic on a public holiday, check if your destination is open and what their hours are. Museums and art galleries are usually closed on Mondays.

January 1	New Years Day
March 17	St. Patrick's Day
(Changeable dates)	Good Friday, Easter Monday
May Day	First Monday in May
June (first Monday)	Bank holiday
August (first Monday)	Bank holiday
October (last Monday)	Bank holiday

| December 25 | Christmas Day |
| December 26 | St. Stephen's Day or Boxing Day |

KEEPING IN TOUCH

Time

Ireland is five hours ahead of Eastern Standard Time, and one hour behind Western Europe. Clocks go ahead one hour for standard time and back for daylight savings time.

TELLING TIME Ireland, like most of the rest of the world outside the U.S., uses the twenty-four-hour clock—in which 1 A.M. is 0100 and 1 P.M. is 1300. Here's a table for the P.M. hours; A.M. hours remains the same as in the U.S.

USA Clock	Twenty-Four-Hour Clock
noon	1200
1 pm	1300
2 pm	1400
3 pm	1500
4 pm	1600
5 pm	1700
6 pm	1800
7 pm	1900
8 pm	2000
9 pm	2100
10 pm	2200
11 pm	2300
midnight	2400

Telephone

Ireland is in the process of converting phone numbers from six to seven digits. At the time of printing not all numbers had been changed, so some phone numbers included in this book still have only six digits. Always check the local directory.

It is very expensive to make a call from a hotel. Usually they charge a service charge even if you are making a collect or credit card call. The most economical way to make a call is to use a phone booth. More and more they are accepting phone cards, although many are still coin operated. Phone cards can be purchased at newsstands, pubs, and the post office. You can direct dial from all areas of Ireland, for operator assistance dial 10. For telephone information for any place in Ireland from the U.S. dial 00. The operator will pick up in the U.S. and connect you to Irish information. The number for **directory assistance in Ireland is** 11811.

To call Ireland from the U.S., dial 011 + the country code 353, then the number with a "1" first + 7 digits for Dublin (011-353-1-234-5678). To call Dublin when in Ireland dial 1 + 7 digits (1-234-5678). Dialing Ireland to the U.S. dial 01 + area code + number (01-212-123-4567).

FOR DIRECT DIAL WITH AT&T, MCI, OR SPRINT for USA Direct from Ireland dial 1-800-550-000 + the number you are calling. The **AT&T** operator will answer and perhaps again request the number you are calling and your calling card number. The same is true for MCI and Sprint. **MCI:** 1-800-551-001 + the number you are calling; **SPRINT:** 1-800-552-001 + the number you are calling.

CELLULAR WORLD RENTAL PHONE, Unit T4, Birch Avenue, Stillorgan Industrial Park, Blackrock, County Dublin, Phone: 1-206-1000, Web site: *www.cellularworld.ie.*

You can rent a phone and Cellular World will deliver it to your hotel or business for a small fee. At this printing the weekly rental is 55.06 IEP Irish pounds and includes VAT + air time.

Mail

POST OFFICE The General Post Office (GPO) on O'Connell Street is open Monday to Saturday 8 A.M.–8 P.M., Sunday 10 A.M.–6:30 P.M. All other post offices are open Monday to Friday 9:30 A.M.–5:30 P.M. Irish postage stamps must be used from the Republic of Ireland and British stamps from Northern Ireland.

Philatelists can buy Irish stamps and get information from GPO, Controller, Philatelic Section, Dublin 1, Republic of Ireland.

POSTAL ADDRESS After the address there is a postal zone or district such as Dublin 1. The odd numbers are north of the River Liffey and the even numbers are south of the River Liffey.

Newspapers

The *Irish Times* (not published on Sunday) and the *Irish Independent* are considered the two best papers in Dublin. The *Evening Herald* is the main evening paper. On Sundays you can get the *Sunday Independent*, the *Sunday Tribune, Ireland on Sunday,* and the *Sunday Business Post.* British and American papers are available at most newsstands. There are also the usual tabloids such as the *Sun* and *Mirror.*

The *Irish Times* has an excellent Web site that includes anything and everything you might want to know about the daily news, weather, sports, movies, theaters, pubs, job hunting, and lots more: *www.irishtimes.com*

Television

In Ireland there are two national channels, RTE1 and Network 2. There is also an independent station, TV3. British channels are available plus satellite and cable TV. Hotels usually have CNN, Sky One, Sky News, BBC News, and other cable stations. There is also the Gaelic speaking station, TG4.

Radio Stations

Radio Telefis Eireann (RTE) is Ireland's national radio company. The main stations are RTE1, broadcasting news in English; RTE 2FM is a popular music station; and 3FM is a classical music station. Raid ío na Gaeltachta broadcasts in Irish. There are other independent stations for news and music. Just move the dial around to find talk radio, news, and a variety of music stations.

RTE Overseas

Radio Telefis Eireann, RTE, Dublin 4, phone: 1-208-2350; fax: 1-208-3031; Web site: *www.rte.ie*

Ireland's national broadcasting station provides services by satellite, shortwave radio, Internet, and telephone for anyone interested in Ireland and its culture.

Internet Access

If you travel with your own laptop you will not have difficulty using it and accessing e-mail. Many hotels now have data and extra phone ports for Internet and fax. If you did not bring your computer you can access e-mail at an Internet café.

Try the following Web site for the name, phone number, and address of the nearest Internet café to you, *www.cybercaptive.com.*

You can also go to the Cyberia Internet Café, Temple Lane South, Temple Bar, Dublin 2, phone: 1-679-7607. Open Monday to Sunday 10 A.M.–10 P.M. Rate: 6IP per hour. If you have a Student or Under-26 ID card you can access voice-mail free of charge.

He who can follow his own will is a king.

♣ —IRISH PROVERB ♣

SAFETY

Take all the usual precautions that you would anyplace in the world; the crime rate in Dublin and its suburbs is on the rise. Dublin is probably a safer city than many others in Europe, but there are pickpockets and purse-snatchers. Don't leave valuables in hotel rooms or cars.

Be alert to your surroundings, be careful at night, do not carry valuables, cash, or wear jewelry. It is not a good idea to walk on any dark side streets or in parks at night. Wear a fanny pack. When you park your car never leave valuables in view. The police in the Republic are known as the Garda Siochana, and can be reached in an emergency by dialing 999. It is a free call and the operator will connect you to the appropriate department. Be sure to make a copy of the front page of your passport and your credit cards and write down traveler check numbers. Leave all the information in your suitcase, do not carry it with you.

The U.S. State Department maintains a twenty-four-hour phone line that provides emergency services and information to U.S. citizens abroad. Phone: 202-647-5225.

DRUGS

As the saying goes, "Don't even think about it." Buying, selling, or using illegal drugs can lead to heavy fines and/or jail time.

TRAVEL INSURANCE

Before leaving home you should always check with your insurance company to see if you are covered for accidents and illness while abroad. Medical evacuation is usually not covered by insurance, but if it is something you are concerned about, check. For suggestions of which medical evacuation company to use, go to *www.travel.state.gov/ medical.html.*

There are many companies that offer overseas medical insurance. Rates vary according to the number of people traveling and the type of insurance you require. Your policy should always include third-party liability for lost luggage, cash, travel delays, or cancellation. Some suggestions are:

ACCESS AMERICA	800-284-8300	*www.worldaccess.com*
INTERNATIONAL SOS	800-523-8930	*www.intsos.com*
GLOBAL EMERGENCY MEDICAL SERVICES	800-860-1111	*www.globalems.com*
MEDEX ASSISTANCE CORP.	800-537-2029	*www.medexassist.com*
TRAVELER'S EMERGENCY NETWORK	800-471-3695	*www.tenweb.com*

Forsake not a friend of many years for the acquaintance of a day.

♣ —IRISH PROVERB ♣

LOST PROPERTY

The most important thing to do if you lose anything or are robbed is to report it to the police/Garda and keep all paperwork including reference numbers, dates, and names given to you by the police, airport, bus, train, or taxi personnel. You will need all of this information for insurance claims.

MEDICAL ASSISTANCE

I think it is always advisable to carry certain "old reliable" items that you might need such as pain relievers and antibiotics, and if you need a special brand of vitamins or calcium pills, bring them. Most important is a letter from your physician if you are carrying syringes for insulin or other medical needs. Always carry important medication on the plane with you: Never put it in your luggage, which might get lost.

Emergencies

PHONE 999 for fire, police, ambulance, lifeboat, and coastal rescue.
AA (Alcoholics Anonymous), 109 South Circular Road, Dublin 8; phone: 1-453-8998
AIDS Helpline, phone: 1-872-4277
Rape Crisis Center, 70 Lower Leeson Street, Dublin 2; phone: 01-661-4911 or 800-778-888

Poison Control, Beaumont Hospital, Beaumont Road, Dublin 9; phone: 1-837-9964

The Samaritans, 112 Marlborough Street, Dublin 1; phone: 1-872-7700. This is an important number for people who are feeling lonesome, depressed, or even suicidal.

Hospitals

Beaumont Hospital, Beaumont Road, Dublin 9; phone: 1-809-3000

Mater Hospital, Eccles Street, Dublin 7; phone: 1-803-2000

Adelaide and Meath Hospital, Tallaght, Dublin 24; phone: 1-414-2000

St. James's Hospital, 1 James Street, Dublin 8; phone: 1-453-7941

Note: Most large hospitals also have accident and emergency departments that are open twenty-four hours a day.

Doctors and Dentists

Eastern Health Board, Dr. Steevens Hospital; phone: 1-679-0700. If you need a doctor and are staying at a hotel ask the concierge for help. Otherwise call this service for local doctors' names.

For dental care, you can also go to the Dental Hospital at Lincoln Place, Dublin 2; phone: 1-612-7000. For emergency dental care you must arrive before 8:30 A.M. or at noon.

EYEGLASS OR CONTACT LENS REPLACEMENT Vision Express, ILAC Centre, off O'Connell Street, Phone: 1-873-2477. Open Monday to Saturday 9 A.M.–6 P.M., Thursdays to 8 P.M., Sundays 2–6 P.M.

LATE-NIGHT PHARMACIES (There are no twenty-four-hour pharmacies in Dublin or at the airport.)

O'Connell's Pharmacy, 55 Lower O'Connell Street, open until 10 P.M.; phone: 1-873-0427

Boots, The Square, Tallaght, open until 11 P.M.; phone: 1-451-4087

Dame Street Pharmacy, 16 Dame Street, open until 10 P.M.; phone: 1-670-4523

> **IAMAT**
> International Association of Medical Assistance to Travellers.
> 417 Center Street, Lewiston, NY 14092, phone: 716-754-4883;
> Web site: *www.sentex.net/~iamat*; E-mail: *iamat@sentex.net*. This is
> a nonprofit organization whose free directory provides a list of
> English-speaking doctors in the country you are visiting. The
> doctors have also been trained in Western countries. Although
> the directory is free, the organization hopes you will make a do-
> nation ($25 suggested), as they rely on that income to exist and
> to publish their splendid materials (including a chart showing
> where you can drink the water, eat the ice cream, and otherwise
> feel safe), which you will also receive if you make a donation.

ELECTRICITY

Electric current is 220V, 50 Hz. Plugs are flat with three square
pins. You must have a converter and an adapter for American appliances such as a hair dryer, travel iron, or electric shaver, otherwise you
risk blowing out the hotel's electricity. Some hotels have dual 220/110
outlets for electric shavers only.

SHOPPING

Most store are open Monday to Friday from 9:30 A.M. to 5:30 P.M.
and are usually open late on Thursday until about 8 P.M., Saturday until 6 P.M., Sunday usually from noon to 4 P.M. *See* Chapter 9: Shopping.

TIPPING

Hotels and restaurants usually include a service charge, but ask if
you are not sure. I usually add an extra tip of 10 percent to 15 percent
for good service, especially to hotel bellboys, waiters, taxis, hair-
dressers, and whomever you feel has done a good and helpful job for
you. It's unneccesary to tip the barman in a pub.

VIDEOS

Ireland uses the PAL 1 (VHF) video system, which is not compati-
ble with the U.S. system. If you buy a video in Ireland you may need to
have it converted for a fee when you get home.

A watched pot never boils.

♣ —IRISH PROVERB ♣

PLACES OF WORSHIP

Ireland is mainly a Roman Catholic country, but most religions do have a place of worship. Please see the list below and call the Tourist Board for more information.

The Saturday edition of the *Irish Times* lists information on religious services.

BUDDHIST 56 Inchicore Road, Dublin 8; phone: 1-453-7247

CATHOLIC CHURCH St. Mary's Pro-Cathedral, Marlborough Street, Dublin 1; phone: 1-874-5441; University Church, 87A St. Stephen's Green, Dublin 2; phone: 1-478-0616

CHURCH OF IRELAND Christ Church Cathedral, Christ Church Place, Dublin 8; phone: 1-677-8099, St. Patrick's Cathedral, Patrick's Street, Dublin 8; phone: 1-475-4817

JEWISH Dublin Hebrew Congregation, 37 Adelaide Road, Dublin 2; phone: 1-676-1734.

METHODIST Dublin Central Mission, 9C Abbey Street Lower, Dublin 1; phone: 1-874-2123

MUSLIM 163 Circular Road South, Dublin 8; phone: 1-453-3242

TRAVELERS WITH DISABILITIES

Dublin is trying hard to accommodate visitors with disabilities. Unfortunately there are still many older hotels that do not have ramps or rooms with wheelchair accessible bathrooms. Prior to planning your trip contact the **National Rehabilitation Board of Ireland,** The Square Shopping Center, Tallaght, Dublin 24; phone: 011-353-1-462-0444. They can supply a list of hotels with the appropriate facilities you may require. They publish two excellent brochures, *Guide for Disabled Per-*

Symbols of Ireland:

The Irish flag: The tricolor, vertically striped flag was first introduced in 1848. Green represents the Catholic majority, orange the Protestant minority, and the center white stripe their unity.

St. Patrick: The patron saint of Ireland, St. Patrick converted the Irish to Christianity in the 5th century. His death on March 17, 460 A.D. is celebrated as St. Patrick's Day.

The Harp: The oldest official symbol of Ireland, it is imprinted on most official documents and coins. In 1862, Guinness began using the harp as its trademark.

The Shamrock: The national plant of Ireland, it derives its name from the Gaelic word *Seamrog*, meaning plant with three leaves. Generally considered good luck, the shamrock is always worn on St. Patrick's Day. Legend has it that St. Patrick explained the holy trinity using this plant.

sons and *Accommodation Guide for Disabled Persons.* They will send them to you free of charge. When reserving a room ask if the facility has wheelchair access and rooms for people with disabilities. It is important to know everything ahead of time. Buses are out of the question; none have wheelchair access.

DISABILITY FEDERATION OF IRELAND, 2 Sandyford Office Park, Blackthorn Avenue, Dublin 18; phone: 1-295-9344. They will send a list of organizations in Ireland that provide services to people with disabilities.

THE IRISH WHEELCHAIR ASSOCIATION, 24 Blackheath Drive, Clontarf, Dublin 3; phone: 833-8241 or 833-5366. They will loan wheelchairs free for travelers in Ireland. A donation is appreciated, but not required. I suggest calling ahead to be sure one is available when you plan to travel.

RAIL TRAVEL Check the Web at: *www.irishrail.ie.* Iarnród Éireann will help passengers if you notify them in advance. Someone will meet you at the station, take you to the train and set up ramps if required. Call the Mobility Impaired Liaison at 1-703-2634, or contact the Department of Transport, 44 Kildare Street, Dublin 2; phone: 670-7444. All DART and train stations have the InterCity Guide for mobility impaired passengers.

CARS WITH HAND CONTROLS Cars with hand controls can be rented from Avis Rent-A-Car, 1 Hanover Street, Dublin 1; phone 1-605-7500; or Hertz, 149 Upper Leeson Street, Dublin 4; phone 1-660-2255.

BISEXUAL, GAY, AND LESBIAN TRAVELERS

It is illegal in Ireland to discriminate against gays and lesbians in work or at accommodations. Unfortunately, once you leave the major cities attitudes are not always the same, and it is also more difficult to find pubs or clubs that cater to gays and lesbians.

Published every two weeks, *In Dublin* and *Gay Community News* has listings for activities in the capital. Also, the free *Event Guide* available at many pubs and cafés is very useful. Check out Ireland's pink pages at *www.dmoz.org/regional/europe/ireland/society_and_culture/gay,_lesbian,_and_bisexual* for a directory full of regional information and helpful links.

GAY SWITCHBOARD Phone 1-872-1055

LESBIAN LINE Phone 1-872-7770

OLDER TRAVELERS

Senior citizens are entitled to many discounts, so be sure to ask when making hotel reservations, going to the theater, traveling on trains, or renting a car. If you have an AARP card or some identification proving your "senior status" it is a good idea to take it with you.

STUDENT TRAVELERS

Youth Hostels

YOUTH HOSTELS ASSOCIATION, An Oige, 61 Mountjoy Street, Dublin 1; phone: 1-830-1766, 1-830-4555; fax: 1-830-5808; Web site: *www.irelandyha.org*

There are more than fifty Youth Hostels run by the Irish Youth Hostel Association in the Republic of Ireland. You must be a member of the association and cards may be obtained in the U.S. or Canada before arriving in Ireland, or at check-in. The An Oige (Irish Youth Hostel Association) card may also be purchased at the An Oige office at the above address or by phone with a credit card. Once you have the card you are entitled to many travel and tour discounts and can get access to the booking network for youth hostels.

There are Web sites for obtaining **International Student ID** cards and Under 26 International Youth Travel Cards in the U.S. and Canada. The ID cards also include free worldwide voice-mail service where family and friends can leave messages. These messages can be accessed at Internet cafés in Dublin. Visit *www.hostels.com* and *www. statravel.co.uk.*

Both of the above Web sites are full of information on obtaining ID cards, low-fare travel, and youth hostels in Ireland. Also included is information on rail passes, insurance policies, and all relevant information on low-budget travel.

WOMEN TRAVELERS:
TOURIST VICTIMS SUPPORT LINE

Women traveling alone must be careful. Use a fanny pack or small bag worn across your chest. Do not carry or wear jewelry, and leave cash and valuables at home or in a hotel safe. Try to travel with a credit card or traveler's checks. If possible travel with a friend. Always have enough cash with you to take a taxi if you have to. Also, know the taxi's phone number so you can call one if necessary. Don't take public transportation alone at night. For more information call the Tourist Victims Support Line, for men and women, twenty-four-hour helpline: 1-478-5295. Open 7 days. Monday–Saturday 10:00 A.M.–6:00 P.M. Sunday noon–6:00 P.M.

> *May you have warm words on a cold evening,*
> *A full moon on a dark night,*
> *And the road downhill all the*
> *Way to your door.*
>
> ♣ —IRISH BLESSING ♣

BEFORE LEAVING HOME

♣ Remember to take your tickets, passport, credit cards, travelers checks, and driver's license (if you plan to drive in Ireland).

♣ Reconfirm your hotel reservation. I always recommend confirming at least the first night with a credit card. Dublin is a very popular destination and hotel reservations are not always easy to obtain.

♣ Bring a converter set if you plan to travel with a laptop computer or anything else that needs to be plugged in. Some hotels are equipped with jacks for e-mail and fax, but others are not. Ireland uses a three square pin plug and 220 volts. Many hotels do have 110-volt shaver outlets, but don't try to put a hair dryer in that outlet—it will burn out. It is strictly for shavers.

♣ Take a pocket calculator for money exchange. Until 2002 Ireland will still be using Irish punts.

ARRIVING IN DUBLIN

By Air

Dublin has one airport and one terminal so arrivals and departures are easy. Dublin Airport is also Ireland's busiest airport with flights to and from the UK, North America, and Europe. There is excellent tax-free shopping to enjoy upon departure from Dublin that sells everything you forgot to buy while in town. There is also a post office for those last-minute post cards, and a bureau de change. The airport is seven miles north of Dublin.

Dublin Bus 59 Upper O'Connell Street, Dublin 1; phone: 1-872-0000, runs twice hourly from the airport to the Bus Terminal in Dublin. There is an express bus service, also run by Dublin Bus, known as **Aircoach,** which operates from 6:30 A.M. until 11 P.M. from the airport to the city center. Phone: 1-844-4900. The trip takes thirty minutes and the fare is more reasonable than a taxi. You can also take a taxi from the airport to your hotel; the taxi queue is directly outside the arrival area. Car rental companies are located in the arrival area also.

AER RIANTA is the Irish airport authority, which manages the airport and information center. Phone: 1-814-1111.

From the U.S.

I always suggest a nonstop flight for the short five-and-a-half-hour overnight trip to Dublin from New York. Check in for international flights at least two hours early—airlines can deny you a boarding pass if you arrive late and can also give your seat away to a person on standby. Check with your airline as to how much luggage you can carry on board; they have become very strict about that recently. Be sure to carry jewelry and medication in your carry-on bag, not the checked luggage.

Airlines

AER LINGUS	800-Irish Air	from Boston, Chicago, JFK, Newark
CONTINENTAL	800-231-0856	from Newark
DELTA	800-241-4141	from Atlanta, JFK

CHARTER TO IRELAND FROM THE U.S. The very best charter company is **Sceptre Tours.** Their charters are flown between JFK, Boston,

Newark, Baltimore, Chicago, and Los Angeles to Dublin, Shannon, or Belfast from the end of April to mid-October, and are operated by Aer Lingus. Phone: 718-738-9400 or toll-free, 800-221-0924; Web site: *www.sceptretours.com*

Check as soon as you know you are traveling; they have good fares and flights. The good fares sell out quickly, and there is a wide range between the lowest and highest fare. There are restrictions as to days of the week that they fly. Sceptre can also arrange hotels, cars, tours, and golf packages. One of their excellent tours for 2000–2001 was round-trip air on Aer Lingus from JFK, Newark, or Boston to Dublin, Cork, Killarney, Belfast, or Galway; four nights at a first-class hotel; a manual car, and full Irish breakfast each day all for $499 + $55 airport tax per person.

If you missed this package check with Sceptre Charter, they always have good deals.

CHARTERS TO IRELAND FROM CANADA

SIGNATURE VACATIONS	800-268-7063
AIR TRANSAT HOLIDAYS	800-587-2672
REGENT HOLIDAYS	800-387-4860

AIRLINES FLYING TO DUBLIN FROM EUROPE

AER LINGUS	1-705-3333 in Dublin
RYANAIR	1-609-7800 in Dublin (Ryanair is a major cost-cutter, no-frills airline that operates out of Dublin. Web site: *www.ryanair.com.* They fly to twenty-three European cities.)
BRITISH AIRWAYS	800-626-747 in Dublin
VIRGIN ATLANTIC	1-873-3388 in Dublin
BRITISH MIDLAND	1-283-0700 in Dublin

WEB SITES FOR LOW AIRFARES Try the following Web sites for lower fares and last-minute bookings. Travel magazines and the travel sections of most newspapers and travel magazines also have Web sites and e-mail addresses for European fares. Some fares have restrictions, so read all the small print. Always pay by credit card just in case there is a problem.

www.bestfares.com
www.travelocity.com
www.expedia.com

www.frommers.com
www.americanexpress.com
www.onetravel.com
www.lastminutetravel.com
www.oconnors.com

EUROPE BY AIR PASS Europe by Air Pass; phone: 1-888-387-2479; Web site: *www.europebyair.com*

Allows travel on seventeen airlines that fly to one hundred and fifty cities in thirty European countries including in and out of Ireland. Offers three travel pass options: You can buy one segment for $99 + airport tax (if you plan on one one-way flight from any European city to Dublin) or a Flight Pass Unlimited for $699 + airport tax (must be used within fifteen days) or the same pass for $899.00 + airport tax (for twenty-one days of unrestricted intra-European travel). You must buy your tickets in the United States; they cannot be bought once you arrive in Europe. Flights can be booked in advance or any time after you begin your trip. Tickets are sent to your U.S. address via FedEx or Priority Mail for a fee.

> *May you live as long as you want*
> *And never want as long as you live.*
> ♣ —IRISH TOAST ♣

By Ferry

Ferries leave daily from Holyhead, Northern Wales, to ports just outside of Dublin. It is easy to reach Holyhead by train, car, or bus from London—it's a six-hour drive from London to Holyhead or a four-and-a-half-hour train trip. If you do take the train from London be sure to check the time the train arrives in Holyhead and that it connects with a ferry. Not all trains connect, and you could have a long wait at the terminal. The same thing is true for the reverse trip; not all ferries connect with trains. It is important to call the ferry company if it is very windy—sometimes the ferries are cancelled under those conditions. The ferries are very comfortable and complete with a casino, bar, restaurant, window seats, lounges, TVs, and a bank, which make the trip pass quickly and pleasantly.

STENA LINE, Ferry Terminal, Dun Laoghaire; phone: 1-204-7700 and 1-204-7777; e-mail: *info.ie@stenaline.com*

The ferry sails from Holyhead to Dun Laoghaire at various times during the day. The trip from Holyhead to Dun Laoghaire on the HSS (high speed service) takes 1 hour, 39 minutes. The HSS has a Club Lounge for an additional 10 IEP pounds per person, which includes reserved seating, waiter service, and complimentary papers and refreshments. From the ferry terminal you can take the DART train, bus, or taxi to the city center.

IRISH FERRIES, DUBLIN OFFICE: 2–4 Merrion Row, Dublin 2; phone: 1-638-3333; fax: 1-661-0743; e-mail: *info@irishferries.ie*; Web site: *www.irishferries.ie.* This office is open daily from 9 A.M.–5:30 P.M., Saturday from 9:15 A.M.–12:45 P.M.

The ferries arrive at Dublin Port where buses connect to the city center. The trip from Holyhead to Dublin takes 1 hour, 49 minutes on the Dublin Swift ferry; the Cruise ferry on the same route takes 3 hours, 15 minutes. A new Irish Ferry, called the *Ulysses*, will sail from Dublin City to Holyhead. It's the world's largest car ferry.

By Bus

Bus companies run buses via the Irish Sea ferries from various locations in England, the Continent, and Wales.

NATIONAL EXPRESS IRISH BUS, Web site: *www.gobycoach.com.* Phone: 01-836-6111 in Dublin; 0990-808080 in London

SLATTERY'S COACH, Phone: 1-662-1611 in Ireland, 270-485-1438 in London

BUS EIREANN, Phone 1-836-6111, Fax: 01873-4534

GETTING AROUND

MAPS Maps for driving or street maps for Dublin and Ireland can be obtained at the Irish Tourist Office when you arrive. If you prefer to be prepared buy **Michelin Map** number 923 of Ireland or the **Bartholomew's** Visitor's Map of Ireland before leaving home.

WALKING (*See* chapter 10, Leisure Activities)
Dublin is a surprisingly compact city and is best explored on foot. Walking in Dublin is very pleasant since most sights are either on the north or south side of the River Liffey. Just plan your walks accordingly. After a few days in Dublin you will start planning your return trip.

By Bus

BUSARAS, Store Street, Dublin 1 is the main bus terminal and is located three blocks east of O'Connell Street and north of the Liffey. **Bus Eireann** is the national bus system that links Dublin with towns and cities all over Ireland and Northern Ireland. Phone: 1-836-6111. The Bus Eireann Web site provides timetables and fares for bus routes throughout Ireland: *www.buseireann.ie*

By Train

IRISH RAIL (Iarnrod Eireann) 35 Lower Abbey Street; phone: 1-836-6222; Web Site: *www.irishrail.ie*

HEUSTON STATION, St. John's Road West, Dublin 8, at the end of Victoria Quay; phone: 1-703-2131.

If you are traveling south or west of Dublin you depart from Heuston Station to places such as Cork, Limerick, Waterford, Tralee, Westport, and Galway.

CONNOLLY STATION, Amiens Street; phone: 1-703-2359.

Trains north to Belfast depart from Connolly Station along with trains to Sligo, Wicklow, and Wexford and Rosslare in the south.

PEARSE STATION, Westland Row, Dublin 2.

Trains from this station go to Dundalk, Drogheda, County Wicklow, and Wexford areas. Trains going north from Pearse Station stop at Connolly Station.

Passes

BRITRAIL U.S. Reservations Center: 226-230 Westchester Avenue, White Plains, NY, 10604; phone: 800-4EURAIL or 888-BRITRAIL; fax: 800-432-1329; Web site: *www.raileurope.com*

Passes *must* be purchased in the U.S.; you cannot buy them in Europe.

The Republic of Ireland is one of seventeen countries where the Eurail Pass can be used. Eurail Pass Web site: *www.eurail.com*

BRITRAIL + IRELAND PASS, includes: any five days of unlimited train travel or any ten days of unlimited train travel with one month to complete travel; round-trip Stena Line service between Britain and Ireland; choice of first- or standard-class rail service. The Stena

Line ferries cross the Irish Sea from Britain. There are many crossings each day, some which connect with trains from London's Euston Station. In 2001 the BritRail + Ireland Pass for five days in one month cost $530 for first-class and $408 standard-class. The ten days in one month fare was $770 for first-class and $570 for standard-class. Don't forget to ask if these fares include any discounts. Children under five travel free.

There are many different types of passes and discounts so you must ask the right questions. There are Youth Passes (under twenty-six), passes for two people traveling together, family passes, senior passes, passes depending on the number of days you will use your pass, passes combined with car passes, and many others. Remember a pass does not guarantee a seat. You must reserve a seat ahead of time, especially during the summer, and sleeping car reservations.

CIE TOURS INTERNATIONAL, 100 Hanover Avenue, P.O. Box 501, Cedar Knolls, NJ, 07927-0501; phone: 800-CIETOUR, 973-292-3438; fax: 800-338-3964; Web site: *www.cietours.com*; E-mail: *helpdesk@cietours.com*

The passes listed below should be ordered at least twenty-one days prior to your trip. Once you receive your voucher for a pass it *must* be exchanged at certain locations in Ireland for the actual pass, which is also the date the pass becomes valid. In Dublin it can be exchanged at the Connolly Train Station or the Irish Rail Travel Center, 35 Lower Abbey Street, Dublin 1. Be sure to reconfirm locations when booking. I am not giving the rates for passes because they change yearly. You can purchase your passes directly from CIE Tours or on their Web site.

These Web sites provide information on fares, deals, timetables; you can plan a trip on Bus Eireann, and buy your passes on-line: *www.irishrail.ie* for rail passes; *www.buseireann.ie* for bus passes.

> ♣ **The Irish Explorer Rail and Bus Passes** for use in the **Republic of Ireland only.** It can be used for unlimited travel on all state and federally run railroad trains and buses.
> ♣ **Combined Rail and Bus:** eight-day pass valid on InterCity, DART, Suburban Rail, Bus Eireann Expressway, Provincial Bus, and City Services in Cork, Limerick, Galway, and Waterford. Good for any eight days out of fifteen.
> ♣ **Rail Only:** five-day pass valid for unlimited travel on InterCity, DART, and Suburban Rail in the Dublin area. Good for any five days out of fifteen.

♣ **The Emerald Card** is good for unlimited **bus** and **train** travel in the **Republic of Ireland** and **Northern Ireland.** Travel can be on Irish Rail, Northern Ireland Rail, Irish Bus, Ulsterbus, local rail service in Dublin, and city bus service in Dublin, Belfast, Cork, Limerick, Galway, and Waterford. Valid for fifteen days in a thirty-day period or eight days in a fifteen-day period.

♣ **Irish Rover Pass—Rail only.** Valid for travel in the **Republic of Ireland** and **Northern Ireland.** Unlimited travel on Irish Rail, Northern Ireland Rail, local rail service in Dublin, and suburban rail service in Northern Ireland. This pass is valid for any five days in a fifteen-day period.

♣ **Road Rambler** is only available in Ireland, and is only for bus travel. It offers eight out of fifteen days of travel.

♣ **Student Travelsave** is a pass for students with an International Student ID Card to receive 50 percent off on Irish Rail and 30 percent off Bus Eireann.

By Car

Traveling by car is one of the best ways to tour Ireland as long as you remember to drive on the left. Also, according to Irish law, all passengers must wear seatbelts. These laws are strictly enforced, so buckle up. Outside of the major cities, most roads are narrow and poorly lit at night so always use caution.

Road Signs are in both English and Irish.

Blue/White Signs indicate motorways. The sign to Dublin will say Ath Cliath as well as Dublin and M7 to indicate the motorway number.

Green/White Signs indicate National roads. A sign to Limerick will say it in English as well as Luimneach (Limerick in Irish). There might also be a square sign indicating a roundabout coming up.

Yellow Signs do not have words, but pictures to indicate children crossing or a slippery when wet road, dangerous bends and junctions.

Red and White signs can be circles, triangles, or the worldwide red Stop sign. They are easy to understand, just always be alert.

Double Yellow Lines mean no parking at any time.

Single Yellow Line means no parking except for the hours indicated on the timeplate. Visiting Dublin during the off-season, you won't have to fight the city traffic and you might even find a parking spot downtown. If you do not find a spot, put the car in a garage. If your car is parked illegally and gets clamped it will cost about 100 IR pounds to get it out.

Car Rentals: Be sure you arrive with a **valid driver's license** from your home state or an **International Drivers License,** or plan to take the bus or train. Most car rental companies do not rent to people under the age of twenty-five or over the age of seventy-five. Be sure to check with the rental agency.

Many Irish and international companies have offices at airports and in the cities. It is always best to reserve ahead for the best rates and discounts. Ask for senior citizen rates, AAA rates, and any discounts you may have from frequent flyer programs or organizations.

Cars must be returned with a full tank to avoid extra charges.

Be sure to check with your credit card company about the CDW or collision damage waiver. Some companies include it with gold and platinum credit cards—then you do not have to take it with the rental and pay twice. VAT is added on to rentals. In Ireland the tax is 12.5 percent.

Cars can be rented in all sizes and with automatic or manual shift. One-way rentals are usually subject to a three-day minimum and/or a drop charge or both. Be sure to ask.

There is a small fee for any extra drivers on a rental.

Drivers and passengers *must* wear seatbelts.

Speed limits: In cities, 30 mph (50 kph); open roads, 60 mph (95 kph); motorways, 70 mph (110 kph).

Don't drink and drive. The laws are very strict.

> 1 mile = 1.6 kilometers
> 1 kilometer = 0.6 mile
> 1 U.S. gallon of gas = 3.78 liters
> 4.5 liters = 1 imperial gallon

Some words to know when you are driving in Ireland:

> car hood = car bonnet
> car trunk = car boot
> detour = diversion
> divided highway = dual carriageway
> scenic view = lay-by
> gas station = petrol station
> traffic circle = roundabout
> parking lot = car park
> give way = yield
> large truck = lorry

Car Rental Companies: This is a listing of a few of the car rental companies that we know are reliable, with their U.S. phone numbers. There are many other companies.

ALAMO	800-522-9696	*www.alamo.com*
AUTO EUROPE	888-223-5555	*www.autoeurope.com*
AVIS	800-331-1212	*www.avis.com*
BUDGET	800-527-0700	*www.budget.com*
DAN DOOLEY	800-331-9301	*www.dan-dooley.ie*
DAN KING	353-61-368-126	*www.DanKing.com*
EUROPE BY CAR	800-223-1516	*www.europebycar.com*
HERTZ	800-654-3131	*www.hertz.com*
KEMWEL	800-678-0678	*www.kemwel.com*
MALONE	800-229-0984	*www.malonecarrental.com*
THRIFTY	800-367-2277	*www.thrifty.com*

The Irish Tourist Board lists dozens of rental car companies in their Web site, *www.ireland.travel.ie*. After getting into the site look under "Getting Around" followed by "Car Hire."

Cell Phones and Car Rentals: If you rent a car from Avis or Hertz consider their convenient cell phone promotions. The phone is mailed to you in the U.S. prior to your trip and is activated the day you arrive in Ireland. You return the phone in a prepaid envelope upon arriving back in the U.S.

Avis: One week free phone. $5.00 per day after the first week. $25.00 one time shipping fee. Plus air time in Ireland: Local: $1.10 per minute. Incoming: $1.54 per minute. Long Distance: $2.42 per minute.

Hertz: One week free phone then $49.00 per week or $7.95 per day. $25.00 shipping fee. Plus air time in Ireland: Any outgoing call, local or long distance: $2.00 per minute. Any incoming call: $1.25 per minute.

Seatbelts and Child Seats: Seat belts are mandatory for all passengers. Child safety seats are also required, and may be rented at the same time you rent a car. Be sure to reserve ahead. No one under twelve may sit in the front seat.

Drinking and Driving: This is a major offense, no nonsense. If you are caught driving and drunk there are fines, jail, or both. There is no talking your way out of it, and they are equally as strict in the Republic as in Northern Ireland.

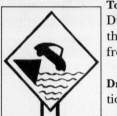

Toll Roads: There are only two toll roads in Dublin, the Dublin East-Link (70p), which crosses the Liffey, and the West-Link (90p), which goes from north to south on the western side of the city.

Driving Services: Driving services are another option if you don't drive.

Carey Limousine International can arrange a driver for you while you are still in the U.S. Phone: 800-336-0646; Web site: *www.careyint.com*

Chauffeur Drive Ireland, Phone: 1-821-1768; mobile: 87-253-5700; mobile fax: 87-201-0440; e-mail: *jimnolan@iol.ie*; Web site: *www.iol.ie~jimnolan/*

Jim Nolan will take you sightseeing by the hour, day, or week in one of his Mercedes Benz cars. His services include meeting you at the airport, ferry terminal, train station, or hotel, and sightseeing tours. Call or e-mail him for his latest rates, which depend on the small or large Mercedes, the number of hours you spend together, and how far your trip takes you. He is very personable and chatty and knows all you need to know about Dublin and Ireland.

Dan Dooley Toll Free in the U.S.: 800-331-9301. This company is not only an Irish car rental company, but also a reliable Irish chauffeur service throughout the Republic of Ireland and Northern Ireland.

Limousine Company, 176 Parnell Street, Dublin 1; phone: 1-872-3003.

Murray's Chauffeur Drive Service, phone: 1-614-2880.

In Dublin

DART Dublin Area Rapid Transit, phone: 1-836-6222. The train schedule is available at all stations and tourist offices.

The DART connects Dublin with Greystones to the south and Howth to the north, with many stops in between. The DART goes along the coast. It is a fast, inexpensive, and clean way to get around County Dublin. It is ideal for getting to the seaside and beach areas. The trains start running at 6:30 A.M. and end at 11:30 P.M. Tickets may be purchased at the train station. If you plan to do a lot of DART train travel look into the variety of tickets available such as family tickets, senior tickets, student tickets, and various passes. If you are going sightseeing north you can take the DART to Howth Junction and change trains to the northern train line to Malahide, Donabate, and many stops all the way to Dundalk. If you are going south you can change at Bray for the South Eastern line going to Wicklow and Arklow. There are also bus connections along the DART line.

> *However long the day it ends with night.*
> ♣ —IRISH PROVERB ♣

NITELINK This is a very helpful service to know if you are out late and need to take a bus to the suburbs. This service operates hourly on Thursday, Friday, and Saturday nights from 12:30 A.M. to 3:30 A.M. departing from College Street, D'Olier Street, or Westmoreland Street. The destinations and bus numbers are located on the front of the buses. Don't forget that the buses returning to the city will say *An Lar*, which is Gaelic for "city center."

> *"Cead Mile Failte"*
> *A hundred thousand welcomes*
> ♣ —IRISH GREETING ♣

TAXIS Taxis can be called to a hotel or restaurant. There are also taxi stands at major sights, the airport, railway stations, and ferry ports. In the city you cannot hail a taxi if you are not near a taxi stand—you must go to a taxi stand or call. If you are alone be sure you have a phone number for a taxi so you are not stranded. If you go to the theater, leave as soon as the show is over so you can be first in line for a taxi. Otherwise you may find you are waiting on a corner and getting nervous. You must pay what the meter says, but remember to tip for late night pickups, extra luggage, waiting time, holidays, etc.

Radio taxi firms

NATIONAL RADIO CABS	Phone: 1-836-5555 for **Northside**
	Phone: 1-454-4070 for **Southside**
PONY CABS	Phone: 1-661-2233
ALL FIVES TAXI	Phone: 1-455-5555
ALL EVENS TAXI	Phone: 1-677-7777
CITY CABS	Phone: 1-872-7272, also have wheelchair accessible cabs
TAXI RADIO LINK	Phone: 1-478-1111
AIRPORT EXPRESS	Phone: 1-836-1111

> *The only cure for love is marriage*
> ♣ —IRISH PROVERB ♣

2. Where to Stay

TYPES OF LODGINGS IN DUBLIN AND IRELAND

B&B

Bed and breakfasts (B&Bs) are very popular in Dublin and Ireland. In the Republic of Ireland, the B&Bs that are government approved display the Shamrock logo at their establishment. B&Bs are usually reasonably priced and the ones I include in this book are all government approved and inspected. Some are very small, but all are good choices.

Camping

There are camping/caravan sites all over Ireland. They too are all regulated and inspected by the government. Bord Failte publishes an excellent guide, "Caravan and Camping Guide" available at all tourist offices. Some sites are open all year and others just during the summer months. There is a central reservations service at 2 Offington Court, Sutton, Dublin 13; phone: 1-832-3776. There you can rent caravans, tents, equipment, and anything else you might need for a camping vacation. Fax: 1-8324126. Will arrange any type of accommodation.

Farmhouses

Farmhouse locations are usually out of town in isolated areas. Many local farmers are now renting a room or rooms at their farms for a "restful" vacation. Meals are usually included. Bord Failte has brochures called "Farmhouse Stays."

Guest Houses

Guest houses are located all over the city and outskirts. They are similar to a hotel or B&B, but usually quite a bit more reasonably priced. They usually include some of the amenities of a hotel such as a TV, but they may not serve meals or have a dining room or bar.

Hostels

The Irish Youth Hostel Organization is known as An Oige. There are many Youth Hostels in Dublin and Ireland, but in order to stay at one you must be a member of the "International Youth Hostel Federation" (*see* Youth Hostels, pages 19–20). It is always advisable to reserve in advance especially during the summer months. They fill up quickly and early.

Self-Catering

All self-catering establishments are registered by Bord Failte, and are members of the "Irish Cottages and Holiday Homes Association." Self-catering is the same as renting an apartment, castle, or cottage. Some come complete with linens, household help, and other deluxe amenities, and others are simple cottages where you supply everything for yourself. See information at the end of this chapter.

Gulliver:
If you arrive in Ireland without reservations you can call this computerized reservation service at 800-398-4376. They can also be reached toll-free from the U.S. at 011-800-668-668-66. This is a free call for credit card reservations. This service operates daily from 8 A.M.–8 P.M., seven days a week. They can reserve hotels, B&Bs, farmhouses, guest houses, hostels, and self-catering establishments.
Web site: *www.ireland.travel.ie*; e-mail: *gulliver@fexco.ie*

DUBLIN HOTELS

Dublin is in the middle of a giant hotel boom. Ireland has become very prosperous and a very popular travel destination. There are many new hotels in the city center and hotels in the surrounding suburbs such as Ballsbridge and Killiney. Be sure to ask all the pertinent questions when booking a hotel room. Hotels will not offer extras when you check in. Are there weekend rates, packages, and senior citizen rates? Is tax included or extra? Most hotels in Ireland add 12.5 percent service charge to the bill. Please ask! Is Continental or Irish breakfast included? Is the hotel wheelchair accessible and is there a dining room or just a breakfast room? If you do not have a car you need to know if the hotel is near a bus or DART or train line. For more information on hotels in Dublin contact *reservations@dublintourism.ie* or visit *www.visitdublin.com*

Many hotels have holiday packages, especially chain hotels. For example, during the Christmas, New Year holiday 2000–01, Jurys Doyle Hotels had a "Get 2 rooms for the price of 1" package starting at IEP 69.

Ireland's Blue Book

Contact Hilary Finlay, Ardbraccan Glebe, Navan, County Meath, Ireland; phone: 011-353-0-46-23416; fax: 011-353-0-46-23292; e-mail: *info@irelands-blue-book.ie* and *bluebook@iol.ie*; Web site: *www.irelands-blue-book.ie*

The year 2000 celebrated the twenty-fifth year of publication of *Ireland's Blue Book*. It is a member of the European Federation of Historic Houses, and represents thirty-five owner-managed country houses, castles, and restaurants. The hotels listed in this book range from grand manors to country homes, but all maintain the same high level of accommodation and food.

Deluxe is IEP 175 and up (approximately $225 and up)
Superior First Class is IEP 155 and up (approximately $200 and up)
First Class is IEP 120 and up (approximately $150 and up)
Moderate First Class is IEP 95 and up (approximately $120 and up)
Note: Moderate First Class and First Class are almost the same rates, and are listed together.
Tourist Class is IEP 50–95 (approximately $90–120)
B&B: Bed and breakfast varies in price.
Guest Houses vary in price.

AIRPORT HOTELS

There are two hotels at Dublin Airport. I prefer to stay in Dublin, but if you have an early flight and don't want to fight the morning traffic, both are good choices. Dublin is seven miles from the airport.

FORTE POST HOUSE, Dublin Airport; phone: 1-844-4211, toll-free in U.S.: 800-225-5843; fax: 1-844-6002.

This is a **moderate first class** hotel. Situated on the grounds of Dublin Airport, this 249-room four- star hotel has all amenities such as trouser press, minibar, and twenty-four-hour shuttle service to the airport and rooms for nonsmokers. There is also a bar and two restaurants on the premises. Be sure to ask for B&B rates, weekend rates, and senior citizen rates. Free parking for hotel guests. Wheelchair accessible.

GREAT SOUTHERN HOTEL, Dublin Airport; phone: 1-844-6000; fax: 1-844-6001; e-mail: *res@dubairport.gsh.ie.*

This is a **first-class hotel.** Located two minutes from the terminal within the airport complex. All amenities available in the rooms include private bath, blow dryer, TV, coffee/tea maker, trouser press, rooms for nonsmokers. There is a restaurant, bar, and lounge. Free parking. Wheelchair accessible.

FORTE TRAVELODGE, Pinnock Hill, Belfast Road, Swords, County Dublin; phone: 1-840 9233; fax: 1-840-9235. This hotel is **inexpensive,** and located close to the airport (not at the airport) on the Dublin-Belfast road. There are very few amenities, but it is clean and reliable.

The truth from a liar is not to be believed.
—IRISH PROVERB

DELUXE HOTELS

BERKELEY COURT HOTEL, Lansdowne Road, Ballsbridge, Dublin 4; phone: 1-660-1711, toll-free in U.S.: 800-42-DOYLE; fax: 1-660-2365; e-mail: *Suzanne.griffin@doyle-hotels.ie*; Web site: *www.jurys.com*

This hotel is a five-minute drive to the city center, and if you are a football fan, it is close to Ireland's Rugby and Soccer Grounds. There are 158 rooms, 24 executive rooms, 5 suites, and a penthouse suite. The hotel has all deluxe amenities, a gym, rooms for nonsmokers, an excellent restaurant, grill, and two bars. Weekend rates available. Free parking. Renovated in 2000 and wheelchair accessible.

CLONTARF CASTLE, Castle Avenue, Clontarf, Dublin 3; phone: 1-833-2321; fax: 1-833-0418; Web site: *www.clontarfcastle.ie*; e-mail: *info@ clontarfcastle.ie*

Located ten minutes northeast of Dublin or the airport by car, taxi, or bus. The castle dates from 1172, but the castle was renovated into a hotel as recently as 1998. The 111 rooms and 4 suites all have private baths, phone, TV, twenty-four-hour room service, restaurant and bar, gym, free-parking and is wheelchair accessible.

CONRAD INTERNATIONAL DUBLIN, Earlsfort Terrace, Dublin 2; phone: 1-602-8900; fax: 1-676-5424; e-mail: *info@conrad-international. ie*; Web site: *www.conrad-international.ie* or *www.hilton.com*

This 191-room, 9-suite hotel is located just off St. Stephens Green and within walking distance of many attractions and shops. All amenities include free in-house movies, trouser press, minibar, twenty-four-hour room service, fitness center, and two restaurants—the Alexandra and Plurabelle Brasserie and the popular Alfie Byrnes Irish Pub. There is also a gift shop and free parking. Both restaurants are wheelchair accessible, as is the hotel. Weekend rates available.

DAVENPORT HOTEL, Merrion Square, Dublin 2; phone: 1-607-3500; fax: 1-661-5663; e-mail: *davenportres@ocallaghanhotels.ie*; Web site: *www. davenporthotel.ie*

This 116-room hotel is located in the heart of Georgian Dublin near Trinity College and other sights. Nonsmoking rooms, all amenities such as twenty-four-hour room service, hair dryer, pants press, TV, fax and computer hookup, gym, free valet parking. Lanyon's Restaurant and the President's Bar are also located at the hotel. Renovated in 2000. Wheelchair accessible.

FITZWILLIAM, St. Stephen's Green, Dublin 2; phone: 1-478-7000; fax: 1-478-7878; e-mail: *enq@fitzwilliamh.com*; Web Site: *www.fitzwilliamh.com*

Be sure to ask for B&B rates, midweek specials, and weekend rates. A new, very modern hotel, the Fitzwilliam just opened in the spring of 1998. Excellently located in the heart of Dublin with St. Stephen's Green on one side and busy Grafton Street on the other. There are two highly regarded restaurants in the hotel.

FOUR SEASONS HOTEL, Simmonscourt Road, Ballsbridge, Dublin 4; phone: 1-665-4000; toll-free in the U.S.: 800-332-3442; fax: 1-665-4099; Web site: *www.fourseasons.com*

Recently opened in February 2001, the Four Seasons is a gorgeous hotel with every possible amenity: health club, spa, swimming pool, salon, twenty-four-hour room service, in-room computer and fax access, meeting rooms, and a restaurant. The 259 rooms and 67 suites are luxurious. Located next door to the Royal Dublin Society, this hotel is perfect if you are attending the Kerrygold Horse Show.

THE MERRION, 21–24 Upper Merrion Street, Dublin 2; phone: 1-603-0600; fax: 1-603-0700; e-mail: *info@merrionhotel.com*; Web site: *www.merrionhotel.com*

The hotel is located in the center of the city within walking distance of Trinity College, Grafton Street, and St. Stephen's Green and the DART station. This 145-room hotel and suites is actually four connected townhouses that have been lovingly restored to its present beautiful state. (The Duke of Wellington was supposedly born in the number 24 townhouse.) The most elaborate rooms are in Monck House (number 22), and Mornington House (number 24), but the entire hotel and its rooms are beautiful. The newer section of the hotel is connected through a covered walkway surrounded by a garden—to one side is the Michelin-starred Patrick Guibaud restaurant. The lobby is large and comfortable and the connecting room with fireplace is used as a bar and afternoon tea area. The rooms are beautiful with all modern amenities, including a fax machine. The hotel has a lower-level restaurant called Morningtons Brasserie, where breakfast and dinner are served. There is also a lower-level pub with live Irish music and drink in the evenings. The hotel has a health club, spa, fifty-nine-foot pool, and treatment rooms. It is wheelchair accessible.

THE SHELBOURNE MERIDIEN HOTEL, 27 St. Stephen's Green, Dublin 2; phone: 1-676-6471; fax: 1-661-6006; toll-free in the U.S. or Canada, 800-225-5843; e-mail: *shelbourneinfo@forte-hotels.com*; Web site: *www.shelbourne.ie*

The Irish Free State's Constitution was drafted at the Shelbourne Hotel in 1922 in room 112. Recently renovated, this 190-room hotel includes many large rooms with spacious bathrooms. Located in the heart of the city overlooking St. Stephen's Green, the hotel is within walking distance of shops and sights. An old Dublin landmark, it is usually overflowing with young people frequenting the bar and pub. Restaurants include the Lord Mayor's Lounge, for breakfast and tea, a dining room, and the famous Horseshoe Bar. The hotel also has a pool, sauna, steam room, Jacuzzi, and exercise equipment. Free parking, wheelchair access.

THE TOWERS HOTEL, Lansdowne Road, Ballsbridge, Dublin 4; phone: 1-667-0033; fax: 1-660-5540.

Adjacent to Jury's Hotel and part of the Jury's Hotel Group. The hotel has 104 rooms and 4 suites, with several rooms for nonsmokers. Some rooms have a phone and TV in the bathroom. Amenities include two restaurants, Irish Pub, the Library Lounge, indoor/outdoor pool, gym, sauna, whirlpool, and free parking. Newly renovated. Wheelchair access.

WESTBURY HOTEL, Grafton Street, Dublin 2; phone: 1-679-1122; fax: 1-679-7078.

Part of Jury's Hotel Group. Room service is available twenty-four-hours a day. This recently renovated 230-room hotel with 8 suites in the city center has beautiful rooms with all amenities including a TV in some of the bathrooms. There are two restaurants, the beautiful Terrace Bar and Lounge, gym, shops, and parking. Wheelchair access and rooms for non-smokers are available.

> *Dance as if no one were watching,*
> *Sing as if no one were listening,*
> *And live every day as if it were your last.*
> ♣ —IRISH PROVERB ♣

SUPERIOR FIRST CLASS

THE ALEXANDER HOTEL, Merrion Square, Dublin 2; phone: 1-607-3700; fax: 1-661-5663; e-mail: *alexanderres@ocallaghanhotels.ie*; Web site: *www.alexanderhotel.ie*

This 103-room, 5-suite hotel is located in the city center near sights, shopping, Trinity College, and St. Stephen's Green. Amenities include private bath, hair dryer, cable TV, twenty-four-hour news channel, rooms for nonsmokers, pants press, voice-mail, gym, and free parking. Caravaggio's Italian Restaurant is located in the hotel as is Winners Bar. Wheelchair accessible.

BURLINGTON HOTEL, Upper Leeson Street, Ballsbridge, Dublin 4; phone: 1-660-5222; toll-free: 800-42-Doyle; fax: 1-660-8496; e-mail: *burlington_hotel@jurysdoyle.com*; Web site: *www.jurysdoyle.com*

This is a very large, convention-style hotel with 451 rooms located just five minutes from the center of the city. There are modern amenities dedicated to serving business people as well as tourists. One of Dublin's best nightclubs, **Annabels,** is located at the hotel and **Doyles Irish Cabaret** operates nightly from Monday to Saturday from May to October. There you can have a three-course dinner followed by Irish coffee that is served at 6:45 P.M. The show starts at 8:15 P.M. The hotel also has a shopping arcade, free parking, two restaurants, a bar, and meeting rooms to accommodate as many as twelve hundred people.

THE CLARENCE, 6–8 Wellington Quay, Dublin 2; phone: 1-407-0800; toll-free in U.S. 800-628-8929; fax: 1-407-0820; e-mail: *Clarence@indigo.ie*; Web site: *www.theclarence.ie*

Opened in 1996 and owned by the band U2, this gorgeous fifty-room hotel is in a building dating from 1852. The hotel overlooks the River Liffey and is located in Temple Bar near Grafton Street and Trinity College. All rooms have amenities such as a minibar, safe, non-smoker's rooms, and twenty-four-hour room service, fax, and computer hookup. There is a restaurant and bar. The restaurant, **The Tea Rooms,** is one of the best restaurants in the city. Rates for hotel rooms start at $250. If you really want to splurge, there is a penthouse deluxe suite at $2000 per night, which includes a baby grand piano, Jacuzzi, and kitchenette. Free parking, wheelchair accessible.

JURYS BALLSBRIDGE HOTEL, Pembroke Road, Ballsbridge, Dublin 4; phone: 1-660-5000; fax: 1-679-7078; e-mail: *info@jurys.com*; Web site: *www.Jurys.com*

A large hotel with three hundred rooms and a newly renovated lobby floor with two restaurants, Dubliner bar and lounge, indoor/outdoor heated pool, gym, and free parking. There are various rates available such as corporate and weekend. Wheelchair accessible.

MORRISON HOTEL, Ormond Quay, Dublin 1; phone: 1-887-2400; fax: 1-887-2499; e-mail: *info@morrisonhotel.ie*; Web site: *www.morrisonhotel.ie*

A new atrium-style, ninety-five-room deluxe hotel, which opened in 1999 and is located on the banks of the Liffey River. If you want a riverview room, request rooms 20 to 23 on each floor. Rates start at $215 double occupancy and go up from there. The designer of this new hotel is from Hong Kong and the colors he uses are black, white, and deep chocolate brown. There are three bars on the ground floor and basement plus the split-level Halo Restaurant. This is definitely a new look in Dublin hotels. (Halo Restaurant: 011-353-1-887-2421. Entrée prices range from $17.00–$26.00.) Nonsmoking and wheelchair accessible rooms are available.

RADISSON SAS ST. HELEN'S HOTEL, Stillorgan Road, Blackrock, Dublin 4; phone: 1-218-6000; toll-free in the U.S.: 800-333-3333; fax: 1-218-6010; Web site: *www.radisson.com*

Located in south Dublin one mile from the Booterstown DART station, three and a half miles from the city center of Dublin. This hotel is surrounded by beautiful gardens, with one hundred fifty rooms and twenty-five suites with all amenities. The lounge/bar located in a glassed-in conservatory overlooks the gardens. There is also an excellent Italian restaurant, fitness room, and free parking, and it's wheelchair accessible.

STEPHEN'S GREEN HOTEL, St. Stephen's Green, Dublin 2; phone: 1-607-3600; fax: 1-661-5663; e-mail: *stephensgreenres@ocallaghanhotels.ie*; Web site: *www.ocallaghanhotels.ie*

Another new hotel to Dublin and part of the O'Callaghan group that owns the Davenport Hotel in Merrion Square, this hotel is located on the corner of Harcourt and Cuffe Streets and overlooks St. Stephen's Green. A combination of two Georgian buildings and a new four-story glass atrium, Stephen's Green has sixty-four rooms and eleven suites, an executive floor, a bistro, bar, and restaurant. The rates vary according to mid-week, weekend, corporate, off-season, and do include tax, but no meals. Limited wheelchair access. Parking charge.

True greatness knows gentleness.
♣ —IRISH PROVERB ♣

FIRST-CLASS AND
MODERATE FIRST-CLASS HOTELS

ACADEMY HOTEL, Findlater Place, Dublin 1; phone: 1-878-0666; fax: 1-878-0600; e-mail: *stay@academyhotel.ie*; Web site: *www.academy-hotel.ie*

This contemporary hotel, which opened in 1998, is well located in the city center near O'Connell Street. All rooms have private bath, air conditioning, TV, minibar, ports for fax and computer, rooms for nonsmokers, restaurant, bar, and free parking. Wheelchair accessible.

BUSWELLS HOTEL, Molesworth Street, Dublin 2; phone: 1-676-4013; fax: 1-676-2090.

This hotel is made up of five Georgian townhouses dating back to 1756 and has all the amenities including rooms for nonsmokers. There is The Grill for an informal lunch or dinner, Buswells Bar with entertainment on Sundays from 4 to 7 P.M., and Trumans for more formal dining. Wheelchair accessible.

CLARION STEPHEN'S HALL HOTEL AND SUITES, 14–17 Lower Leeson Street, Dublin 2; phone: 1-638-1111; fax: 1-638-1122; e-mail: *stephens@premgroup.com*; Web site: *www.premgroup.com*

Located downtown, this is an excellent choice for families since all the rooms are either one- or two-bedroom suites, all with living rooms, dining area, bath, TV, phone, fax, CD player. Nonsmoking suites available. Free garage parking, and completely new and renovated restaurant, and new bar. The hotel is wheelchair accessible with elevators to all floors.

GRAFTON CAPITAL HOTEL, Johnsons Place, Dublin 2; phone: 1-475-0888; fax: 1-475-0909; Web site: *www.capital-hotels.com*; e-mail: *info@grafton.capital-hotels.com*

Ideally located in the center of the city close to Grafton Street, St. Stephen's Green, shopping, Trinity College, museums, and restaurants. Rooms with all amenities included. There is a Tex-Mex restaurant called Break for the Border right next door, a bar with live music on Fridays and Saturdays, and parking with a charge. Wheelchair accessible.

GRESHAM HOTEL, O'Connell Street, Dublin 1; phone: 1-874-6881; fax: 1-878-7175; e-mail: *ryan@indigo.ie*; Web site: *www.ryan-hotels.com*

A three-hundred-room historic landmark hotel built in 1871, one hundred new rooms were added in 1998. Located near major sights, theaters, and shops in the center of the city. The rooms have all amenities, but request a new room, which is air-conditioned and has queen-size beds. There is a gym, business center, valet parking, restaurant, two bars, and a lounge. Wheelchair accessible.

HERBERT PARK HOTEL, Ballsbridge, Dublin 4; phone: 1-667-2200; fax: 1-667-2595; e-mail: *rward@herbertparkhotel.ie*; Web site: *www. herbertparkhotel.ie*

Contemporary-style hotel built in 1996 next to the Royal Dublin Showgrounds and perfect if you are attending any horse shows at the RDS. All amenities included such as a small gym, restaurant, bar, and free parking. Wheelchair accessible.

HIBERNIAN HOTEL, Eastmoreland Place, Ballsbridge, Dublin 4; phone: 1-668-7666, toll-free in U.S.: 800-525-4800; fax: 1-660-2655; e-mail: *info@hibernianhotel.com*; Web site: *www.slh.com/hibernia*

This is a small forty-room hotel located in a Victorian manor house with all amenities including fax and computer access, cable TV, ten junior suites, and free parking. You almost get the feeling of being in a friend's home as opposed to a hotel. There is the Patrick Kavanagh Restaurant located in the hotel serving Irish specialties. Wheelchair accessible.

HILTON DUBLIN HOTEL, Charlemont Place, Dublin 2; phone: 1-402-9988, toll-free in U.S.: 800-HILTONS; fax: 1-402-9966; Web site: *www.hilton.com*

Overlooking Dublin's Grand Canal, this hotel has all of the amenities you would expect in a Hilton hotel including free parking.

MERCER HOTEL, Mercer Street Lower, Dublin 2; phone: 1-478-2179; fax: 1-478-0328; e-mail: *stay@mercerhotel.ie*; Web site: *www.mercerhotel.ie*

This is a boutique-style twenty-one-room hotel that opened in 1997 and is located in the city center near St. Stephens Green and Grafton Street. Currently open year-round except for Christmas. All amenities are included such as air-conditioning, in-room dataport, free overnight parking, VCR, CD player, and French-style bistro restaurant. Wheelchair accessible.

PARAMOUNT HOTEL, Parliament Street and Essex Gate, Temple Bar, Dublin 2; phone: 1-417-9900; fax: 1-417-9904; e-mail: *paramount@ iol.ie*; Web site: *www.paramounthotel.ie*

A new seventy-room hotel located in the heart of Temple Bar. All the rooms have private baths and all amenities. Weekend packages available starting at 90 IR per person for a double room. There is a bistro restaurant and a bar.

QUALITY CHARLEVILLE HOTEL AND SUITES, Lower Rathmines Road, Dublin 6; phone: 1-406-6100; fax: 1-406-6200; e-mail: *charleville@charleville.premproup.ie*; Web site: *www.premgroup.ie*

Located in the suburb of Rathmines village—an ideal location for families. It is a twenty minutes walk to the city center, but if you have a car there is free underground parking. Most of the rooms are suites with a sitting room area, kitchenette, and all amenities such as a fax machine, CD player, and data port. There is a Brasserie restaurant and bar. Wheelchair accessible.

THE MONT CLARE HOTEL, Merrion Square, Dublin 2; phone 1-607-3800; fax 1-661-5663; e-mail *montclareres@ocallaghanhotels.ie*; Web site *www.montclarehotel.ie*

Located in a Georgian building in downtown Dublin near Trinity College, Grafton Street, and many sights. All amenities include twenty-four-hour room service, restaurant, pub, and free parking.

THE MORGAN HOTEL, 10 Fleet Street, Temple Bar, Dublin 2; phone: 1-679-3939; fax: 1-679-3946; e-mail: *sales@themorgan.com*; Web site: *www.themorgan.com*

The rooms in this sixty-one-room boutique hotel located in the heart of the Temple Bar area are nicely decorated, but sparse. All amenities include fax/computer hookup, minibar, in-room safe, gym. Some rooms have balconies, and nonsmoking rooms are available. Charge for parking. Located close to tourist sights and shopping. The Irish artist Siobhan McDonald did the paintings for the rooms and the hotel. Needless to say there is a lively pub on the ground floor of the hotel. Only breakfast is served although there is a room-service dinner menu. Limited wheelchair access.

THE RIVER HOUSE HOTEL, 23–24 Eustace Street, Temple Bar, Dublin 2; phone: 1-670-7655; fax: 1-670-9629; e-mail: *riverhousehotel@compuserve.com*; Web site: *www.visunet.ie/riverhouse*

A three-star hotel with rates starting at IR 90 per double room per night, including full Irish breakfast. Amenities include items such as TV, in-room bath, phone, and a tea/coffee maker. The hotel also has a bar with food service and late-night music, and a nightclub, the Mission Night Club, with dance music played by a D.J. Open Tuesday through Saturday 11 P.M.–2:30 A.M. Pay for parking.

THE RUSSELL COURT HOTEL, 21–25 Harcourt Street, Dublin 2; phone: 1-478-4066; fax: 1-478-1576.

Breakfast is included in the rate. Built by joining three Georgian townhouses, the Russell Court has forty-eight-rooms and is near St. Stephen's Green, Grafton Street, and shops and sights. If you want to stay at this little gem you had better book early; it is usually full with repeat clients. The rooms are large, furnished well, and include non-smoking rooms, cable TV with movies, tea/coffee maker, parking. There is a restaurant, Dicey Reilly's Pub, and a beer garden, which is wonderful during the summer. Four nights a week there is live music, mostly Irish. Wheelchair accessible.

TEMPLE BAR HOTEL, Fleet Street, Temple Bar, Dublin 2; phone: 1-677-3333; fax: 1-677-3088; e-mail: *templeb@iol.ie*

This hotel opened in 1993 in the wonderful Temple Bar area of Dublin and is in walking distance of sights, pubs, restaurants, and shops. The rooms are modern with all amenities. The hotel has a restaurant, café, and pub. Charge for parking.

TOURIST CLASS HOTELS

ASTON HOTEL, 7–9 Aston Quay, Dublin 2; phone: 1-677-9300; fax: 1-677-9007; e-mail: *stay@aston-hotel.com*; Web site: *www.aston-hotel.com*

This is a small twenty-eight-room hotel located in Temple Bar, near all sights, pubs and restaurants. The hotel has a restaurant, which serves breakfast only, and is wheelchair accessible.

BEWLEY'S HOTEL AT NEWLANDS CROSS, Newlands Cross, Naas Road, Dublin; phone: 1-464-0140; fax: 1-464-0900; e-mail: *res@bewleys hotels.com*; Web site: *www.bewleys-hotels.com*

This is a 257-room hotel with large rooms, well furnished, in a new building. It is a great location if you are headed south or west. It is also convenient if you are leaving from Dublin Airport. Open all year, enclosed parking. The restaurant is open for breakfast by 7 A.M., and closes after dinner at 10 P.M., 9:30 P.M. on Sunday. Wheelchair accessible.

BEWLEY'S PRINCIPAL HOTEL, 19/20 Fleet Street, Dublin 2; phone: 1-670-8122; fax: 1-670-8103; e-mail: *bewleys@tinet.ie*; Web site: *www.bewleysprincipalhotel.com*

Located behind the Bewley's Westmorland Street café, this hotel is in the Temple Bar area and has seventy rooms all with in-room bath, TV, phone, and complimentary tea and coffee. The Bewley's excellent central city location, one block from the O'Connell Bridge, is its major attraction. The hotel is small as are the rooms, which are all similarly furnished.

BLOOMS HOTEL, Anglesea Street, Temple Bar, Dublin 2; phone: 1-671-5622; fax: 1-671-5997; e-mail: *blooms@eircom.net*; Web site: *www.blooms.ie*
    Well located in the Temple Bar area. Rooms are less expensive midweek and have heating, in-room baths, TV, restaurant, and bar, but no air-conditioning.

CENTRAL HOTEL, 1–5 Exchequer Street, Dublin 2: phone: 1-679-7302; fax: 1-679-7303; e-mail: *reservations@centralhotel.ie*
    This old-fashioned hotel has a wonderful location in the heart of the city with rooms that have high ceilings and nice décor. There is a restaurant and library bar.

CHIEF O'NEILL'S HOTEL, Smithfield Village, Dublin 7; phone: 1-817-3838; fax: 1-817-3839; e-mail: *reservations@chiefoneills.com*; Web site: *www.chiefoneills.com*
    A new seventy-three-room hotel located in Smithfield Village not far from the city center. All the rooms have private baths, TV, in-room movies, and a CD player. Suites have Jacuzzis. There is a rooftop garden, executive floor, restaurant, and bar with live entertainment.

CLIFTON COURT HOTEL, 11 Eden Quay, Dublin 1; phone: 1-874-3535; fax: 1-878-6698, e-mail: *cliftoncourt@eircom.net*
    The hotel overlooks the River Liffey at the O'Connell Bridge. Amenities include an elevator, TV, phone in each room, restaurant/café, and **Lanigan's Pub,** one of Dublins oldest and most famous, which was opened in 1822. There is traditional Irish music every night.

GEORGE FREDERIC HANDEL HOTEL, 16–18 Fishamble Street, Dublin 2; phone: 1-670-9400; fax: 1-670-9410; e-mail: *reservations@handelshotel.com*; Web site: *www.handelshotel.com*
    Located in Temple Bar, this hotel is at the site where Handel's *Messiah* was performed in 1742. This is a new forty-room hotel with small rooms and friendly staff. Breakfast is the only meal served, but there is a bar and bar food is served all day. Wheelchair accessible.

GEORGIAN HOUSE HOTEL, 18 Lower Baggot Street, Dublin 2; phone: 1-661-8832; fax: 1-661-8834.

Located near St. Stephen's Green. This is a small forty-seven-room hotel in a two-hundred-year-old Georgian building. The rooms have baths, phones, and color TV. There is a bar with music, a seafood restaurant and free parking.

JURY'S CHRISTCHURCH INN, Christchurch Place, Dublin 8; phone: 1-454-0000; fax: 1-454-0012; e-mail: *chanel-malone@jurys.com*; Web site: *www.jurys.com*   € 105

This is a large 182-room hotel located in medieval Dublin opposite Christchurch Cathedral. The rooms are cheerful with all amenities including nonsmoking rooms, restaurant, and pub. Charge for parking. Wheelchair accessible.

THE MESPIL HOTEL, Mespil Road, Dublin 4; phone: 1-667-1222; fax: 1-667-1244; e-mail: *mespil@leehotels.com*; Web site: *www.leehotels.com*

The hotel is a modern five-story apartment-style hotel overlooking the Grand Canal and a short walk to Grafton Street and Dublin sights. Front rooms face the canal and I would definitely try for one of those. Amenities include room service, fax and computer access, restaurant, bar, and free parking. Wheelchair accessible.

NUMBER EIGHTY-EIGHT, 88 Pembroke Road, Ballsbridge, Dublin 4; phone: 1-660-0277; fax: 1-660-0291.

Located near the American Embassy, Herbert Park, and for those attending the annual Horse Show, the Royal Dublin Society. This is a fifty-room hotel with rooms for nonsmokers, private bath, computer/fax access, free parking, and breakfast only. There are many restaurants in the area within walking distance. Wheelchair accessible.

B&B'S

ALBANY HOUSE, 84 Harcourt Street, Dublin 2; phone: 1-475-1092; fax: 1-475-1093.

Open all year. Breakfast is the only meal served in this friendly B&B. If you want to have tea or coffee later in the day they will serve it for a small charge. Rates start at IR 90 for double room with bath. What I love about this B&B is its wonderful location just off St. Stephen's Green within walking distance of most of Dublin's sights and near the DART. The thirty-two rooms all have bathrooms, but the rooms and baths do vary in size. They are all nicely furnished.

www. byrne-hotels-ireland.com/
albany@indigo.ie   albany-accommodation.htm

ANGLESEA TOWN HOUSE, 63 Anglesea Road, Ballsbridge, Dublin 4; phone: 1-668-3877; fax: 1-668-3461.

Open all year except Christmas. Enclosed car park. Each of the seven rooms in this delightful B&B have a private bath. Breakfast is the only meal served, but after eating it you may not have to eat again until the next day. It is huge and delicious with choices from omelets, bacon, eggs, and yogurt with fruit, fresh juices and coffee. There are many restaurants in the area for dinner. Not wheelchair accessible.

DUN AOIBHINN, 30 Sutton Park, Sutton, Dublin 13; phone: 1-832-5456; fax: 1-832-5213; e-mail: *marymcdonnell@ireland.com*

Open all year except during the Christmas holiday. Located six miles northeast of Dublin and a five-minute walk to the DART train, this B&B is an ideal location for sightseeing in Dublin. Each room in the three-bedroom home has its own bathroom and is well furnished. The house also has a lounge, TV, video, tea and coffee maker, and breakfast is included.

MERRION SQUARE MANOR, 31 Merrion Square North, Dublin 2; phone: 1-662-8551; fax: 1-662-8556.

Closed for Christmas. This is a restored Georgian townhouse, beautifully furnished in an excellent location near Grafton Street, Trinity College, and the National Gallery. There are double and twin beds and single rooms all with private baths, phones, TV, hair dryers, pants pressers, and tea/coffee makers. A buffet breakfast is served in a lovely dining room.

MOYTURA HOUSE, Saval Park Road, Dalkey, County Dublin; phone: 1-285-2371; fax: 1-235-0633; e-mail: *giacomet@indigo.ie*

Located near the center of the village of Dalkey in a residential area within walking distance of the DART train to the city center of Dublin, many restaurants, and the James Joyce Tower. There are three double rooms with private bath furnished in excellent taste. Breakfast is included plus the use of a sitting room. Open April–October, no pets and no smoking.

NUMBER 31, 31 Leeson Close, Dublin 2; phone: 1-676-5011; fax: 1-676-2929; e-mail: *number31@iol.ie*; Web site: *www.number31.ie*

Open all year, no dinner at hotel, but many restaurants in the area. Parking at hotel. A twenty-room hotel with excellent service, lovely rooms all with en suite bathrooms, and delicious breakfasts, which in-

clude cranberry bread, eggs, cereal, and our favorite potato pancakes.
No wheelchair access.

GUEST HOUSES

ABERDEEN LODGE, 53–55 Park Avenue, off Ailesbury Road, Ballsbridge, Dublin 4; phone: 1-283-8155; fax: 1-283-7877; e-mail: *Aberdeen
@iol.ie*; Web Site: *www.irishmanors.com*

This is a four-star rated restored Edwardian guest house with
twenty rooms with full Irish breakfast included. All credit cards accepted. Located near the center of Dublin by car or DART. The guest
house in-room amenities include private bathrooms and showers, a
trouser press, TV, phone, some rooms have four-poster beds, and the
suites have whirlpool spas in the bath. There is also free guest parking.
The dining room overlooks the garden and has good food, service,
and wine.

ARIEL HOUSE, 52 Lansdowne Road, Ballsbridge, Dublin 4; phone: 1-
668-5512; fax: 1-668-5845.   *95€*

Closed December 23 to January 9. This is a government-rated four-
star guest house in a restored Victorian mansion. Breakfast is included. All rooms are beautifully furnished and have private baths. It
is three-minute DART ride to the center of Dublin and all its sights.
Free parking. There is a wheelchair ramp available for the ground-
floor rooms, but no elevator for the upper-floor rooms or suites.

BROWNES TOWNHOUSE, 22 St. Stephen's Green North, Dublin 2;
phone: 1-638-3939; fax: 1-638-3900; e-mail: *info@brownesdublin.com*;
Web site: *www.brownesdublin.com*

This twelve-room 1790s town house opened in 1997 with its great
location and views (if you have the front rooms overlooking St.
Stephens Green). There are ten rooms and two suites all with air conditioning, and TV. The Lord Shelbourne Suite does not have a view,
but the Thomas Leighton Suite overlooks the Green. Browne's
Brasserie is on the main floor. (*See* Chapter 3, "Where to Eat and
Drink.") Not wheelchair accessible.

BUTLERS TOWN HOUSE, 44 Lansdowne Road, Ballsbridge, Dublin
4; Phone: 1-667-4022; fax: 1-667-3960; e-mail: *info@butlers-hotel.com*;
Web site: *www.butlers-hotel.com*

This is a twenty-room town house hotel beautifully restored with individually decorated rooms and an old-world feeling. Full Irish breakfast is included with the room price. The rooms have air-conditioning and central heating and private baths. There is room service for a light lunch or dinner, a lounge, and free parking. Closed from December 24 to January 3. One wheelchair accessible room and bath.

EIGHTY-EIGHT GUEST HOUSE, 88 Pembroke Road, Ballsbridge, Dublin 4; phone: 1-660-0277; fax: 1-660-0291.

A reasonably priced and elegant guest house well located for visiting the center of Dublin, the RDS, local restaurants, and sights.

GREY DOOR, 22–23 Upper Pembroke Street, Dublin 2; phone: 1-676-3286; fax: 1-676-3287; e-mail: *info@greydoor.ie*

A government-rated four-star guest house, the Grey Door is located near Grafton Street and St. Stephen's Green. There are seven deluxe rooms with baths, two restaurants with Irish cuisine, and Irish music in a less formal Pier 32 restaurant. Not wheelchair accessible. Closed December 24–29. Rates start at IR 75. Weekend rates available. All credit cards accepted.

KILRONAN GUESTHOUSE, 70 Adelaide Road, Dublin 2; phone: 1-475-5266; fax: 1-478-2841. www.dublinn.com/kilronan.htm

Wonderfully located within walking distance of St. Stephen's Green, Trinity College, and many other Dublin sights, the guest house has well-decorated bedrooms with private shower, phone, TV, hair dryer, and free parking. Mastercard and Visa accepted. Rates start at IR 30. Open all year.

KINGSWOOD COUNTRY HOUSE, Naas Road, Clondalkin, Dublin 22; phone and fax: 1-459-2428; e-mail: *kingswoodcountryhs@tinet.ie*

Located on the N7 toward Naas, west and southwest of Ireland. Seven double rooms with shower, TV and phone. Restaurant serves Irish cuisine. Closed December 24–27. Rates start at IR 45. Weekend specials are available. All credit cards accepted. The guest house is not accessible for wheelchairs, but the restaurant is.

LANSDOWNE MANOR, 46–48 Lansdowne Road, Ballsbridge, Dublin 4; phone: 1-668-8848.

Located near the Lansdowne Rugby stadium, this is a lovely guest house created from two Victorian mansions. The furnishings are Victorian-style chintzes, all rooms with private bath. Breakfast is excellent and the only meal served here. Closed one week at Christmas.

RAGLAN LODGE, 10 Raglan Road, Ballsbridge, Dublin 4; phone: 1-660-6698; fax: 1-660-6781.

A seven-room restored Victorian house dating from 1861, the rooms here are decorated with loving care and have a bath or shower, TV, phone, and central heating. There is a breakfast room and lounge. There are many restaurants in the area. Private parking.

TRINITY LODGE, 12 South Frederick Street, Dublin 2; phone: 1-679-5044, 1-679-5182; fax: 1-679-5223.

This seven-room, three-suite guest house is open all year and usually busy due to its excellent location near Trinity College, Grafton Street, shops, bridges, pubs, restaurants, and sights. The rooms are well furnished and very pretty all with private bath, TV, air conditioning, phone, hair dryer and pants-presser. The suites can sleep six people.

CAMPING

CAMAC VALLEY TOURIST CARAVAN AND CAMPING PARK, Naas Road, Clondalkin, Dublin 22; phone: 1-464-0644; fax: 1-464-0643; e-mail: *camacmorriscastle@eircom.net*

Open all year. Located thirty-five minutes from downtown Dublin this is the newest park for campers and caravans (trailers). The facilities are all new.

SHANKILL CARAVAN AND CAMPING PARK, Shankill, County Dublin; phone: 1-282-0011; fax: 1-282-0108; e-mail: *Shankillcaravan@ eircom.net*

Open all year. Located thirty-five minutes from Dublin and twenty minutes from Dun Laoghaire and the ferry terminal. There is a bus to Dublin that stops at the entrance to the park every fifteen minutes, and the DART is also nearby at Shankill.

UNIVERSITY HOUSING

TRINITY COLLEGE, phone: 1-608-2358; fax: 1-671-1267; e-mail: *reservations@tcd.ie*

The accommodations at Trinity College are not deluxe by any means, but they are reasonably priced and conveniently located right at the end of Grafton Street. Not all have private baths or kitchens, but some do. If you plan to spend the summer in Dublin and especially if you are studying there, it is an ideal place. You can walk almost anyplace in Dublin center, or take public transportation.

HOTELS NEAR DUBLIN

Dun Laoghaire (South of Dublin)

HOTEL PIERRE, 3 Victoria Terrace; phone: 1-280-0291; fax: 1-284-3332. **Superior Tourist Class.**

This hotel has forty-three rooms and five suites overlooking Dublin Bay and is within walking distance to the DART station. The rooms have a bath or shower, TV, phone, room service, and free parking. There is a restaurant and bar in the hotel.

ROYAL MARINE HOTEL, Marine Road; phone: 1-280-1911, toll-free in U.S.: 800-448-8355; fax: 1-280-1089; Web site: *www.ryan-hotels.com.* **First Class.**

A one-hundred-four-room, eight-suite hotel that overlooks Dublin Bay with beautiful gardens and a modern addition to the original Victorian hotel. Amenities include private bath, hair dryer, phone, TV, room service, pants press, free parking. The hotel also has a restaurant, bar, and lounge and is wheelchair accessible.

Howth (North of Dublin)

DEER PARK HOTEL, Howth; phone: 1-832-2624, toll-free in U.S.: 800-44-UTELL; fax: 1-839-2405. **Superior Tourist Class.**

This seventy-eight-room hotel is located on the Howth Castle grounds and includes the largest golf complex in Ireland. There are two nine-hole courses, one twelve-hole course, an eighteen-hole course, and an eighteen-hole Pitch and Putt course. Most rooms have a sea view. Amenities include private bath, phone, TV, tea/coffee maker, room service, restaurant, coffee shop, swimming pool, and bar. Free parking. Wheelchair accessible.

Killiney (South of Dublin)

THE COURT HOTEL, Killiney Bay, Killiney; phone: 1-285-1622, toll-free in U.S. and Canada: 800-44-UTELL; fax: 1-285-2085; e-mail: *book@killineycourt.ie*; Web site: *www.killineycourt.ie*

This beautiful **First Class** hotel is located twenty minutes from Dublin by DART and overlooks Killiney Bay. In this eighty-six-room Victorian Mansion, most rooms have a sea view along with private bath, hair dryer, cable TV, fax hook-up, tea/coffee maker, twenty-four-hour room service, and free parking. There is a beautiful restaurant with Irish and French food, a grill room for steaks and seafood, and a bar and lounge. There is a Jazz brunch on Sundays. It is wheelchair accessible, and non-smoking rooms are available.

FITZPATRICK CASTLE HOTEL, Killiney; phone: 1-230-5400, toll-free in U.S.: 800-367-7701; fax: 1-230-5430.

This is a beautiful **First Class** hotel with 113 rooms and eight suites. Part of the hotel is a castle built in 1741 with a new addition. The hotel overlooks Dublin Bay and is only nine miles from the center of Dublin. Amenities include private bath, tea/coffee maker, room service, some rooms with fax (request it on booking if it is a requirement), nonsmoking rooms, fitness center with indoor pool, gym, steam room, and sauna. Free parking. Restaurant and bar are also available.

Malahide (North of Dublin)

GRAND HOTEL, Malahide; phone: 1-845-0000; fax: 1-845-0987.

This one-hundred-room **First Class** hotel is located five minutes from the Dublin Airport and twenty minutes from the Dublin City center. You do need a car to stay here. Amenities include private bath, TV, free parking, restaurant, two lounges, and a leisure center. There is golf and fishing nearby, which can be arranged by the hotel. Wheelchair accessible.

Sutton (North of Dublin)

MARINE HOTEL, Dublin Road, Sutton Cross, Dublin 13; phone: 1-839-0000; fax: 1-839-0442.

This is a small, twenty-six-room, **Moderate First Class** hotel located seven miles from Dublin Airport. It is within a five-mile radius of eight golf courses. If you are going to play golf every day and want a moderately priced hotel you might want to stay here. Amenities include private bath, hair dryer, cable TV, some rooms with balconies, free parking, rooms for nonsmokers, restaurant, bar, lounge, indoor pool, sauna, and private beach.

HOME EXCHANGE

Exchanging homes has become very popular and very easy to do. You list your home or apartment with an exchange company and/or Web site and for a small fee you receive a book listing others who wish to exchange homes too. Then you contact those people and send photos, letters, e-mail, and faxes.

HomeLink International, Box 650, Key West, FL 33041; phone: 305-294-7766, toll-free 800-638-3841; fax: 305-294-1448; e-mail: *homelink@swapnow.com*; Web site: *www.swapnow.com*

International Home Exchange Network, Box 915253, Longwood, FL 32791; phone: 407-862-7211; Web site: *www. homexchange.com*

The yearly fee to list a property in the Web site is $29.95, and you can make unlimited changes in your listing

Intervac U.S., 30 Corte San Fernando, Teburon, CA 94920; phone: 800-756-4663; fax: 415-435-7440; Web site: *www.intervacus.com*; e-mail: *info@intervacus.com*

Intervac U.S. offers a "Web only" membership for $50; you can have your home listed on the Web and have access to others interested in exchanging homes. There is also a printed book membership. The rate for the book entry starts at $93 plus the additional cost for including a photo, and postage. There may be other charges so it is best to contact them directly.

As you slide down the banister of life
May the splinters never face the wrong way!

♣ —IRISH TOAST ♣

SELF-CATERING (HOME RENTALS)

One excellent way to get the flavor of any country is to stay in one place for more than a few days. If you are lucky enough to stay in Ireland for a week or more in one location you might consider a rental. The country is small, and you can easily use one location as a headquarters for extensive sightseeing. Beyond the practical benefits, rentals enable you to become part of the neighborhood and perhaps make some new friends.

There are many accommodations with the wheelchair symbol that are approved for people with disabilities. Rentals are available all year, but like air travel, rental rates are best off-season. When renting whether through the Irish Tourist Board catalogs or privately, be sure to ask all the questions so as not to be disappointed with your rental. You will want to know if it is one floor or two, has an elevator, attached housing, yard, maid service, linen and amenities supplied, and anything else you need to know. The big thing is to ask, don't wait to be advised.

Most companies will have lists ranging from small cottages to manor houses, castles and apartments. The Irish Tourist Board publishes many catalogs on home rentals. One excellent catalog is *Ireland, Self-Catering Guide*. This guide lists hundreds of rentals throughout Ireland along with photographs of the rentals and descriptions of the area. Another guide is *Irish Farmhouse Bed and Breakfast*. That catalog can be ordered through the *Irish Farmhouse Holidays Association*, 2 Michael Street, Limerick, Ireland; phone: 011-353-61-400-700; fax: 011-353-61-400-771.

AT HOME IN IRELAND, 111 Anglesea Road, Dublin 4; phone: 1-668-3139; fax: 1-668-3824.

This company publishes a guidebook of rentals for luxury castles, country homes, cottages and apartments. Call, fax, or write for their catalog, which was $10 at the time I wrote this book.

COUNTRY COTTAGES, 2300 Corporate Blvd., NW # 214, Boca Raton, FL, 33431; phone: 561-988-4000; fax: 561-988-0016; reservations: 800-674-8883; e-mail: *cottages@worldnet.att.net*; Web site: *www. europvacationvillas.com*

Country Cottages is a company that arranges travel packages including airfare, car rental and accomodation in a villa, apartment, mansion, B&B, or cottage. Their Thanksgiving and St. Patrick's Day packages are especially appealing.

ELEGANT IRELAND, Contact: Geraldine Murtagh, Elegant Ireland, P.O. Box 6080, Dublin 8, or 15 Harcourt Street, Dublin 2; phone: 011-353-1-475-1632, 1-475-1665; fax: 011-353-1-475-1012; e-mail: *info@ elegant.ie*; Web site: *www.elegant.ie*

This is an Irish company that represents owners of country houses, castles, and cottages that can be rented for short or long term both in Dublin and throughout the country. Some properties can be rented for as few as three nights. Elegant Ireland can also arrange self-drive or chauffeur-driven cars, golf, and other activities.

HOME AT FIRST, Family Vacation Specialists: P.O. Box 193, Springfield, PA 19064; phone: 800-523-5842; fax: 610-543-4970

This company can plan your entire vacation. They can arrange a complete package of air, cottage or apartment, sightseeing, and a car, or a land-only package. If you wish they could also arrange golf tee times; for anglers they arrange to have your fishing license ready plus rental equipment and a guide. Hikers can have a trip prepared with maps and a guide. All rentals include weekly linen change and cleaning, guide books, and maps of the area, airport meeting and transfer if you are on an air package, car rental and an overnight stay in the city of arrival before you pick up the car.

IRISH COTTAGE HOLIDAY HOMES, 4 Whitefriars, Aungier Street, Dublin 2, Ireland; phone: 011-353-1-475-1932; fax: 011-353-1-475-5321; e-mail: *info@irishcottageholidays.ie*; Web site: *www.ichh.ie*

This brochure offers moderately priced cottages and apartments that can be rented for a few days or a few weeks. They are all self-catering and are located throughout Ireland. The off-season rates are excellent. These rentals are available twelve months a year.

KEITH PROWSE & CO. LTD., 234 West 44th Street, New York, NY 10036; phone: 800-669-8697; fax: 212-302-4251.

This company represents various companies in Ireland. You may request their brochure.

TRIDENT HOLIDAY HOMES, 15 Irishtown Road, Irishtown, Dublin 4, Ireland; phone: 1-668-3534; fax: 1-660-6465

The Irish tourist board approves all the homes listed with this company. During the summer season from June to September all rentals start and end on Saturday. During the rest of the year they are flexible. Trident offers cottages, holiday homes, and city townhouses for rent in the east, south, and west of the country. They will arrange for babysitting, boat or bicycle rentals, fishing trips, and tours in the area you are in.

> *I have been three years in this country and*
> *Never found a dull man.*
>
> ♣ —LADY RANDOLPH,
> MOTHER OF WINSTON CHURCHILL ♣

3. Where to Eat and Drink

DUBLIN RESTAURANTS AND PUBS

There are excellent restaurants serving wonderful fresh seafood, Irish cheeses, delicious Irish brown bread, and of course potatoes in all price ranges throughout Dublin. Definitely try a potato pancake, known as boxty, before you leave. Most pubs still serve a dish called colcannon, which is potato, scallions, and kale. Needless to say, try Irish Stew made with mutton, potatoes, and onions. It can be found on menus in pubs as well as deluxe restaurants.

The following restaurants are listed in alphabetical order. Be sure to look at the $ sign for approximate dinner prices. Prices do change and restaurants do go out of business so call ahead for reservations whenever possible. I suggest trying an expensive restaurant at lunchtime when the food and service is equally good and the prices usually half that of dinner.

Money saving hints

TOURIST MENU Many restaurants have a sign in the window saying they have a Tourist Menu. That means a three-course dinner at a lesser price than ordering each item individually. There are also early bird menus that you must order before a specific time, usually 6 P.M. Some hotels and restaurants offer Pre-theater dinners, which are served by 6 P.M.

TRINITY COLLEGE They have excellent homemade soups and salads or sandwich lunches accompanied by a concert or play performance at modest prices. Several times, I've enjoyed a tasty lunch accompanied by Irish music.

Prices in Restaurants

These rates are per person for an appetizer, main course, and dessert. This does not include drinks or gratuity.

$$$$	Very Expensive	approximately IEP 30 and up per person
$$$	Moderate to expensive	approximately IEP 20–30 per person
$$	Moderate	approximately IEP 15 per person
$	Inexpensive	approximately under IEP 15 per person

Pub Prices

$ or $$	prices range from a pint of Guinness to lunch or dinner

RESTAURANTS

$$$ AYA, behind Brown Thomas Department Store, Clarendon Street, Dublin 2; phone: 1-677-1544; e-mail: *mail@aya.ie*; Web site: *www.aya.ie*

Everything is possible here from a traditional Irish breakfast and Japanese grill breakfast to take-out food, sushi bar, tempura, and yakitori. Wheelchair accessible. Open daily for breakfast, lunch, and dinner.

$$$ AYUMI-YA, Newpark Center, Newtownpark Avenue, Blackrock, County Dublin; phone: 1-283-1767; Fax: 01 288 0478; e-mail: *info@ayumiya.ie*; Web site: *www.ayumiya.ie* Open daily for dinner, Japanese and vegetarian.

Although this restaurant is located south of the city, I mention it because it has become a must for lovers of Japanese food. Yoichi Hoashi owns both this and AYA in Dublin. You can enjoy dinner at the typical low Japanese tables or regular restaurant tables. The food served here is yakitori, tempura, sashimi, sushi, vegetarian dishes and dishes cooked right at your table such as sukiyaki and shabu-shabu.

$ BAD ASS CAFÉ, 9–11 Crown Alley, phone and fax: 1-671-2596.

Located behind the Central Bank, this café is busy, loud, and fun for all ages. The food is simple such as pizza, salads, burgers, grilled chicken and steaks, children's specials.

$ BESHOFF'S RESTAURANTS, 6 Upper O'Connell Street; phone: 1-872-4400, and 14 Westmorland Street, Dublin 2; phone: 1-677-8026.

Ivan Beshoff settled in Dublin in 1913 from Russia and started his fish business that eventually turned into fish and chips restaurants. There are at least twenty varieties of fish served and delicious chips.

 **$ BEWLEY'S CAFES,** Bewley's is a Dublin tradition for a quick breakfast before work, a cup of tea in the afternoon, to meet a friend for lunch or dinner or in today's times to pick up some take-out food. They also sell their famous tea and coffee in tins as well as souvenir cups, tea-pots and coffeepots. **Locations:** 11–12 Westmoreland Street, 13 South Great George's Street, and the famous one at 78 Grafton Street.

$ BLAZING SALADS, Powerscourt Townhouse Centre, 59 S. William Street, Dublin 2.

This is a vegetarian restaurant serving everything from fat-free, dairy-free, sugar-free, yeast-free, gluten-free, but definitely not taste-free.

$ BREAK FOR THE BORDER, Lower Stephen's Street, Dublin 2; phone: 1-478-0300.

Located next door to the Grafton Capital Hotel. This is a very lively Tex-Mex restaurant, bar and nightclub with a Western theme. Open nightly with live rock and country bands from Wednesday through Saturday.

$$ BROWNES BRASSERIE, 22 St. Stephen's Green, Dublin 2, phone: 1-638-3939.

This is a reasonably priced restaurant with excellent food and a great location.

$$ BRUNO'S, 30 East Essex Street, Temple Bar, Dublin 2; phone: 1-670-6767.

The service and food here were of a very high quality for a simple Temple Bar restaurant. The fish chowder, filled with a variety of fresh fish, is delicious. They also serve beef dishes and simple fresh grilled fish dishes, French and Italian dishes, good desserts and a reasonable wine list. Look for a new Bruno's opening on Kildare Street.

$ CAFÉ EN SEINE, 40 Dawson Street, Dublin 2; phone: 1-677-4369. Open daily from 10 A.M., closed Good Friday and December 25.

This café opened in 1993 and is still very popular. You can have dinner outside in nice weather, and also enjoy a Sunday jazz brunch.

$ CAPTAIN AMERICAS, 44 Grafton Street, Dublin 2; phone: 1-671-5266. Open daily for lunch and dinner.

This is a large, fun restaurant serving simple food like burgers, salads, and vegetarian entrees.

$ CASA PASTA, 12 Harbour Road, Howth, County Dublin; phone: 1-839-3823. Open Monday through Thursday 6 to 11 P.M., Friday through Sunday, lunch and dinner. During the winter they do not serve lunch on Tuesday, Wednesday, or Thursday.

This is an Italian bistro serving up good food and live music.

$$-$$$ CHAPTER ONE, 18–19 Parnell Square, Dublin 1; phone: 1-873-2266; fax: 1-873-2330. Located in the basement of the Dublin Writers Museum. Open Tuesday to Friday for lunch, Tuesday to Saturday for dinner, closed Sunday, Monday, and bank holidays.

Their menu offers an impressive selection of fresh local fish, Irish dishes, and game.

$$$$ COMMONS RESTAURANT, Newman House, 85-86 St. Stephen's Green; phone: 1-478-0530; fax: 1-478-0551. Closed Saturday lunch and Sunday, two weeks at Christmas, and bank holidays.

Located in the historic eighteenth-century courtyard townhouse where James Joyce once studied. The chef provides an inventive menu of goose with honey, bass with caviar, and quail, among other fish and meat dishes.

$$ COOKES AND THE RHINO ROOM, 14 South William Street, Dublin 2; phone: (Cookes) 1 679 0536, (Rhino Room) 1-670-5260; e-mail: *cookes1@iol.ie*

What I love about these restaurants (the Rhino Room is upstairs from the café) is the simple delicious cooking. Upstairs the chef is a little fancier, but not overdone. Black bean soup with lime is a particular favorite. Right off Grafton Street, this is a perfect lively lunch place.

$$-$$$ COOPERS CAFÉ, Sweepstake Centre, Ballsbridge, Dublin 4; phone: 1-660-1525; fax: 1-660-1537; e-mail: *coopersrestaurant@tinet.ie*
Located right across the street from the Royal Dublin Society, it is popular and busy especially during event times. Open for lunch Sunday through Friday, dinner daily, closed December 25, 26, Good Friday. Wheelchair accessible. The menu here mixes Mediterranean style with fresh fish and meat, delicious salads, and pasta dishes.

$$$ DISH, 2 Crow Street, Temple Bar, Dublin 2; phone: 1-671-1248; fax: 1-671-1249; e-mail: *dish@indigo.ie* Open daily from 12:30 P.M.– 11:30 P.M. Not wheelchair accessible.
Located in the heart of Temple Bar, the menu bursts with unusual dishes such as sweet potato and pear bisque as well as simple fish and meat dishes. The good food is complemeted by fun-filled atmosphere.

$$ DOBBINS WINE BISTRO, 15 Stephen's Lane, Phone: 1-661-3321; fax: 1-661-3331. Closed: dinner Monday, lunch Saturday, Sunday, bank holidays, and Christmas week.
There is a small patio for warm summer days. This is a bistro-style restaurant and reservations are a must. Try the smoked wild Irish salmon as an appetizer. It is delicious especially with the excellent bread. As a main course try the breaded lamb, breast of duck, or fish.

$ DYFLIN RESTAURANT, Bedford Row, Temple Bar, Dublin 2; phone: 1-677-8528. Open daily for lunch and dinner on a first-come, first-served basis, no reservations.
This is an informal restaurant that serves salads, pastas, pizzas, chicken, lamb, and pork.

$$$ EDEN, Meeting House Square, Temple Bar, Dublin 2; phone: 1-670-5372; fax: 1-670-3330. Not wheelchair accessible. Open Monday to Friday 12:30 P.M.–3 P.M., Saturday and Sunday noon to 3 P.M., Monday to Sunday 6 P.M.–10: 30 P.M. Reservations recommended.
A very trendy contemporary Irish restaurant with an open-view kitchen overlooking Meeting House Square, Eden serves pork, lamb shank, venison, stew beef, and fish dishes, as well as delicious mashed potatoes.

$$ ELEPHANT AND CASTLE, 18 Temple Bar, Dublin 2. Phone: 1-679-3121; Fax: 1-679-1399. Open daily for breakfast, lunch, and dinner. Wheelchair access.

A very busy American-type restaurant, serving delicious chicken wings, hamburgers, omelets. They also have a nice wine list.

$$$ ERNIE'S, Mulberry Gardens, Donnybrook; phone: 1-269-3300; fax: 1-269-3260. Closed Sunday and Monday. Wheelchair accessible.
Serving modern French cooking, the surroundings here are as nice as the food. The walls are covered with works of Irish painters.

$$ FITZERS CAFE, In town: Dawson Street, phone: 1-677-1155; Temple Bar Square, phone: 1-679-0440.
Both Fitzers serve very good continental food.

$ GALLAGHER'S BOXTY HOUSE, 20 Temple Bar; phone: 1-677-2762.
Boxty is a traditional Irish potato pancake and Gallagher's serves them with a variety of different stuffings.

$$ THE GREY DOOR IRISH RESTAURANT, 22/23 Upper Pembroke Street, Dublin 2; phone: 1-676 3286; fax: 1-676-3287; e-mail: *info@ greydoor.ie* Open: Dinner Monday to Saturday. Closed December 24 for one week and bank holidays.
This is an exceptional Irish restaurant serving a variety of fresh local fish.

$$$$ HALO, Morrison Hotel, Ormond Quay, Dublin 1, Phone: 1-878-2999; Fax: 1-887-2499; e-mail: *info@morrisonhotel.ie* Open daily 12:30 P.M.–2 P.M., 7 P.M.–10: 30 P.M., wheelchair access.
Beautiful, trendy and expensive, this is definitely one of the "in" places in town. The menu is pleasingly varied with items such as curried scallops, monkfish with saffron, salmon and sushi.

$ ITSABAGEL, Epicurean Food Hall, Lower Liffey Street, Dublin 1; phone: 1-874-0486; fax: 1-874-0489; Web site: *www.itsabagel.com*; e-mail: *info@itsabagel.com* Open Monday to Friday 8:30 A.M.–6 P.M., Saturday 10 A.M.–6 P.M.
So you thought you could only get New York bagels in New York? Wrong. Delivered from New York partially cooked and frozen, these bagels are delicious. You can even call or fax your order before noon and it will be ready for lunchtime pickup. Slather it with cream cheese and smoked salmon or any of their other many toppings. They also have a large selection of soups and salads.

$-$$ JUICE, 9 Castle House, South Great George's Street, Dublin 2; phone: 1-475-7856.

This is probably the best vegan restaurant in Dublin. Serving only non-meat, dairy-free, and organic dishes, the menu includes home-made butter bean and black olive pâte, Irish brown bread and crudités, and spinach and ricotta cheese cannelloni.

$ THE KILKENNY SHOP, 6 Nassau Street; phone: 1-677-7066. Open 9 A.M.–5: 30 P.M., closed Sunday and holidays.

This self-serve restaurant is located above the Kilkenny Shop and is usually busy at lunchtime. Get there early if you want to enjoy their home-cooked Irish stew, casseroles, and delicious scones and cakes.

$$$ KING SITRIC, East Pier, Harbour Road, Howth, phone: 1-832-5235. Closed Sunday.

This lovely two-story harborside restaurant with gorgeous views of the sea offers excellent fresh seafood such as Dublin prawns, salmon, oysters, sole, and other local fish caught the night you eat it. Try the to-die-for desserts as well. The night I ate there the ocean liner *QE2* passed right by the big windows. King Sitric is now a small hotel as well as a restaurant.

$$$ LA STAMPA, 35 Dawson Street, Dublin 2; phone: 1-677-8611, open Monday to Friday 12:30 P.M.–2 P.M., Monday to Thursday and Sunday 6:30 P.M.–11:15 P.M., Friday and Saturday 6:30 P.M.–11:45 P.M. Not wheelchair accessible.

Very good food, including fricassee of warm oysters and a variety of pasta, poultry, and fresh local fish, is served in this gorgeous dining room. Their wine list is well rounded and not outrageously priced.

$$ LATCHFORDS BISTRO, 100 Lower Baggot Street; phone: 1-676-0784. Closed Saturday lunch and Sunday.

This is an upscale French/Irish bistro located in a Georgian town-house. The food is mostly Irish fish with a French twist. Poultry and meat are also served.

$$$$ LE COQ HARDI, 35 Pembroke Road, Ballsbridge, Dublin 4; phone: 1-668-9070; fax: 1-668-9887. Open lunch and dinner, Monday to Saturday. Closed Sunday and two weeks in August. No wheelchair access.

Located in a beautiful townhouse, this restaurant serves French and Irish food in a more formal setting. The service is excellent, as is the food. To start, you might order white Clonakilty pudding and continue with Irish salmon or roast venison. Also on the excellent menu is quail with foie gras and Howth lobster. The wine list is expensive and offers a wonderful selection.

$$$ L'ECRIVAIN, 109a Lower Baggot Street, Dublin 2; phone: 1-661-1919; fax: 1-661-0617; e-mail: *enquiries@lecrivan.com*

The restaurant is wheelchair accessible on the first floor only. Open for lunch Monday to Friday 12:30 P.M. to 2 P.M., and dinner Monday to Saturday 7 P.M. to 11 P.M. Located in the heart of Georgian Dublin within walking distance of St. Stephen's Green. The chef/owner, Derry Clarke, prepares both modern Irish and Continental food. You might try excellent baked rock oysters, coconut soup, scallops, or breast of Ailsbury duck plus other wonderful fresh Irish fishes. He also serves Clonakilty black pudding and Dublin Bay prawns. Finish you dinner with an assortment of delicious Irish cheeses or ice cream.

$ LEFT BANK BAR AND RESTAURANT, 18–21 Anglesea Street, Temple Bar, Dublin 2; phone: 1-671-1822.

This restaurant/bar is known for its seafood and live music.

$$$ LES FRERES JACQUES, 74 Dame Street; phone: 1-679-4555; fax: 1-679-4725, closed December 25 to January 2, Sunday, Saturday lunch, and bank holidays.

Superbly prepared duck and fish dishes and delicious desserts make this restaurant a treat. Modest wine list.

$$$ LOCKS RESTAURANT, 1 Windsor Terrace, Portobello, Dublin 8; phone: 1-454-3391; fax: 1-453-8352. Closed Saturday lunch, Sunday, end of July to early August.

A cozy neighborhood restaurant with a fireplace. They serve many excellent dishes, including my favorite Dublin Bay prawns and venison with lentils.

$$ MANGETOUT, 112 Lower Baggot Street, Dublin 2; phone: 1-676-7866; fax: 1-676-7821. Not wheelchair accessible. Open Tuesday to Friday 12:30 P.M.–2:15 P.M., Tuesday to Saturday 7 P.M.–11 P.M.

This low-key restaurant occupies the original space of L'Ecrivain, which moved up the street. The food is very good with interesting touches such as pan-fried cod with a cassoulet of beans.

$$$ MERMAID CAFÉ, 69 Dame Street, Dublin 2; phone: 1-670-8236. Open daily for lunch and dinner.

A highlight of this charming café is the Giant Atlantic Seafood Casserole.

$$ ODESSA, 13 Dame Court, Dublin 2; phone: 1-670-7634. Open Monday to Wednesday 5–11 P.M., Thursday to Sunday noon–midnight.

This restaurant has an interesting menu of Californian, Mexican, and Mediterranean dishes.

$$$ OLD DUBLIN RESTAURANT, 91 Francis Street, Dublin 8; phone: 1-454-2028, 1-454-2346; closed Sundays.

Serving mostly Russian and Scandinavian dishes with a smattering of simple Irish dishes, this pleasant restaurant is a unique choice,

$ OLIVER ST. JOHN GOGARTY, 58–59 Fleet Street, Temple Bar, Dublin 2; phone: 1-671-1822, 1-671-1170; fax: 1-671-7637. Open daily.

A traditional Irish restaurant serving Irish food bar/pub or restaurant. Irish music plays from 4–7 P.M. and 9–11 P.M. There is also an Irish breakfast accompanied by music served on Sundays from noon–2:30 P.M.

$ O'SHEA'S MERCHANT, 12 Lower Bridge Street, Dublin 8; phone: 1-679-3797; fax: 1-679-3797. Open daily from 10 A.M. to midnight.

This pub/restaurant caters to everyone. They have early-bird dinners, children's menus, and hearty pub food with music and dancing nightly.

$ PASTA FRESCA, 3–4 Chatham Street, Dublin 2; phone: 1-679-2402. Open daily for lunch and dinner, Sunday for lunch, closes at 6 P.M. Located near Grafton Street, St. Stephen's Green, and the Gaiety Theatre.

Start with an antipasto or carpaccio. The menu naturally has many freshly made pasta dishes such as spaghetti alla Bolognese, cannelloni, or lasagna, but they also serve veal and steak. It is an ideal restaurant for a meal before attending a show at the Gaiety.

$$$$ PEACOCK ALLEY, at the Fitzwilliam Hotel, 109 St. Stephen's Green, Dublin 2; phone: 1-677-0708; fax: 1-478-7025, one Michelin star. Closed December 25, 26, January 1, Sundays, and bank holidays. Wheelchair accessible.

Specialties are lobster tortellini, grilled fish, and scrumptious desserts.

$/$$ THE PORTERHOUSE, 16 Parliament Street, Dublin 2; phone: 1-679-8847, open daily except Good Friday and Christmas day.

At Dublin's first microbrewery try different beers while enjoying a meal in the pub or restaurant.

$$$$ RESTAURANT PATRICK GUILBAUD, The Merrion Hotel, 21 Upper Merrion Street, Dublin; phone 1-676-4192; fax: 1-661-0052. Closed Sunday and Monday.

This is a two-star Michelin restaurant. The service here is superb as is the food prepared by chef Patrick Guilbaud. On a nice day you can have lunch under a bright yellow awning in the beautiful hotel garden. The French/Irish cooking includes poached Connemara lobster, local Irish fish such as Dublin Bay prawns in pastry, Irish beef, rabbit, quail, and squab.

$$ ROLY'S BISTRO, 7 Ballsbridge Terrace, Dublin 4; phone: 1-668-2611; fax: 1-660-8535. Wheelchair access. Open noon to 3 P.M., 6 P.M.–10 P.M. Monday to Sunday. Closed Good Friday, December 25, 26.

This is a warm, cozy two-story restaurant bistro with excellent Irish food such as Irish lamb stew, Irish potpies, Dublin Bay prawns, lobsters, loin of pork with Guinness and Clonakilty black pudding.

$$$ RUBICON RESTAURANT, 6 Merrion Row, Dublin 2; phone: 1-676-5955; fax: 1-676-1999. Open for lunch Monday to Saturday 12–3 P.M., dinner Monday to Saturday 5:30 P.M. until everyone has gone home, Sundays 5–10 P.M.

Downstairs there is a large open fireplace where pre-dinner or after-dinner drinks can be served. The ground floor houses the restaurant, which serves Irish and international cuisine. Located in the center of Dublin near the Shelbourne and Merrion Hotels and opposite O'Donoghue's Pub.

$$ RYAN'S, 28 Parkgate Street, Dublin 8; phone: 1-677-6097; fax: 1-671-3590. Open Monday to Friday for lunch, Tuesday to Saturday for dinner, closed Sunday, Monday dinner.

Located near the city center and Phoenix Park, this restaurant serves a variety of skillfully prepared Mediterranean and Irish dishes.

$$ TALAVERA ITALIAN RESTAURANT, Radisson SAS St. Helen's Hotel, Stillorgan Road, Blackrock, Dublin 4; phone: 1-218-6000; fax: 1-218-6010.

A pleasant, casual restaurant serving typical Italian dishes. Before dinner you can have a drink in the pretty garden room in the lobby of the hotel.

$$$ THE TEA ROOM, The Clarence Hotel, 6–8 Wellington Quay, Temple Bar, Dublin 2; phone: 1-670-9000. Open Monday to Friday for breakfast, lunch, and dinner; Saturday and Sunday for breakfast and dinner.

The perfect place for a romantic evening. The food here is excellent—try the corn-fed chicken with morel cream or confit of duck.

$$$$ THORNTON'S, 1 Portobello Road, Dublin 8; phone: 1-454-9067; fax: 1-453-2947; e-mail: *thorntons@iol.ie* Closed Saturday lunch, Sunday, and Monday. One Michelin star.

This is Irish cuisine at its best. Game is served in season. Irish fish dishes, such as confit of salmon and roast scallop, are served fresh daily. I love the marinated salmon with cucumber and caviar. The menu also includes delicious terrines, ratatouille, and roast pig, suggesting a French influence. Be sure to end your meal with homemade ice cream or chocolate mousse.

$$ TOSCA, 20 Suffolk Street, Dublin 2; phone: 1-679-6744. Open daily from noon to midnight. The brother of Bono (lead singer of U2), owns this very popular restaurant. There are early-bird specials as well as late dinners. The food ranges from pasta to steak and fish.

$$$ UNICORN RESTAURANT, 12b Merrion Court, Merrion Row, Dublin 2; phone: 1-676-2182. Open for lunch Monday to Saturday 12:30–5 P.M., dinner Monday to Saturday 6 P.M.–11: 30 P.M. Ten percent service charge for groups over six.

There is an extensive, excellent menu in this pretty Italian restaurant with nightly specials, a good wine list, plus a very good house wine.

Encourage youth and it will prosper.
♣ —IRISH PROVERB ♣

PUBS

Most pubs are open from Monday to Saturday, 10:30 A.M.–11: 30 P.M., Sunday 12:30 P.M.–2 P.M., 4 P.M.–11 P.M. All pubs are closed on Good Friday and Christmas Day. There is not a street or a neighborhood without a few pubs, so pop in and have fun. Some are quiet and relaxed while others are bursting with patrons singing, dancing, and listening to traditional music. Even if you are not a beer drinker, try a Guinness at least once. But don't feel obligated—pubs are great for people-watching even if you don't imbibe. Guinness publishes a **Dublin Pub Trail** map, which is free at the tourist office. It lists over thirty pubs in the Dublin area. The other alternative is the **Literary Pub Crawl,** which is a wonderful group tour that goes to pubs that boasts visits from famous Irish authors.

AULD DUBLINER PUB, 17 Anglesea Street, Dublin 2; phone: 1-677-0527. This is an old-style pub with good food and traditional Irish music Sunday to Thursday from 9–11 P.M.

BAGGOT INN, 143 Lower Baggot Street, Dublin 2; phone: 1-676-1430. This is a two-story bar with music, although it is usually rock, not traditional Irish music.

THE BRAZEN HEAD, 20 Lower Bridge Street, Dublin 8; phone: 1-679-5186. This is Dublin's oldest pub—built in the 1660s—and it is always busy and touristy. There is traditional music and singing.

CAFÉ EN SEINE, 40 Dawson Street, Dublin 2; phone: 1-677-4369. This is a pub/French café with great atmosphere and good food.

DAVY BYRNE'S, 21 Duke Street, Dublin 2; phone: 1-677-5217. This is where Leopold Bloom had a gorgonzola sandwich with mustard and a glass of Burgundy wine in James Joyce's *Ulysses*. They also serve delicious Irish coffee and lunch.

DOHENY & NESBITTS, 5 Lower Baggot Street, Dublin 2; phone: 1-676-2945. One of Dublin's oldest pubs well located near Leinster House. It is always busy with lawyers, journalists, and politicians.

DUKE, 9 Duke Street, Dublin 2; phone: 1-679-9553. The Literary Pub Crawl starts here at 7:30 each evening.

KEHOE'S, 9 South Anne Street, Dublin 2; phone: 1-677-8312. This pub was a favorite of the writer Brendan Behan. It is said that he was a "drinker with a writing problem." It has a beautiful preserved '50s bar that always seems to be busy.

MOTHER REDCAP'S TAVERN, 40–48 Back Lane, Dublin 8; phone: 1-453-8306. Located next to Mother Redcap's Market. This pub opened in 1988.

MULLIGAN'S, 8 Poolbeg Street, Dublin 2; phone: 1-677-5582. This is a busy pub for journalists and locals. A real old-fashioned pub, it was featured in the Irish film *My Left Foot.*

O'DONOGHUE'S, 15 Merrion Row, Dublin 2, Phone: 1-660-7194. The famous "Dubliners" got their start at this busy pub in the 1960s. Today people are still singing and spilling out onto the street.

O'DWYER'S, 7 Lower Mount Street, Dublin 2; phone: 1-676-2887. A busy, trendy pub.

O'NEILL'S, 2 Suffolk Street; phone: 1-679-3656. This is one of Dublin's best-known and most popular pubs with excellent food served from noon until 2:30 A.M.

O'SHEA'S MERCHANT, 12 Lower Bridge Street, Dublin 8; phone: 1-679-3797. A rowdy pub with nightly singing and set dancing sessions. The food is traditional Irish.

SCRUFFY MURPHY'S, 1–2 Powers Court, Lower Mount Street, Dublin 2; phone: 1-661-5006. Open for lunch and dinner. Located near the city center and the Shelbourne and Merrion Hotels.

STAG'S HEAD, 1 Dame Street, Dublin 2; phone: 1-679-3701. Opened in 1770, an exceptional pub known for its good food and friendly staff.

SEAN O'CASEY, 105 Marlborough Street, Dublin 1; phone: 1-874-8675. Located next to the Abbey Theatre. Named for the great Irish playwright who wrote *Juno and the Paycock* and *Plow and the Stars,* this pub is decorated with theater memorabilia. From 9 P.M. on most nights there is traditional Irish music.

THE OLD STAND, 37 Exchequer Street, Dublin 2; phone 1-677-7220. A traditional Irish pub with traditional food such as Irish stew and cabbage dishes.

THE TEMPLE BAR, 48 Temple Bar, Dublin 2; phone: 1-677-3807. This new, but made-to-look-old pub is always bursting with people, especially in good weather.

WHELAN'S, 25 Wexford Street, Dublin 2; phone: 1-478-0766 or 1-476-2420. The second oldest pub in Dublin recently received a facelift. The music here always draws a crowd.

Afternoon Tea

This is an occasion that should not be missed in Ireland. You can almost skip dinner if you have a full tea. Afternoon tea can range from a cup of tea and a scone at Brewley's to a major event in a hotel, which might include tea sandwiches of ham, egg salad, smoked salmon and cheese, a scone with cream and jam, pastries, and a choice of brewed teas. A full tea is a great idea if you are going to the theater and don't want to rush through dinner to make a 7:30 P.M. show. Afternoon tea is served from 3 until 5:30 P.M. Usually hotels serve full afternoon teas in beautiful surroundings, sometimes accompanied by music.

Late Night Snacks or Early Breakfast

JURY'S COFFEE DOCK, Jury's Hotel, Pembroke Road, Ballsbridge, Dublin 4; phone: 1-660-5000. Open twenty-three hours a day, seven days a week. For those who like to stay up late or get up very early, this is an ideal spot at all hours. They serve a full Irish breakfast and continue serving all day and until the wee hours of the morning.

For a Unique Experience

It is best to do this if you have a car because there is no public transportation to this fun restaurant/pub, and it is forty minutes from Dublin. Taxis are available, but are very expensive.

$$ JOHNNIE FOX'S PUB, The Dublin Mountains, Glencullen, County Dublin; phone: 1-295-5647; fax: 1-295-8911. Open seven nights per week, no children after 7 P.M. Closed December 25 and Good Friday; e-mail: *7nights@johnniefoxs.com*; Web site: *www.johnniefoxs.com*
  Their motto is "There are no strangers here—only friends who

have not met yet." This is an excellent seafood restaurant serving prawns, crabs, mussels, fresh salmon, oysters, lobsters, and caviar. The nightly show including traditional Irish songs and dance similar to *Riverdance* make this an unforgettable experience.

RECIPE FOR IRISH COFFEE

Put two teaspoons of brown sugar into a warmed glass; add one-third Irish whiskey and two-thirds hot, strong black brewed coffee. Fill glass almost to the top leaving just enough room to float fresh whipped cream on the top. Do not stir. Sip without stirring or using a spoon.

4. The Calendar:
Festivals and Special Events

Dublin is crowded with events throughout the year—following are the ones I find unique. A complete list of local events is available at the Irish Tourist Board. Remember that dates do change from year to year although the months of the events usually do not.

JANUARY

JANUARY 1, New Year's Day is a public holiday.
DUBLIN INTERNATIONAL THEATRE SYMPOSIUM, Trinity College, Dublin 2; phone: 1-280-0544. e-mail: *panpan@iol.ie.* Year-round.
JANUARY SALES, be at your favorite store early for the best buys.
JANUARY 6, Christmas lights of Dublin are turned off.
CONCERTS at the National Concert Hall, Earlsfort Terrace, Dublin 2; phone: 1-417-0000, fax: 1-475-1507; Web site: *www.nch.ie*
HORSE RACES Leopardstown Racecourse operates most of the year with twenty-three meetings, and continues through March 31. Phone: 1-289-3607; fax: 1-289-2634; Web site: *www.leopardstown.com*

FEBRUARY

SIX NATIONS RUGBY INTERNATIONAL CHAMPIONSHIPS, 62 Lansdowne Road, Ballsbridge, Dublin 4. Call or fax the Irish Rugby Football Union. Phone: 1-668-4601; fax: 1-660-5640. The six nations are Ireland, Scotland, England, Wales, France, and Italy.

MARCH

ARKLOW MUSIC FESTIVAL, Arklow, County Wicklow, near Dublin
ST. PATRICK'S DAY celebrations are held all over Ireland on March
17. There are usually parades, bands, floats, and fun. For information,
phone: 1-676-3205; fax: 1-676-3208; e-mail: *info@paddyfest.ie*; Web site:
www.paddyfest.ie A fun-filled St. Patrick's Day Web site: *www.guinness.com*
Includes drink recipes, games, and details on winning a pub in Ireland. Another Web site for this special day is *www.marlo.com.* This one
enables you to send St. Patrick greeting cards via the Web. It even includes green fireworks.
**GUINNESS TEMPLE BAR FLEADH FESTIVAL OF TRADITIONAL
MUSIC,** Temple Bar Information Center; phone: 1-671-5717. This is a
three-day traditional music festival in honor of St. Patrick's Day. Many
performances are indoors, but some are held outdoors and most are
free.
IRISH KENNEL CLUB'S ST. PATRICK'S DAY DOG SHOW, National
Show Centre, Cloghran, near Dublin Airport; Phone: 1-453-3300. This
is a very popular event with judging beginning at 9 a.m.
FEIS CEOIL is a classical music festival and competition for singers
and musicians. For information call 1-676-7365; fax: 1-676-7429, or
contact the Feis Ceoil Office, 37 Molesworth Street, Dublin 2.
MALAHIDE FOOD AND DRINK FESTIVAL, north of Dublin

APRIL

EASTER RACING FESTIVAL AT FAIRYHOUSE RACECOURSE, Ra-
toath, County Meath, near Dublin (held on Easter Monday).
GAELIC FOOTBALL LEAGUE FINALS, Dublin
DUBLIN FILM FESTIVAL, 1 Suffolk Street, Dublin 2. This is the very
best in Irish film-making and international film-making with many
films plus lectures. Phone: 1-679-2937; fax: 01-679-2939; e-mail:
dff@iol.ie; Web site: *www.iol.ie/dff/*
IRISH NATIONAL HUNT FESTIVAL, Punchestown Racecourse,
Naas, County Kildare, near Dublin
IRISH GRAND NATIONAL, Fairyhouse Racecourse, Ratoath, County
Meath, near Dublin.
DUBLIN GRAND OPERA SOCIETY SPRING SEASON, Dublin

MAY

INTERNATIONAL MUSIC FESTIVAL, Dublin
1,000 & 2,000 GUINNESS RACE MEETING, the Curragh Racecourse, County Kildare, near Dublin
EVENING RACE MEETING, Fairyhouse Racecourse, County Meath, near Dublin
BANK OF IRELAND PROMS at the Royal Dublin Society, Dublin
GARDEN FESTIVAL AT ROYAL HOSPITAL, Kilmainhan, County Dublin
DUBLIN MARITIME FESTIVAL, Dublin
SPRING SHOW, Royal Dublin Society Showgrounds, Dublin
COUNTY WICKLOW GARDEN FESTIVAL, throughout County Wicklow. See information in "June" below

JUNE

ADIDAS/EVENING HERALD WOMEN'S MINI MARATHON. For information call 1-670-9461. Over 30,000 women compete in this ten-kilometer charity event. It is the largest all-women race in the world. Participants can walk or run.
MUSIC IN GREAT IRISH HOUSES FESTIVAL. Throughout Ireland, classical music concerts held in the great houses.
BLOOMSDAY CELEBRATIONS, June 16, Dublin; Phone: 1-878-8547; fax: 1-878-8488; Web site: *www.jamesjoyce.ie* This day celebrates twenty-four hours in the life of Leopold Bloom, the main character in James Joyce's *Ulysses.* The exact date was June 16, 1904, and each year on that date ceremonies are also held at the James Joyce Tower in Sandycove and throughout Dublin, plus guided tours of special James Joyce sights.
IRISH DERBY WEEKEND, the Curragh Racecourse, County Kildare, near Dublin
DUBLIN ORGAN AND CHORAL FESTIVAL, Dublin
COUNTY WICKLOW INTERNATIONAL GARDENS FESTIVAL, held throughout County Wicklow in May and June. This festival is also held in the fall. Phone: 404-66058; e-mail: *wctr@iol.ie*; Web site: *www.wicklow.ie* This festival gives you the opportunity to see heritage homes and gardens that are not usually open to the public.
MARACYCLE. Thousands bike ride between Dublin and Belfast.
GARDEN OF IRELAND FESTIVAL, Arklow, County Wicklow, near Dublin

JULY

IRISH OPEN GOLF CHAMPIONSHIP. Check locations with tourist board. In 2001 it will be held in Fota Island, County Cork.

IRISH OAKS, the Curragh Racecourse, County Kildare, near Dublin

DUN LAOGHAIRE FESTIVAL, this festival is a lot of fun with its crafts sales, concerts, bands, sports events, and talent competitions.

SUMMER SCHOOL. Contact the Irish Tourist Board. Sessions are held in July and August all over Ireland and in Dublin. The Dublin sessions include Irish studies at Trinity College, acting studies at theaters and colleges, language studies, and much more.

JAMES JOYCE SUMMER SCHOOL, two weeks of lectures and seminars on Joyce's work. Newman House, 85 St. Stephen's Green, Dublin 2; phone: 1-706-8480.

JULY 4TH BARBEQUE, held at the Royal Dublin Society to celebrate American Independence Day. Ballsbridge.

GUINNESS BLUES FESTIVAL, three-day festival of Irish and international blues held all around Dublin. Phone: 1-497-0381.

EUROPEAN GOLF TOURNAMENT, K CLUB, County Kildare, near Dublin

AUGUST

EVENING RACE MEETING, Fairyhouse Racecourse, County Meath, near Dublin

RIVER LIFFEY POWERBOAT RACE, Dublin Regatta, Dublin

ROYAL DUBLIN HORSE SHOW, Kerrygold Dublin Horse Show, in the RDS (Royal Dublin Society), Ballsbridge, near center Dublin. Phone: 1-668-0866; fax: 1-660-4014. Horse lovers come from all over the world to see over two thousand horses competing in dressage and jumping. Other special events include ladies' day, awards, and grand balls held in the evening.

WICKLOW REGATTA FESTIVAL, County Wicklow, near Dublin

FATHER AND SON WORLD INVITATIONAL GOLF TOURNAMENT, County Kerry, Ireland

FLEADH CHEOIL is the major Irish summer festival for traditional music. Competitions are held for singing and instruments.

SUMMER MUSIC FESTIVAL. Free lunchtime concerts and afternoon plays held at St. Stephen's Green. Check dates with the Irish Tourist Office.

SEPTEMBER

IRISH ANTIQUE DEALER'S FAIR. This is an annual event held at the RDS Showgrounds in Ballsbridge. Contact the Irish Antique Dealer's Association, Adare, County Limerick. Phone: 61-396-409; fax: 61-396-733.

ALL-IRELAND FINALS, Gaelic Athletic Association, Croke Park, Jones Road, Dublin 3; phone: 1-836-3222. If you are interested in attending the finals, call or write for tickets the minute you read this. They sell out months in advance.

NATIONAL HERITAGE WEEK is held throughout Ireland in early September. These events highlight Ireland's national heritage sites. During the week there are lectures, exhibits, walks, and free admission to some sights.

SEARCHING FOR YOUR IRISH ANCEStors is held in both Dublin and Belfast annually. It includes researching your ancestors, lectures, tours, and entertainment.

OCTOBER

DUBLIN THEATER FESTIVAL is an outstanding festival of new plays by Irish authors. Held at theaters in Dublin during the first two weeks of October. Write to Mr. Tony O'Dalaigh, Director, 47 Nassau Street, Dublin 2; phone: 1-677-8439; fax: 1-679-7709.

DUBLIN CITY MARATHON is held the last Monday in October. Runners from Ireland and anyplace else can participate in this run through the Dublin streets. Write for entry forms: Dublin Marathon Office, 2 Clare Street, Dublin 2; phone: 1-623-2250; fax: 1-626-3757; Web site: *www.dublincitymarathon.ie*

WEXFORD OPERA FESTIVAL. Wexford is eighty miles south of Dublin. Held during the last two weeks of October, the festival features opera, classical music, and recitals.

WICKLOW MOUNTAINS AUTUMN WALKING FESTIVAL. Held the third weekend in October, experienced local guides conduct this walking festival. Call the tourist office for information, 404-66058.

OSCAR WILDE AUTUMN SCHOOL is held in Bray, County Wicklow, in late October. It celebrates the life of the Irish playwright and poet.

SAMHAIN OR HALLOWEEN PARADE. Dancers, dragons, monsters, ghosts, and more parade through the city center.

NOVEMBER

IRISH NATIONAL STAMP EXHIBITION is held early November
CHRISTMAS LIGHTS are turned on for the holiday season

DECEMBER

DUBLIN GRAND OPERA, Gaiety Theater, South King Street, Dublin 2; phone: 1-677-1717.

CHRISTMAS HORSE RACING FESTIVAL, Leopardstown Racetrack in Dublin. Phone: 1-289-3607. Five days of racing between Christmas and New Year's.

NATIONAL CRAFTS FAIR OF IRELAND. Irish craftsmen display their works at this fair held at the Royal Dublin Society. Phone: 1-867-1517; fax: 1-878-6276

DECEMBER 25 Christmas Day

DECEMBER 26 St. Stephen's Day

2002

In 2002, the accession of Brian Boru to the High Kingship of Ireland a thousand years ago will be commemorated. If you are interested in this event phone: 61-376149; fax: 61-375251; e-mail: *kincorahouse@ eircom.net*

> *There is not a way into the woods*
> *for which there is not a way out of it.*
>
> ♣ —IRISH SAYING ♣

5. Theater, Music, and Nightlife

Dublin has an active nightlife, so be sure to save some energy at the end of the day for a visit to the theater and nightclubs that pepper the city. Buy the local papers or pick up the free *Dublin Event Guide,* the *In Dublin Guide,* or the *Events of the Week Guide* for a complete list of movies, theater, clubs, music, and other city activities.

BUSKERS

Buskers—street performers—are very common around the city. Mostly poets, artists, and singers, they perform free, but appreciate contributions. Grafton Street is a popular location for groups of singers, since it is a busy pedestrian street.

NIGHTCLUBS

Hint: If you are interested in clubbing, go early. Pubs close at 11 P.M. so the clubs get very crowded with locals as well as visitors. Nightclubs usually serve until 2 or 3 A.M.

GAIETY THEATRE, South King Street, Dublin 2; phone: 1-677-1717; Open 11 P.M.–2:30 A.M. Friday and Saturday. This is a unique club with movies, and three bars with cabaret, jazz, DJs, and Latin music.

THE KITCHEN, Located next to the Clarence Hotel (of U2 fame), 6–8 Wellington Quay in Temple Bar, and it is very popular. Phone: 1-677-6178. The club is open from 11 P.M.–2 A.M. Considered one of the best clubs in the city; people like to see and be seen here.

LILLIE'S BORDELLO, Adam Court, off Grafton Street; phone: 1-679-9204. This club is popular with models, rock stars, and those who can afford the steep prices.

LOBO, Ormond Quay; phone: 1-887-2400. Open late, a fun spot for eating and people-watching.

POD (PLACE OF DANCE), 35 Harcourt Street; phone: 1-478-0225. This huge and beautiful dancehall is always filled with lively young people.

RENARDS, 23–25 South Frederick Street, Dublin 2; phone: 1-677-5876, open 11 P.M.–3 A.M. With a bouncer and velvet rope at the door, the club has that exclusive feel that is popular with business types. Open an hour later than many clubs.

RIRA, (Irish for "uproar") Dame Court, Dublin 2; phone: 1-671-1220; open 11 P.M.–2:30 A.M. A trendy crowd but laid-back vibe make this club worthwhile. Different music on different nights keeps it interesting.

SUGAR CLUB, 8 Lower Leeson Street; phone: 1-678-7188 features swing and salsa bands in a beautiful yet crowded setting.

TICKET BROKERS

HMV TICKET SHOP, 65 Grafton Street, Dublin 2; phone: 1-679-5334. Open Monday to Saturday 9 A.M.–6 P.M. They are agents for all popular music events in the city.

TICKETMASTER, phone: 1-456-9659. This is a twenty-four-hour phone service for all events that require tickets.

GOLDEN DISC, 1 Grafton Arcade, Dublin 2; phone: 1-677-1025.

THEATERS

DUBLIN THEATRE FESTIVAL AND FRINGE FESTIVAL The Dublin Festival and Fringe Festival are held annually in September or October. Events are held around the city in places such as art galleries, stadiums, pubs, and warehouses, and tickets can usually be obtained at the last minute. Phone: 1-874-8525 for reservations and tickets.

Dublin's "Off-Broadway"

We call it Off-Broadway; in Ireland it is the alternative to the traditional theater. There are new and excellent shows being offered at lower prices in smaller theaters.

ANDREWS LANE THEATRE, 9–17 Andrew's Lane, Dublin 2; phone: 1-679-5720

SAMUEL BECKETT CENTRE, Trinity College; phone: 1-679-3488

THE PROJECT, East Essex Street, Temple Bar, Dublin 2; phone: 850-260-027

TIVOLI THEATRE, Francis Street, Dublin 8; phone: 1-454-4472

Traditional Theater

Ireland and especially Dublin has a great number of theaters with an extraordinary variety of shows. Some people go to London or New York to see as much theater as possible. Now you can include Dublin. *Riverdance* was first performed there to enormous crowds and acclaim before it traveled the world. *Dancing at Lughnasa,* another huge Broadway success, originally opened in Dublin. Now is your chance to experience Irish theater before it hits the States.

ABBEY THEATRE, 26 Lower Abbey Street, Dublin 1; phone 1-878-7222. Web site: *www.abbeytheatre.ie.* Box Office: Monday to Saturday 10:30 A.M.–7 P.M., Shows: Monday to Saturday 8 P.M., Saturday matinees at 2:30 P.M. The Abbey opened in 1904 under the direction of W.B. Yeats. It is the home of Ireland's national theater company, and most of the performances are of Irish plays. In 1951 the theater burned down and was rebuilt and reopened in 1966. Many shows that originate at the Abbey go on to New York or London's West End theaters. The Abbey also houses the smaller **Peacock Theatre,** phone: 1-878-7222. The Peacock is a 150-seat theater, which stages plays of a more experimental nature. They also perform plays in Irish.

ANDREWS LANE THEATRE, 9–17 Andrews Lane, Dublin 2; phone: 1-679-5720. A fairly new theater presenting contemporary Irish works. There is also a smaller theater that stages more experimental work.

CITY ARTS CENTRE, 23–25 Moss Street, Dublin 2; phone: 1-677-0643; Web site: *www.iol.ie/cityarts*. Presents dance, music, and theater productions.

GATE THEATRE, 1 Cavendish Row, Parnell Square; phone: 1-874-4045. Box Office: Monday to Saturday 10 A.M.–7 P.M. Shows: Monday to Saturday 8 P.M. The Gate Theatre and the Abbey Theatre are considered on an equal par, both presenting modern and classical plays. The theater was founded in 1928.

GAIETY THEATRE, South King Street, Dublin 2, Phone: 1-677-1717. This theater usually has musical comedy, drama, and Opera Ireland concerts. On Friday and Saturday nights from 11:30 P.M. (when the doors open) the fun begins with noisy and exciting concerts. Call ahead for the schedules. *See* "Nightclubs."

HQ @ THE HOT PRESS HALL OF FAME, 57 Middle Abbey Street, Dublin 2; phone: 1-878-3345. Open 7:30 P.M.–2 A.M. This is a new club hosting Irish and international acts.

THE NATIONAL CONCERT HALL This is the home of the National Symphony Orchestra of Ireland. Earlsfort Terrace, Dublin 2; phone: 1-417-0077; fax: 1-417-0078; e-mail: *info@nch.ie*; Web site: *www.nch.ie* For box office reservations, phone 1-417-0000, open 11 A.M.–7 P.M. There is wheelchair seating for four people—when making reservations advise the ticket agent if you need one of the seats. Located on the southeast corner of St. Stephen's Green on the former grounds of the University College of Dublin, it became the National Concert Hall in 1981. This magnificent concert hall is home to the National Symphony Orchestra and the Concert Orchestra plus visiting international orchestras and artists. Along with classical music they host Gilbert and Sullivan evenings, opera, and jazz concerts.

Pre-concert dinner is served at the beautiful Terrace Restaurant Monday to Friday at 6 P.M. Lunch is served Monday to Friday from 11 A.M. to 2:30 P.M.

OLYMPIA THEATRE, 72 Dame Street; phone: 1-677-7744. This theater is Dublin's oldest—it opened in 1749 as the "Star of Erin Music Hall." Performances of ballet, music, drama, and vaudeville are held here. On Friday nights from midnight to 2 A.M. they have "Midnight at the Olympia" featuring country, disco, rock, or jazz music.

THE POINT THEATRE, East Link Bridge, North Wall Quay, Dublin 1; phone: 1-836-3633. This new theater has seats for three thousand people and holds rock and pop concerts and international performers.

ROYAL DUBLIN SOCIETY (RDS), Merrion Road, Ballsbridge, Dublin 2; phone: 1-668-0866. The box office is open at different times depending on the event. The RDS is best known for its annual Dublin Horse Show held each August. The arena can hold more than six thousand people and is used for major concerts.

> *May the face of every good news and the back of*
> *Every bad news be towards us.*
> ♣ —IRISH BLESSING ♣

TRADITIONAL IRISH MUSIC

Music and singing are an important part of Irish life. Some pubs and hotels have music sessions every evening. Usually informal with fiddlers, flautists, pipers, and bodrhan players, feel free to join in and sing if you know the words. Some pubs charge a cover but others just expect you to buy some drinks. Always ask so you won't be surprised when your check arrives.

THE TRADITIONAL MUSIC ASSOCIATION: COMHALTAS CEÓLTOIRÍ ÉIREANN, 32 Belgrave Square, Monkstown; phone: 1-280-0295; fax: 1-280-3759. There are regular events held here, but call for the schedule, which changes often. They also organize traditional Irish dance sessions called **Ceilis** every Friday night at 9:30 P.M. Dancing lessons (for a small fee) begin at 8 P.M. so you can be ready to dance by 9:30.

CEOL—IRISH TRADITIONAL MUSIC CENTRE, Smithfield Village, Smithfield, Dublin 7; phone: 1-817-3820; fax: 1-817-3821, e-mail: *info@ceol.ie*; Web site: *www.ceol.ie.* Open daily all year Monday to Saturday 9:30 A.M.–6 p.m., Sundays noon–6 P.M. Buses and trains go to Smithfield Village from the city center. *Ceol* is the Irish word for "music." Admire the instruments on display and listen to musicians playing them. The center's film presentation shows the types of music played in each part of Ireland and is especially informative. Be sure to stop by the research area for information on where you can hear traditional music in Ireland. Attached to Ceol is Chief O'Neill's café and bar, which serves traditional Irish food.

Some Well-known Places to Hear Good Traditional Irish Music

ABBEY TAVERN, Howth, Dublin; phone: 1-839-0307. It is touristy but lots of fun and they are always busy, so you must reserve ahead. You can also have dinner here, but make reservations. You can book for dinner, dinner and the show, or just the show.

BURLINGTON HOTEL, Upper Leeson Street, Dublin 2; phone: 1-660-5222. Dinner begins at 7 P.M. and the show follows at 8 P.M. nightly from May to October. Ask about the four-course dinner and show package.

COMHALTAS CEOLTÓIRÍ EIREANN, 32 Belgrave Square, Monkstown, Dublin; phone: 1-280-0295. No reservations required for the performances held here. This is the home of the Irish Cultural Organization and they work to encourage Irish traditional music and Ceili dancing. During the summer, authentic Irish shows are performed with traditional music, song, and dance.

JURY'S IRISH CABARET, Pembroke Road, Ballsbridge, Dublin 4; phone: 1-660-5000. Call for reservations for dinner and the show or just the show. This is Ireland's longest-running show that features Irish music, Broadway tunes, ballads, and stories, and the audience is encouraged to join in. It's great fun.

O'DONOGHUE'S, 15 Merrion Row, Dublin 2; phone: 1-660-7194. Located near St. Stephen's Green and Merrion Street. There is usually singing every night at this always-busy pub. The famous Dubliners singing group first started singing here in the 1960s.

OLIVER ST. JOHN GOGARTY, 58/59 Fleet Street, Dublin 2, Temple Bar; phone: 1-671-1822. You can hear traditional music nightly from 9 P.M.–11 P.M., Saturday from 3:30 P.M.–7 P.M. and Sunday from 12:30 P.M.–3 P.M.

SEAN O'CASEY, 105 Marlborough Street, Dublin 1; phone: 1-874-8675. Traditional Irish music played and sung almost nightly from 9 P.M. This pub is only one street away from the Abbey Theatre, so be sure to stop by after the show.

MUSICAL PUB CRAWL, Oliver St. John Gogarty's (upstairs) at the corner of Fleet and Anglesea Streets in Temple Bar, 7:30 P.M. every night in summer from the first Friday in May to the last Saturday in October. During the winter months of November, February, March, and April the Pub Crawl is held on Friday and Saturday nights only. Purchase your ticket when you meet the group or at the Dublin Tourist Office. E-mail: *info@musicalpubcrawl.com*. Two professional musicians who sing and tell stories of Irish music lead the Musical Pub Crawl. The tour visits several pubs and lasts two and a half hours.

MOVIE THEATERS AND FILM

Old classic Irish films and more recent releases are shown throughout the city. The excellent ones that have been exported to the United States and the world include *In the Name of the Father, My Left Foot, Michael Collins, The Crying Game, Waking Ned Devine, The Field,* and *The Butcher Boy*. Three of the old classics are *Ryan's Daughter, The Quiet Man,* and *The Informer,* which was filmed in Dublin.

VIRGIN MULTIPLEX, Parnell Centre, Parnell Street; phone: 1-872-8400. This is a twelve-plex theater.

IMAX CINEMA, phone: 1-817-4200; shows documentaries on a huge screen.

IRISH FILM CENTRE, 6 Eustace Street, Temple Bar; Phone: 1-679-3477; shows classic films as well as new and independent Irish films. There is also a bar, bookshop, and café in the complex.

SAVOY CINEMA, Upper O'Connell Street; Phone: 01 874 6000

6. Sights

Dublin is one of the great cities of Europe with many "must see" sights including wonderful walks, bridges, parks, museums, restaurants, pubs, churches, and castles. A week in Dublin gives you a taste for a return trip. If you are traveling with children you may have to eliminate some sights but there is plenty for families to enjoy (*see* chapter 11).

♣ Before heading out to see these wonderful sights please be sure that what you want to see is open on that day. Many museums are closed on Mondays.

♣ The River Liffey divides the city into north and south sides. I have organized this section accordingly. You may consider paying the small fee for one of the many excellent guided walking tours offered through hotels and tourist companies.

IF YOU HAVE ONE DAY IN DUBLIN

Start your first day in Dublin with one of the excellent local one-hour **bus tours** to get an overview of the city. Then head out on your own.

Begin with a walking tour on the **south side of the Liffey** at **Trinity College.** Trinity College is the oldest university in Ireland, dating from 1592. See the priceless **Book of Kells** with its magnificent illustrated manuscripts, the **Long Room Library,** wander the campus, go to the bookstore, and if there is a guided tour on the day you visit, I suggest taking it. The tour is conducted outside and the guide points out the statues and describes the history of the college. Have a pub lunch next or perhaps lunch at the famous Bewley's Oriental Café on Grafton Street. After lunch continue to **The Bank of Ireland** across the street from Trinity College. This is one of the great eighteenth-century landmarks. Continue along Dame Street to **Dublin Castle,** which dates back to the thirteenth century. Then see Dublin's two beautiful cathedrals, **St. Patrick's Cathedral** and **Christ Church Cathedral.** If you have time and energy stop and see the **Dublinia** Exhibit at Christ Church. Walk up the pedestrian **Grafton Street** past lovely shops, bookstores, an open-air flower market, and then stop for a well-deserved cup of tea at the famous Dublin institution **Bewley's Oriental Café** on Grafton Street. Walk to the end of Grafton Street toward **St. Stephen's Green**. Continue to the end of the street and make a left going toward the famous **Shelbourne Hotel** where the Irish Constitution was signed. Continue on a few more streets to **Merrion Square** with its beautiful Georgian buildings. Walk to the end of the square to see the full-size statue of **Oscar Wilde** reclining on a boulder. If you are staying overnight try to see something at the **Abbey Theatre.**

> *Let your anger set with the sun*
> *And not rise again with it.*
> ♣ —IRISH PROVERB ♣

IF YOU HAVE TWO DAYS IN DUBLIN

After the busy first day you will need to take it a bit easier. Today do whatever you missed on the first day (a bit more leisurely), but add the following:

Wander around the **Temple Bar** area. Temple Bar is one of the oldest parts of the city, which has recently been renovated from a run-down section to a cultural and very "in" place. There are new and expensive apartments, hotels, pubs, restaurants, cafés, galleries, theaters, art centers, and the Irish Film Centre. **The Ark,** a cultural center for children, is also located there, as is the DesignYard, with galleries and craft shops. Try to stop in a bookstore or two, and do a little shopping in the new, trendy shops. Stop for lunch at a local pub or a drink at the Clarence Hotel. If you are staying overnight be sure to have reservations for dinner and/or theater tickets.

IF YOU HAVE THREE DAYS IN DUBLIN

Be sure you have seen all of Day One and Day Two sights and then set off for the **north side of the Liffey.** Start your day at **O'Connell Street,** named after Daniel O'Connell, Ireland's nineteenth-century leader. See the statue of Parnell. Visit the **GPO,** the General Post Office, and send a postcard or two. Look for the bullet marks on the wall from the Easter Rising of 1916. If you are looking for souvenirs this is the street to stop and buy a Dublin T-shirt, or anything else that looks interesting in one of the many shops along the way. Continue on to the **Dublin Writers Museum,** the **Gate Theatre,** and perhaps the **Hugh Lane Art Gallery.** After lunch visit the **James Joyce Center,** then **St. Mary's Pro Cathedral** and the **Abbey Theatre.** There is still a lot more to do, but maybe you want to relax and wander through one of the outstanding museums. Or just stroll. That's one of my favorite things to do because it gives you a chance to people-watch and perhaps find something special on your own. By the third day you have a feel for your surroundings and I think it is fun not be programmed, but to start experimenting. If you do need an idea of what to do next, you can continue your sightseeing at the **Custom House,** the **Old Jameson Distillery,** perhaps on to a museum, or afternoon tea in a beautiful hotel.

IF YOU HAVE FOUR DAYS OR MORE IN DUBLIN

Be sure you have seen all the above sights. There are many more things to see that are described in this book, but you cannot do it all on one trip. See what interests you, or perhaps rent a car or plan your day with a train trip, a local bus tour or a location reached via the **DART.** See the following section and chapter 12 ("Day Trips") for additional information. It's nice to get out of town once you have seen a city. It gives you an entirely different outlook and opinion of the country. Here are some suggestions for nearby activities for Day Four and beyond:

Take the DART train and go **south** to the suburbs of **Dun Laoghaire, Sandycove** with its James Joyce Martello Tower, have lunch in a pub then continue to **Dalkey** and **Killiney.**

Or go **north** on the DART to the fishing village of **Howth,** have lunch, and continue on to **Malahide** with its castle, **Donabate** and **Newbridge House,** and then back to Dublin.

The more days you have the farther afield you can go. I have given you sights, but if you are in Dublin and love sports, consider a round of golf, the races, or fishing. It's all possible in this compact and interesting city and country.

Do not resist getting old, many are denied the privilege.
♣ —IRISH PROVERB ♣

SIGHTS

South Side of the Liffey

BANK OF IRELAND, Foster Green (near College Green), opposite Trinity College, Dublin 2; phone: 1-671-1488. Open Tuesday to Friday 10 A.M.–4 P.M. This is now a museum with exhibits of Irish banking and Irish history spanning the last two hundred years. The building was built in 1729 for the House of Commons and the House of Lords. Visit the chambers that were the House of Lords to see the tapestries, carved oak paneling, and eighteenth-century crystal chandelier. The tapestry depicts the Protestant victories in Londonderry in 1689 and the Battle of the Boyne in 1690. The original Bank of Ireland opened on June 25, 1783, and was located at Mary's Abbey. It moved to the ex-Parliament house to become the Bank of Ireland in 1804. Noted Dublin writer Eamonn MacThomais conducts guided tours on Tuesdays. Tours are conducted at 10:30, 11:30, and 1:45 every Tuesday. Arrive ten minutes before the tour is scheduled to begin. Reservations are not required. There is a branch of the Bank of Ireland located in the banking hall plus an exhibit entitled "The Story of Banking."

THE CHESTER BEATTY LIBRARY AND GALLERY OF ORIENTAL ART. Located in the Clock Tower of Dublin Castle, Dublin 2; phone: 1-407-0750; fax: 1-407-0760; e-mail: *info@cbl.ie*; Web site: *www.cbl.ie*. Open Tuesday to Friday 10 A.M.–5 P.M., Saturday 11 A.M.–5 P.M., Sunday 1 P.M.–5 P.M. Admission free. The Silk Road Café and shop are open during gallery hours. Sir Alfred Chester Beatty, an American of Irish descent, moved back to Ireland in 1953 and in 1956 donated this outstanding collection of rare books, Islamic and Chinese art, early Christian manuscripts, paintings, and other works to the Irish nation. It is one of the world's great private art collections with more than twenty-two thousand pieces. The manuscripts in the collection are old and rare including copies of the Koran. There are works dating from the third century, and parts of the Books of Numbers and Deuteronomy that date from A.D. 150. There are also snuff bottles from China made of mother-of-pearl, jade, and porcelain.

CHRIST CHURCH CATHEDRAL, *See* chapter 7, "Museums and Churches"

CITY HALL, Lord Edward Street, Cork Hill, Dublin 2; phone: 1-679-6111; open weekdays 9 A.M.–1 P.M., 2:15 P.M.–5 P.M. The City Hall was originally the Royal Exchange and was built between 1769 and 1779. In 1852 it was taken over by the Dublin Corporation, where the City Council has conducted its meetings ever since. The Corporation has been in existence since 1192. Lord Mayors of Dublin have been elected annually since 1665 and each July the City Council members elect the mayors. The Rotunda, which houses statues of Daniel O'Connell and Henry Grattan and other famous historic Irish figures, is open to the public. During the Easter Rising City Hall was seized by the insurgents.

DUBLIN CASTLE, Dame Street, Dublin 2; phone: 1-677-7129; fax 1-679-7831. Open Monday to Friday 10 A.M.–5 P.M., Saturday, Sunday, and bank holidays 2–5 P.M. On the instructions of King John the building of Dublin Castle began in 1205 and was completed in 1213. Dublin Castle was the center of English rule over Ireland for centuries, until Ireland became independent in 1922. Guided tours are conducted through the grounds and **State Apartments** of the Castle. It is well worth taking a tour to see the beautiful rooms with Waterford crystal chandeliers hanging over gorgeous Donegal carpets. The tour is the only way to see the apartments. There are paintings, mirrors, and ornate furniture to literally feast your eyes on. The apartments were the homes of the British Viceroys. The last Viceroy was Lord Fitzalan in 1922. A few of the outstanding apartments are the **Apollo Room,** the **Round Room,** and the **Wedgwood Room.** Don't miss **St. Patrick's Hall** with its hand-painted ceiling and pillars. The ceiling paintings show the relationship between England and Ireland. Irish presidents are inaugurated in St. Patrick's Hall. Today Dublin Castle is used for government offices. While at the Castle be sure to visit the **Royal Chapel,** also called the **Church of the Holy Trinity.** It is on the Castle grounds. The chapel was completed in 1814 and was originally an Anglican Church. In 1943 it became a Catholic Church.

DUBLIN CIVIC MUSEUM, *see* chapter 7, "Museums and Churches"

DUBLINIA, Christ Church Place at High Street, Dublin 8; phone: 1-679-4611. Open: April to September daily 10 A.M.–5 P.M., October through March, Monday to Saturday 11 A.M.–4 P.M., Sunday 10 A.M.–4:30 P.M. Wheelchair accessible. Café and souvenir shop. Admission charge includes entrance to Christ Church Cathedral. Christ Church Cathedral is linked by a bridge to the Synod Hall, which now houses Dublinia, the exhibition of Old Dublin's history from Strongbow's time up to the sixteenth century (1170–1540). The exhibits include an illuminated Medieval Maze complete with sights, sounds, and smells from the arrival of the Anglo-Normans in 1170 to the 1530s, when the monasteries were closed. Then there are exhibits of the daily life of the times. You can climb the ninety-six steps to the top of the Church of St. Michael's Tower for a view of the city.

FITZWILLIAM SQUARE Located south of Merrion Square and east of St. Stephen's Green, it is the smallest and last-built (between 1791 and 1825) of Dublin's beautiful Georgian squares. It is also the most residential. Only residents of the square can use the beautiful gardens.

 **GRAFTON STREET** Grafton Street is a beautiful pedestrian street that runs from College Green to St. Stephen's Green. It became a pedestrian street in 1982; prior to that it was a busy traffic street. After closing it to vehicular traffic it was repaved with redbrick. Now Grafton Street is lined with beautiful shops, department stores, restaurants, and smaller streets that go off the main street. The smaller streets are Duke, South Anne, Nassau, Clarendon, and Wicklow. They too are lined with beautiful shops. Along Grafton Street you will find street performers, musicians, and a flower market. Some of the department stores on Grafton Street are Arnotts, Brown Thomas, Marks and Spencer, and Weir's Jewelers. Also on Grafton Street is the Beweley's Oriental Café. Be sure to stop there for a cup of tea or coffee and a scone. You can also buy packages of tea and coffee, teapots, and other souvenirs to take home. The "tart with the cart," Molly Malone stands at the College Green end of the street.

GUINNESS HOPSTORE, Crane Street, off St. James Street. Open Monday to Friday 10 A.M.–4:30 P.M. all year. Closed Christmas and bank holidays. Admission charge. This building is a converted nineteenth-century warehouse. There is an audiovisual show, bar, and shop.

GUINNESS STOREHOUSE, St. James Gate, Dublin 8; phone: 1-408-4800; fax: 1-408-4965, Web site: *www.guinness.ie*; e-mail: *dublinhopstore @guinness.com* Wheelchair accessible. The storehouse is located at St. James Gate and the Hop Store is on Crane Street just off St. James Street. Open January through September Monday to Saturday 9:30 A.M.–5 P.M., Sunday and bank holidays 10:30 A.M.–4: 30 P.M. Phone for

opening times, October through December. Arthur Guinness founded
the brewery in 1759, and it has remained in the family ever since. At
one time Guinness was the largest brewery in the world. The Guinness
family has been very philanthropic and over the years has helped to
restore many of the city's parks and hospitals. The new storehouse,
opened late 2000, is located in the six-story fermentation building.

**IRISH MUSEUM OF MODERN ART/ROYAL HOSPITAL KILMAIN-
HAM,** *See* chapter 7, "Museums and Churches"

IRISH HERALDIC MUSEUM, *See* chapter 7, "Museums and
Churches"

KILMAINHAM GAOL, Inchicore Road, Kilmainham, Dublin 8;
phone: 1-453-5984; fax: 1-453-2037. Open daily April through September 9:30 A.M.–6 P.M., October through March, Monday to Friday
9:30 A.M.–5 P.M. Wheelchair accessible. Admission by guided tour
only. There is an audiovisual show and an excellent museum, which
gives an overview of the history of uprisings in Ireland. *In the Name of
the Father* was filmed here. The jail, or gaol, was opened in 1796, and
by 1798 political prisoners including rebellion leaders were already
joining criminals such as debtors. The prison was overcrowded and
cold, and more than 140 prisoners were executed here. Leaders of all
the 1798, 1803, 1848, 1867, and 1916 uprisings against the British
were confined in this jail. Fourteen of the fifteen executions that took
place in 1916 between May 3 and May 12, after the Easter Uprising,
took place here. The last political prisoner was Eamon de Valera, who
later served as Ireland's prime minister and president. The prison
closed in 1924 and it fell into disrepair. In 1960 a group of veterans
from the 1916 Uprising decided it should be restored. The restoration took twenty years to complete and it was finally opened as a national monument. In the main courtyard is the *Asgard,* which was the
yacht owned by Erskine Childers, author of *Riddle of the Sands* and a
Republican who was executed during the Civil War in 1922. The *Asgard* was used to smuggle rifles from Germany to Howth for the Irish
Volunteers in July 1914, and many of those rifles were used in the
1916 Uprising.

LEINSTER HOUSE, Kildare Street, Dublin 2; phone: 1-618-3166.
Open when parliament is not in session. Located next to the National
Library and the National Museum, Leinster House was designed by

Richard Cassels and built between 1745 and 1747 for James Fitzgerald, the twentieth Earl of Kildare. In 1766 the earl became the first duke of Leinster. **Ireland's parliament,** Oireachtas na hEireann, meets here. Leinster House is where the Irish Lower House of Representatives (Dail Eireann) and the Upper House Senate (Seanad Eireann) meet. Parliament meets for ninety days a year. If you want to see a debate and they are in session, you can obtain tickets at the Kildare Street gates. You must produce your passport and go through security in order to enter.

THE LIBERTIES The Liberties was an area outside the walls of medieval Dublin, which is now a walk through Dublin's earliest history. The area is south and west of Christ Church Cathedral, Fishamble Street, Werburgh Street, Bride Street, and Bridgefoot Street. Within this neighborhood are the two major cathedrals, St. Patrick's and Christ Church; St. Werburgh's and St. Audoen's Churches; Marsh's Library and many other interesting sights including the Iveagh and Mother Redcap Markets. During the nineteenth century much of this area became slums, but recently it has been semi-restored with new housing.

MANSION HOUSE, Dawson Street. Not open to the public except for special events. If you are in Dublin during one of these events, try to go since it is the only way to see the beautiful interior of the mansion. The Mansion House was built in 1705 by Joshua Dawson and was eventually sold by him to the Dublin Corporation for 3,500 pounds. It became the official residence of the Lord Mayor of Dublin in 1713. The Round Room of the mansion is where the first Irish Parliament met on January 21,1919.

MARSH'S LIBRARY, St. Patrick's Close, Dublin 8; phone and fax: 1-454-3511; Web site: *www.marshlibrary.ie*; e-mail *keeper@marshlibrary.ie*. Open Monday, Wednesday, Thursday, and Friday from 10 A.M.–5 P.M., Saturday from 10:30 A.M.–12:45 P.M. Closed Sunday and Tuesday. Donation requested. Located behind St. Patrick's Cathedral. This is a *must* for anyone who loves books. The Archbishop of Dublin, Narcissus Marsh, founded Ireland's oldest library in 1701, which opened in 1707. Archbishop Marsh died in 1713 and was buried in St. Patrick's Cathedral. Sir William Robinson designed the library as well as the Royal Hospital Kilmaninham. There are more than 25,000 books and rare manuscripts on view in this beautiful library. Many of the books are on theology, medicine, maps, ancient history, and French literature, as well as books in Hebrew, Greek, Arabic, Russian, and Latin. The library also has some of the first books printed in England.

There is also a collection of manuscripts including one written in Latin in 1400 on *Lives of the Irish Saints.*

(**Hint:** The library is kept cold to protect the manuscripts, so bring a sweater.)

Delmas Conservation Bindery is located at the library. They restore, repair, and rebind rare books, maps, and manuscripts.

 **MERRION SQUARE** Merrion Square was built in 1762 and is the most beautiful Georgian square in Dublin. Today there are plaques on many of the doors indicating who lived there and when. Daniel O'Connell lived at number 58 Merrion Square; Oscar Wilde lived at number 1 from 1855 to 1878. It is now the American College in Dublin. W. B. Yeats lived at numbers 52 and 82. The square has beautiful green, blue, yellow, and red Georgian doors, ornate door-knockers, and now houses many offices. Opposite the west side of the square is **Leinster House** with an obelisk commemorating the founders of the Irish State (*see* "Leinster House" on pages 93–94). **Merrion Square Gardens,** adjacent to Merrion Square, are beautiful with walks, flowers, a playground, statues, and memorials. The most interesting statue is the one of Oscar Wilde located at the corner of the garden. He is reclining on a rock and is dressed in a blue suit with red collar and cuffs. **The National History Museum** and **Government Buildings** are also located in Merrion Square. **The Government Buildings** are on Upper Merrion Street. Tours are given on Saturday from 10:30 A.M.–3: 30 P.M. This building houses the offices of the Taoiseach (pronounced tea-shock), the Irish Prime Minister. **The National Gallery** is also on Merrion Square. (*See* chapter 7 "Museums and Churches.")

NATIONAL LIBRARY OF IRELAND, Kildare Street, Dublin 2; phone: 1-603-0200; fax: 1-676-6690; Web site: *www.nli.ie.* Free admission. Open January through October, December, Monday 10 A.M.–9 P.M., Tuesday, Wednesday 2–9 P.M., Thursday, Friday 10 A.M.–5 P.M., Saturday 10 A.M.–1 P.M. Closed Sunday and the month of November. Opened in 1890, this is an outstanding library filled with volumes of Irish literature, first editions, and archives of Irish history. As so much else in Dublin this library is featured in James Joyce's *Ulysses.*

NATIONAL PHOTOGRAPHIC ARCHIVE, Meeting House Square, Temple Bar, Dublin 2; phone: 1-603-0371; e-mail: *photoarchive@nli.ie*; Web site: *www.nli.ie/fr_arch.htm.* Free admission. This library opened in 1997 to house the photographic archives of the National Library. It currently has over one million photographs from the Irish countryside, towns, cities, individuals, and political events. It also has photographic exhibitions.

NEWMAN HOUSE, 85–86 St. Stephen's Green, Dublin 2; phone: 1-706-7422; fax: 1-706-7211. Call for opening days and times. There is an admission fee, which includes a tour and a video presentation on the history of Newman House. Newman House is made up of two Georgian houses, which have been restored and are gorgeous. The first national synod of Catholic Bishops to be convened since the seventeenth century was held in Thurles in 1850, and it was decided to establish a Catholic University in Dublin, which opened in 1853. Dr. John Henry Newman, later to become Cardinal Newman, was asked to become its first rector. The University was under the control of the Jesuits until 1908, when it became part of the National Universities of Ireland and it is now part of University College, Dublin. James Joyce was a student at Catholic University from 1899–1902. Other famous students were Padraig Pearse, a leader of the 1916 Uprising, and Eamon de Valera, who became president of Ireland. **Iveagh Gardens:** Open daily. This is a little gem of a garden located behind the Newman House and reached via Earlsfort Terrace or Harcourt Street. Unfortunately, many overlook it because of the high walls surrounding it.

POWERSCOURT TOWNHOUSE, *See* chapter 9, "Shopping"

SHELBOURNE HOTEL, 27 St. Stephen's Green; phone: 1-676-6471. The Shelbourne Hotel is a deluxe hotel in the center of Dublin. *See* chapter 2, "Where to Stay," for hotel description. I mention the Shelbourne in this section because the Irish Constitution was drafted there in 1922. The staff is used to people just walking into the lobby to look around. I recommend it. If you have time or tired feet, stop in the lounge for a cup of tea or a drink. Although newly renovated, this is a wonderful, old hotel. Coming out of the front door of the hotel, turn left toward Merrion Square and you will pass a small **Huguenot Cemetery,** established in 1693 for the French Protestant refugees who settled in Dublin.

ST. ANNE'S CHURCH, *See* chapter 7, "Museums and Churches"

St. Audoen's Churches, *See* chapter 7, "Museums and Churches"

St. Patrick's Cathedral, *See* chapter 7, "Museums and Churches"

St. Stephen's Green, Originally an open common and enclosed in 1663, it was opened to the public in 1877. Sir Arthur Guinness paid for the landscaping in 1880. There is a memorial arch known as Fusiliers Arch at the top of Grafton Street, which commemorates the 212 Royal Dublin Fusiliers who fought in the Boer War, which began on October 11, 1899, and ended with the Peace of Vereeniging on May 31, 1902. There are also memorials dedicated to W. B. Yeats, James Joyce, Countess Markievicz, Wolfe Tone, and also to those who died during the great potato famine. There is a playground, a lake with ducks to feed, a Victorian bandstand for free summer concerts, and a wonderful garden with the names of the plants in Braille. On the north side of the Green is the Shelbourne Hotel and on the south side is Newman House.

St. Werburgh's Church, *See* chapter 7, "Museums and Churches"

Sweeney's Pharmacy, Lincoln Place. Just a bit of trivia: This pharmacy, still in business and has been since 1904, is where Leopold Bloom, the main character in James Joyce's *Ulysses,* bought a bar of lemon soap. Pick one up for yourself.

Tailor's Hall, Back Lane, Dublin 8; phone: 1-454-1786. Saved from being demolished by the National Trust, Tailor's Hall is located near Christ Church Place and is Dublin's last remaining guildhall. The assembly hall has a plaque listing the members of the guild from 1491–1841. It now houses *An Taisce,* the Irish National Trust.

Temple Bar, Dublin 2. Temple Bar Information Center, 18 Eustace Street. Open daily all year. Phone: 1-677-2255; fax: 1-677-2525; e-mail: *info@temple-bar.ie*; Web site: *www.temple-bar.ie.* Call for up-to-date listings on what's happening in the area.

Temple Bar is considered the Left Bank or Greenwich Village of Dublin. This area has become the entertainment and cultural center of Dublin. Located here are recording studios, film centers, music shops, very trendy restaurants, theaters, pubs, art galleries, loads of busy shops, boutiques, and the Hotel Clarence owned by the rock band U2. There are new and old hotels, over 150 shops, many types of ethnic restaurants, cafés, and pubs. There are also new apartment buildings in the area. Fifteen years ago Temple Bar was a rundown neighborhood, which has been completely changed to one of the trendier areas. A few of the highlights in this area are The Book Market, held every Saturday from 11 A.M.–6 P.M.; Meeting House Square with its Temple Bar Music Center; Arthouse, which is a multimedia center for the arts; Gallery of Photography; the Irish Film Center and the Irish Film Archive; the Gaiety School of Acting; the Ark, which is a cultural center for children; and the National Photographic Archive. There is also a Food Market, which takes place every Saturday from 9:30 A.M. till late afternoon. Even if you don't plan to buy any food it is worth seeing. Monies from the Irish government and the European Union have been spent in the area to build up and encourage major artistic groups to move there, and they have succeeded.

Temple Bar is well located between Trinity College and Christ Church Cathedral. For information on galleries, shows, exhibitions and all activities in the area, get in touch with the Temple Bar Information Center.

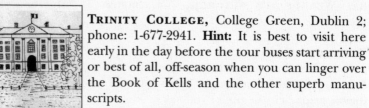

TRINITY COLLEGE, College Green, Dublin 2; phone: 1-677-2941. **Hint:** It is best to visit here early in the day before the tour buses start arriving or best of all, off-season when you can linger over the Book of Kells and the other superb manuscripts.

Trinity College is Ireland's oldest university, founded in 1592 by Queen Elizabeth I. On March 13, 1591, Thomas Smith, the mayor of Dublin, laid the first stone of Trinity College. Admission was for Protestants only, but Catholics could attend if they renounced their faith. In 1873 Trinity College lifted its religious restrictions, but Catholics did not begin attending classes there until the 1970s. Women were admitted as students to Trinity College in 1903. A few of the famous students were Douglas Hyde, Jonathan Swift, Oscar Wilde, Wolfe Tone, JM Synge, Samuel Beckett, and Bram Stoker. There are two statues at the main front entrance of the college. One is of the statesman Edmund Burke, the political writer born in 1729, and the other is of Oliver Goldsmith, the poet and playwright born in 1728.

The oldest buildings on campus are the **Rubrics,** a range of redbrick apartment buildings dating from 1700 and now used for student housing. One of the many highlights at Trinity College is the **Book of Kells** located in the **Trinity College Old Library.** The Old Library building dates from 1732, although the collection started in 1601. The library contains over half a million books and well over two thousand manuscripts. The Act of 1801 gives Trinity College the right to own a copy of every book printed in Ireland and Britain, although most are stored and not displayed. The Book of Kells is the illuminated medieval manuscript created by monks in A.D. 800. It is one of the oldest books in the world. You need a separate ticket to see this exhibit, where the pages of the book are turned daily in order to keep it in its perfect condition. It is in an enclosed case and only a certain number of people are permitted into the exhibit at a time. There is an excellent exhibition, **"Turning Darkness into Light,"** that tells about the Book of Kells and how it was produced, preparing the vellum to write on to the inks, drawings, lettering, pens, and brushes. The price of the admission also includes a visit to the **Long Room,** which contains over 200,000 of the college's oldest books. The Long Room library has one of the few remaining copies of the **1916 Proclamation of the Republic of Ireland.**

The Douglas Hyde Gallery, phone: 1-608-1116 is located in the Arts Building in Trinity College. Open Monday, Tuesday, Wednesday, and Friday 11 A.M.–6 P.M., Thursday 11 A.M.–7 P.M., Saturday 11 A.M.–4: 45 P.M. Admission free.

The Dublin Experience is located in Trinity College's Davis Theatre, phone: 1-608-1688. Open from May to October. Admission Charge. The Dublin Experience is a forty-five-minute audiovisual show tracing Dublin's history from the Vikings to the present time.

Trinity College Walking Tour. Tours are conducted May through October, Monday to Saturday 9:30 A.M.–4:30 P.M., Sunday noon–4 P.M. Tickets for the tour are approximately $8.00. As you enter Trinity College at the front entrance there are tour guides and a tour booth so you can immediately join a tour. They depart every fifteen minutes from that area and include an outdoor tour of the grounds plus entrance to the Colonnades to see the Book of Kells.

There is much to see at Trinity College, including its excellent bookstore. Stop there after seeing everything else. They sell postcards, posters, jewelry, souvenirs, and books by all the great Irish authors.

WHITEFRIAR STREET CARMELITE CHURCH, *See* chapter 7, "Museums and Churches"

North Side of the Liffey

ABBEY THEATRE, 26 Lower Abbey Street; phone: 1-878-7222. W. B. Yeats, Lady Augusta Gregory, and Edward Martyn founded the Abbey Theatre in 1904. It was originally known as the Irish National Theatre. After a fire destroyed the theater it reopened in 1966, and promotes the work of new Irish writers as well as the classics.

CUSTOM HOUSE VISITOR CENTRE, Custom House Quay, Dublin 1; phone: 1-878-7660; fax: 1-878-8013. Open year-round. James Gandon, who was also the architect of the Four Courts in Dublin, built this architecturally beautiful Georgian building in 1791. Republicans set fire to the building in 1921 and the interior was badly damaged. It reopened in 1926. The building is used for government offices and is *not open to the public*. Only the visitor center, with exhibitions on the history of the Customs House and an audiovisual video showing the history of the house, is open to tourists. A statue of Commerce by Edward Smyth is on top of the copper dome of the building. The sculptures facing the river that represent the Atlantic Ocean and the thirteen main rivers of Ireland were done by Smyth. A beautiful view of the building is from the south side of the Liffey at night when it is lit up.

DUBLIN WRITERS MUSEUM, *See* chapter 7, "Museums and Churches"

FOUR COURTS, Inns Quay; phone: 1-872-5555; free admission only when the court is in session. The Four Courts is the seat of the High Court of Justice of Ireland. The first stone was laid by the Lord Lieutenant, the Duke of Rutland on March 13, 1786 and was opened on November 3, 1796. The Four Courts actually refers to the original courts of Chancery, King's Bench, Exchequer, and Common Pleas. There are statues of Moses, Wisdom, Justice, and Mercy at the courthouse.

GATE THEATRE, *See* chapter 5, "Theater, Music, and Nightlife"

GENERAL POST OFFICE, Always referred to as the **GPO.** O'Connell Street, Dublin 1; Phone: 1-705-7000; e-mail: *pressoffice@anpost.ie*; Web site: *www.anpost.ie*. Open daily from 8 A.M.–8 P.M., Sundays from 10:30 A.M.–6: 30 P.M. This is the main post office in Dublin and the only one open on Sunday. Construction started on the GPO in 1815 and was completed in 1818. The new Republic was declared from the steps of the GPO by Patrick (Padraic) Pearse on Easter Monday 1916. Read his words on a plaque in the GPO: "We hereby proclaim the Irish Republic as a Sovereign Independent State, and we pledge our lives and the lives of our comrades-in-arms to the cause of its freedom, of its welfare, and of its exaltation among the nations."

Everyone who signed the proclamation was executed in Kilmainham Prison. In the fighting that followed the GPO was destroyed by shelling. There are still bullet holes on the facade of the GPO. The building was not reopened until July 11, 1929.

HUGH LANE MUNICIPAL GALLERY OF MODERN ART, *See* chapter 7, "Museums and Churches"

IRISH FILM CENTRE, 6 Eustace Street, Temple Bar, Dublin 2; phone: 1-679-5744; box office open from 1:30 P.M.–9 P.M., phone: 1-679-3477. Centre is free of charge from Monday through Saturday 10 A.M.–11 P.M. Films are shown daily for a fee from 2–11 P.M., **Flashback,** a film telling the history of Irish film since 1896, is free of charge and shown June to mid-September, Wednesday through Sunday at noon. The film center opened in 1991 with two movie theaters, a film archive, library, bookshop, and bar.

JAMES JOYCE CENTER, *See* chapter 7, "Museums and Churches"

MOORE STREET, Moore Street is a busy market street where Dublin traders have had open stalls for generations. During the Irish Famine there were still shops here selling food and meat. At number 20 Moore Street there was once the "Dublin Infirmary for Curing Diseases of the Skin." It opened in 1818 and closed in 1837 due to lack of funds. At number 16 Moore Street there is a plaque that commemorates where Patrick Pearse decided to surrender to the British instead of incurring more loss of civilian life during the 1916 Easter Rising.

MOUNTJOY SQUARE, One of Dublin's five Georgian Squares, Mountjoy was once considered one of the most beautiful areas in Dublin. In recent years, it has fallen into disrepair, unlike Merrion or Fitzwilliam Squares. It was built between 1792 and 1818.

O'CONNELL STREET, O'Connell Street dates from the 1700s and is one of the widest streets in Europe. The O'Connell Bridge over the

River Liffey is the major link between the north and south sides of the city. The bridge was named for Daniel O'Connell in 1882. O'Connell was a lawyer who helped to bring about the Catholic emancipation. There is also a statue of O'Connell near the bridge. There is a pedestrian island in the center of the street with many monuments. The Anna Livia Millennium Fountain was unveiled in 1988 to celebrate Dublin's Millennium. At Parnell Square and O'Connell Street is a monument to Charles Stuart Parnell.

OLD JAMESON DISTILLERY, Bow Street, Smithfield, Dublin 7, around the corner from St. Michan's Church. Tours are held daily except Christmas and Good Friday. Open 9:30 A.M.–6 P.M. Last tour is at 5 P.M. For reservations, rates, and directions, phone: 1-807-2355. Admission charge. There is a distillery tour center, which opened in 1997, to show how whiskey was invented and distilled. After the one-hour tour you get the added attraction of a glass of Jameson's Irish whiskey. After the whiskey tasting you receive a personalized certificate stating that you are an "official" taster. The tour also includes a video presentation. There is a gift shop and restaurant.

PARNELL SQUARE, This was the second Georgian Square and built in 1755. Lord Charlemont bought land here in 1762 and built his mansion. Today that home is the **Hugh Lane Municipal Gallery of Art.** Near the Gallery is the **Dublin Writers Museum.** On the south side of this square is the original **Rotunda Hospital.** The east side of the square houses the **Gate Theatre.** On the north side of the square is the **Garden of Remembrance**, which commemorates the 1916 Easter Rising. The statue by **Oisin Kelly** at the end of the garden represents the **Children of Lir.** (*See* "Statues" later in this chapter.)

PRO CATHEDRAL, (Also known as St. Mary's Pro Cathedral) *See* chapter 7, "Museums and Churches"

ROTUNDA HOSPITAL, Parnell Square, phone: 1-873-0700. The Rotunda Hospital, formally known as the Lying-in Hospital, is considered to be the oldest maternity hospital in the world, founded in the 1700s by Dr. Bartholomew Mosse. He took up midwifery in Dublin in 1742 to prevent the large number of women from dying in childbirth. The famous Gate Theatre, which was known as the Assembly Rooms when it was completed in 1786, was part of the Rotunda Hospital.

ST. MARY'S ABBEY, *See* chapter 7, "Museums and Churches"

ST. MARY'S CHURCH, *See* chapter 7, "Museums and Churches"

ST. MICHAN'S CHURCH, *See* chapter 7, "Museums and Churches"

ST. FRANCIS XAVIER CHURCH, *See* chapter 7, "Museums and Churches"

> *In some parts of Ireland the sleep which knows*
> *No waking is always followed by a wake, which knows*
> *No sleeping.*
>
> ♣ —MARY WILSON LITTLE ♣

Other Wonderful Sights

THE CHIMNEY AT SMITHFIELD VILLAGE, Smithfield Village, Dublin 7; phone: 1-676-9575; fax: 1-676-9518. Open daily Monday to Saturday 9:30 A.M.–6 P.M., Sunday 10:30 A.M.–6 P.M. Admission charge. This is Dublin's only observation tower with a 360-degree panoramic view of the city. There are two glass-enclosed observation decks reached by a glass elevator.

DRIMNAGH CASTLE, Long Mile Road, Drimnagh, Dublin 12; phone: 1-450-2530. Located 3 miles southwest of Dublin. Open April 1 to October 31 Wednesday, Saturday, and Sunday noon to 5 P.M., November 1 to March 31 Wednesday noon to 5 P.M., Sunday 2–5 P.M. Open other days by appointment only. Admission charge. If you want to see a real castle, moat and all, this is the place. Until 1954 Drimnagh Castle was the oldest continually inhabited castle in Ireland. It is the only castle in Ireland to be surrounded by a flooded moat. At the castle you can still see the Great Hall, the battlement tower with lookout posts, stables, a coach house and a formal seventeenth-century garden. Behind the garden are peacocks, hens, and a variety of birds.

BRIDGES: There are fourteen bridges spanning the River Liffy; the oldest remaining bridge dates from 1768. They were originally named for the Lords of England, but after Independence many were renamed for Irish heroes. The ones listed here are the major bridges although there are many more.

Ha'Penny Bridge, (pronounced hay penny) was the only pedestrian bridge over the River Liffey until the **Millennium Bridge** opened on December 20, 1999. The name comes from the toll that was charged to cross the bridge in the old days. It was built in 1816 and its original name was the Wellington Bridge. When you cross this or any other bridge over the Liffey you are either on the north or south side of the

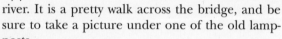

river. It is a pretty walk across the bridge, and be sure to take a picture under one of the old lamp-posts.

Another famous bridge over the Liffey is the **O'Connell Bridge.** The O'Connell Bridge had its foundation laid in 1791 and was completed in 1794. It is named for Daniel O'Connell, who fought for the emancipation of the Catholics. He helped the Catholics get the right to be elected to parliament and to be part of the government of Ireland. It was originally called the Carlisle Bridge, but was renamed in 1882.

The oldest bridge crossing the Liffey is probably the **Father Mathew Bridge.** It dates from 1014. It was repaired and replaced in 1210, 1428, and 1816. This bridge also went through three name changes and became the Father Mathew Bridge in 1938.

The **Liam Mellows Bridge** was opened in 1768 as the Queens Bridge only because Queens Street runs down to it. In 1942 it was renamed after Liam Mellows who was executed in 1922 during the Civil War.

The **East Link Toll Bridge** opened in 1985. Near this bridge is the Point Theatre, one of Dublin's newest and largest theaters, which was converted from a former shipping depot.

The **Matt Talbot Memorial Bridge** opened in 1978, and it marks the westernmost limits for shipping in the Liffey. The only other bridge between this and the sea is the East Link Toll Bridge, which can be raised to allow ships through.

CANALS: There are two canals in Dublin both built in the eighteenth century to provide passage from Dublin to the River Shannon and the middle of the country. The canals are the **Royal Canal** and the **Grand Canal.**

The construction of the **Grand Canal** started in 1756 and was completed in 1796. The canal was built to transport freight and passengers between Dublin and Shannon Harbour. The distance is about one hundred miles. The Grand Canal also links Dublin with the River Barrow. In 1960 the canal was closed to commercial traffic because the railroads took over the job of transporting goods. The canal is still used by boaters, fishermen, and pedestrians along the banks. All of the locks on the canal are still in good working order. The **Royal Canal** was completed in 1817 and also used for transport of freight and passengers. Its route was through the northern outskirts of Dublin to the Shannon. Both canals became less used after the railroad links were completed from Dublin to Shannon. The Royal Canal closed in 1961, but you can still walk along its towpaths.

For more information about the waterways of Ireland call the Irish Tourist Board and visit the Waterways Visitors Center.

Waterways Visitor Center, Grand Canal Quay, Pearse Street; phone: 1-677-7510. Open June through September daily from 9:30 A.M.–6:30 P.M., October through May Wednesday to Saturday 12:30 P.M.–5 P.M. Admission fee. Wheelchair access to ground floor only. Located near the Grand Canal Docks and built as an exhibition center showing the construction and operation of Irish waterways and canals. There is a video showing the role the canals play, plus a model of a barge working its way through the locks. The canals have also been reclaimed for pleasure cruisers. In nice weather you can take an hour or day trip along the canals.

PARKS: Hint: Don't walk in any park after dark. Like any park in the world, it is a good idea to always take precautions.

Phoenix Park, Open daily from 6:30 A.M.–11 P.M. Phoenix Park was laid out in the middle 1700s. It is the largest enclosed city park in Europe and covers 1,760 acres. Chesterfield Avenue, the main road through the park, is lighted by natural gas lamps, the only gas lights in Dublin. The president of Ireland lives in a house inside Phoenix Park called **Aras an Uachtarain.** It was built in 1751. It is now open to the public for visits on Saturday mornings at 9:30 A.M. The tour departs from the Phoenix Park Visitors Centre. Tickets are free on a first-come, first-served basis. For information, phone 1-617-1000. Also inside Phoenix Park is the residence of the American Ambassador to Ireland, the **Dublin Zoo, Ashtown Castle,** which is the oldest building in the park and is now a visitor's center. The Apostolic Nuncio lived there for many years. There are also gardens, a lake, and sports fields for football and cricket, and polo grounds. Deer also roam the park. there is the **Papal Cross** indicating where Pope John Paul II held mass when he visited Ireland in 1979. Over one million people attended the mass. There is also a monument to **General Wellington,** who was born in Dublin, which was built in 1861 to celebrate his victory at Waterloo.

Dublin Zoo, located in Phoenix Park. *See* chapter 11, "Dublin for Children"

Marlay Park, Grange Road, Rathfarnham; phone: 1-493-4208; open daily. This park begins the Wicklow Way walk. It is located in the city's southern outskirts. On Saturdays from 2–5 P.M. children can have a ride on the model steam railway located in the park. There are nature walks and crafts workshops. The shops include jewelry making, bookbinding, and furniture making.

> *May good luck be your friend,*
> *In whatever you do,*
> *And may trouble be always a*
> *Stranger to you.*
> ♣ —IRISH PROVERB ♣

Merrion Square Archbishop Ryan Park, open daily during daylight hours, located in the center of Merrion Square with gardens, fields of flowers, old Dublin street lamps, and sculptures including the full-size Oscar Wilde.

St. Anne's Park and Rose Gardens, located five miles north of Dublin. It is a very pretty park, which was once the home of the Guinness family. There are footpaths, woodlands, temples hidden between the greenery, and when you come out of the park onto the coast road you have beautiful views of North Bull Island and Howth Head. The rose gardens are in bloom from June through September.

St. Audoen's Park, located between High Street and Cook Street near Christchurch Cathedral and next to St. Audoen's Church. Open daily. This is a small park newly developed in 1987. Of interest is its boundary with the old city wall and city gates, which date from the twelfth century.

St. Edna's Park, Grange Road, Rathfarnham. The Pearse Museum is located here. (*See* chapter 11, "Museums and Churches.") A lake and nature trail are also on the park grounds.

St. Stephen's Green, *See* page 97.

Statues: There are some wonderful statues in Dublin, which you cannot miss as you walk around the city. Stop and look at them, and take a photograph in front of your favorite.

Molly Malone, Lower Grafton Street. The fishmonger supposedly lived in Dublin until she died in 1734. Dubliners know her as " the tart with the cart."

Oscar Wilde, Merrion Square. This is one of my favorites. This is a full-size color statue of Oscar Wilde reclining on a huge rock.

Children of Lir, Garden of Remembrance, Parnell Square East. The garden is dedicated to those who died fighting for Irish independence. It was built to celebrate the fiftieth anniversary of the 1916 Easter Rising. The statue by Oisin Kelly depicts the Irish fairytale about four children turned into swans by a cruel stepmother. The Garden of Remembrance is open daily.

Countess Markievicz, St. Stephen's Green. Born Constance Georgina Gore-Booth in 1868, she was the first woman elected as a member of Parliament. She became Minister of Labor in Eamon de Valera's first cabinet. She fought for the poor all her life even though she was born to great wealth. She also fought in the Easter Rising and spent time in jail on five different occasions. When she died in 1927 over a hundred thousand people filed past her coffin and de Valera gave the funeral oration at Glasnevin Cemetery.

Cuchulainn, inside the GPO on the O'Connell Street side. Irish children hear stories of Cuchulainn, a legendary Irish warrior; he is a hero. Just outside the GPO are three more statues representing **Mercury, Hibernia,** and **Fidelity.**

Ireland's Famine Memorial, Custom House Quay. This series of six life-size figures tells the story of the Great Famine of 1845–49 in Ireland. More than one million men, women, and children died during the famine and another million and a half emigrated. If you wish to contribute or want information about the famine or the fund, contact The Irish Famine Commemoration Fund, 7–9 Sweetman's Ave., Blackrock, Dublin; phone: 1-668-5355, toll-free from the U.S.: 888-854-7055; e-mail: *irishfamine@indigo.ie*; Web site: *www.irishfaminefund.ie*

Meeting Place, north end of the Ha'penny Bridge is the statue of two women shoppers sitting on a bench with their bags. In Dublin they are known as "the hags with the bags."

Anna Livia Millennium Fountain, located on the center island across from the GPO on O'Connell Street. It symbolizes the River Liffey. This statue is also known as " the floozie in the Jacuzzi."

Father Mathew Statue, Father Mathew also has a bridge named after him. He was called the "Apostle of Temperance" due to his Pioneer Total Abstinence Movement founded in 1838. He tried to convince the Irish not to drink whiskey.

Fusilier's Arch, northwest corner of St. Stephen's Green, also known as "The Traitors Arch." Commemorates the men of the Royal Dublin Fusiliers who died during the Boer War.

James Joyce Statue, located on the corner of North Earl Street.

Nelson's Pillar: the first stone of Nelson's Pillar was laid by Charles, Duke of Richmond, and Lennox, the Lord Lieutenant, on February 15, 1808. This 135-foot statue was built in memory of Lord Nelson, who died on October 21, 1805. It was blown up on the night of March 8, 1966 by a group of Irish loyalists who did not appreciate this statue being in the city center. The explosion took place fifty years after the 1916 Easter Rising. You can see the head at the Dublin Civil Museum. In 2001, a 400-foot monument of light designed by Ian Richie and called "The Spike" by Dubliners will be erected where Nelson's Pillar once stood.

Parnell Monument, O'Connell Street. Erected in 1907 in memory of Charles Stewart Parnell, one of Irelands great national leaders.

> *You'll never plough a field by turning it over in your mind.*
> ♣ —IRISH PROVERB ♣

Universities In Dublin:

Trinity College, Dublin (*See* Trinity College, this chapter)

University College Dublin, Belfield, Dublin 4; phone: 1-716-7777; Web site: *www.ucd.ie*

Dublin City University, Glasnevin, Dublin 9; phone 1-700-5000; fax: 1-700-5888

Royal College of Surgeons, 123 St. Stephen's Green, Dublin 2. Located on the west side of St. Stephen's Green, and built between 1825 and 1827. There is now an addition behind the original building on York Street.

7. Museums and Churches

Heritage Card:
This card gives unlimited admission for one year to over sixty-five sites throughout Ireland. Some of the Dublin sites include: Chester Beatty Library, Irish Museum of Modern Art, National Concert Hall, National Gallery of Ireland, National Library of Ireland, and the National Museum of Ireland. Fee: Adult IR 15.00, seniors IR 10.00, children or students IR 6.00, and families IR 36.00. For complete information contact:
  Heritage Card
  The Heritage Service, Education and Visitors Service
  51 St. Stephens Green
  Dublin 2
  fax: 1-661-6764
  Web site: *www.heritageireland.ie*
  e-mail: *info@heritageireland.ie*

Ireland at a Glimpse Card:
This is a mostly two-for-one coupon book on admissions to tourist sites such as museums, castles, caves, distilleries, zoos, parks, craft centers, gardens, and much more. You can purchase it for $14.95 (2000 price) from Irish Books and Media, 1433 East Franklin Avenue, Minneapolis, MN, 55404-2135; phone: 612-871-3505; fax: 612-871-3358.

MUSEUMS

BANK OF IRELAND AND HOUSE OF LORDS, 2 College Green, Dublin 2; phone: 1-677-6801. Open Monday to Friday 10 A.M.–4 P.M., Thursday 10 A.M.–5 P.M., Closed Saturday, Sunday, and bank holidays. Admission and tours are free. Built in 1728 as the first Irish parliament building, it became the Bank of Ireland in 1803. The tour is of the former parliament's upper chambers. Also in this building is the working Bank of Ireland, and that is located in the gorgeous old banking hall.

BANK OF IRELAND ARTS CENTER, Foster Place, Dublin 2; phone: 1-671-1488. Admission charge. Open Tuesday to Friday 10 A.M.–4 P.M., Saturday and Sunday by prior arrangement. Wheelchair accessible. This is an interactive museum reflecting both banking and Irish history over the past two hundred years. This building is the old bank armory building. It also traces the history of the adjoining College Green building, one of the landmarks of Georgian Dublin.

CHESTER BEATTY LIBRARY, *See* chapter 6, "Sights"

DRIMINAGH CASTLE, *See* chapter 6, "Sights"

DUBLIN CIVIC MUSEUM, 58 South William Street, Dublin 2 (next to the Powerscourt Townhouse Center); phone: 1-679-4260; fax: 1-677-5954; Open 10 A.M.–6 P.M. Tuesday to Saturday, 11 A.M.–2 P.M. on Sunday. Admission free. Located in the old City Assembly House and opened to the public in 1953, this is a small museum focusing on the history of Dublin from medieval times to now. They exhibit old maps, prints, street signs, Viking artifacts, and the head of Lord Nelson that was part of the statue that was blown up in 1966. There are also temporary exhibitions.

DUBLIN WRITERS MUSEUM, 18–19 Parnell Square North, Dublin 1; phone: 1-872-2077; fax: 1-872-2231. Open Tuesday to Saturday 10 A.M.–5 P.M., Sunday and holidays 11:00 A.M.–5 P.M. Open Mondays during July and August. There is wheelchair access to the first floor only. This museum opened in 1991 in a restored eighteenth-century Georgian townhouse. It was the home of John Jameson of Irish whiskey fame. If you love rare manuscripts, diaries, and first editions of books and photographs this is the place to spend half a day. There is also an excellent bookshop to get lost in for an hour or two and a café. The bookstore has the works of the writers represented in the museum plus others. The museum exhibits personal items, letters, books, and mementos of many writers including Jonathan Swift, James Joyce, George Bernard Shaw, Oscar Wilde, JM Synge, W. B. Yeats, Samuel Beckett, Joseph Sheridan, and many others. You can see an 1804 edition of Jonathan Swift's *Gulliver's Travels* and an 1897 first edition of Bram Stoker's *Dracula.* Next door is the Irish Writer's Center where today's writers meet to talk and give readings.

EARTH SCIENCE MUSEUM, phone: 1-661-8811. At this writing the museum is closed until 2003 for renovation, but when it reopens it will exhibit fossils, dinosaurs, and geological collections.

FINDLATER MUSEUM, 10 Upper Hatch Street, Dublin 2; phone: 1-475-1699. Open Monday to Saturday 10 A.M.–5:30 P.M. Admission charge. This museum traces the history of a Dublin merchant family over the last 170 years.

GUINNESS HOP STORE AND MUSEUM, *See* chapter 6, "Sights"

HUGH LANE MUNICIPAL GALLERY OF MODERN ART, Charlemont House, Parnell Square North, Dublin 1; phone: 1-874-1903; fax: 1-872-2182; e-mail: *exhibitions@hughlane.ie*; Web site: *www.hughlane.ie* Open Tuesday to Thursday 9:30 A.M.–6 P.M., Friday and Saturday 9:30 A.M.– 5 P.M., Sunday 11 A.M.–5 P.M. Admission free. Shop and café located in the museum. Located next to the Dublin Writers Museum in a restored eighteenth-century house known as Charlemont House, and considered one of Dublin's most beautiful Georgian houses, it was built in 1765. The gallery opened in 1908 and was named for the Irish art collector, Sir Hugh Lane, who died when the *Lusitania* was sunk in 1915. In his will he divided his excellent art collection between both Ireland and the National Gallery in London. The collection includes paintings from the Impressionist and Post-Impressionist periods, plus sculptures by Rodin and works by modern Irish artists. There is also a Stained-Glass Room containing works by noted Irish artists.

IRISH HERALDIC MUSEUM, 2 Kildare Street, Dublin 2; phone: 1-603-0311; fax; 1-662-1062; e-mail: *herald@nli.ie*; Web site: *www.nli.ie*. Open Monday to Friday 10 A.M.–4: 30 P.M., Saturday 10:30 A.M.–12: 30 P.M. Admission free. There is no other museum like this one. Located in the Genealogical Office, the museum exhibits thirteenth-century coins of Dublin, banners, stamps, old seals, a small display of armor, and some British and papal decorations. For a fee you can make an appointment with Ireland's Chief Herald. The building was originally the Kildare Street Club, founded in 1782. There are columns outside the building with carvings of monkeys playing billiards and bears playing violins. You have to look up carefully, but you can't miss them.

THE IRISH HISTORICAL PICTURE COMPANY, 5 Lower Ormond Quay, Dublin 1; phone: 1-872-0144. Open daily from 9 A.M.–6 P.M. Located opposite the Clarence Hotel on the Liffey Quays, this museum has a collection of over ten thousand prints of nineteenth-century villages and towns in Ireland. You can really see Ireland the way it once was.

IRISH JEWISH MUSEUM, 3–4 Walworth Road, Dublin 8; phone: 1-453-1797. Not wheelchair accessible. Open by appointment and October through April, Sunday 10:30 A.M.–2:30 P.M., May through September, Tuesday, Thursday, Sunday 11 A.M.–3:30 P.M. For appointments phone: 1-467-0773 or 1-475-8388. Admission free, donation is appreciated. There is a small shop with a few items for sale such as pens, writing paper, envelopes, and a few photographs. Dublin-born Israeli President Chaim Herzog and son of the first Chief Rabbi of Ireland opened this museum in 1985. Rabbi Herzog's home at 55 Bloomfield Avenue has a plaque on it with the dates he lived there. The Irish Jewish museum is housed in an old synagogue used only as a museum now. The museum displays photographs, Torah scrolls with their handles and covers, an Ark Cover dating from the 1700s, prayer shawls, candlesticks, letters, and memorabilia from Dublin's Jewish families. There is also a reconstruction of a typical turn-of-the century kitchen from a Jewish home. Today there are about two thousand Jews in Ireland, and only one synagogue remains in Dublin, but they trace their presence in Ireland back to 1067. Dublin has had two Jewish Lord Mayors, father and son. Robert Briscoe was mayor from 1956–1957 and 1961–1962. His son Benjamin held office from 1988–1989.

IRISH LABOUR HISTORY SOCIETY MUSEUM, Beggars Bush, Haddington Road, Dublin; phone: 1-668-1071

IRISH MUSEUM OF MODERN ART/THE ROYAL HOSPITAL KILMAINHAM, Royal Hospital, Military Road, Kilmainham, Dublin 8; Phone: 01 612-9900; Fax: 01-612-9999; email: *info@www.modernart.ie*; Web site: *www.modernart.ie*. The museum is wheelchair accessible except for the Ground Floor East Wing Gallery. Admission free. Open Tuesday to Saturday 10 A.M.–5:30 P.M., Sunday and bank holidays noon–5:30 P.M. Closed Mondays and December 24–26. Garden and bookshop open the same hours as museum. Guided Heritage tours are available on Sundays at 2:30 P.M. and 3:30 P.M. or by appointment. Guided tours of the exhibitions are conducted on Wednesday and Friday at 2:30 P.M., Saturday 11:30 A.M. Tours can also be pre-booked by calling: 01-612-9900. Foreign-language Tours can also be pre-booked. The museum also hosts concerts.

The Irish Museum of Modern Art is housed in the Royal Hospital Kilmainham. It is considered one of the best examples of seventeenth-century architecture in Ireland. The Royal Hospital was founded in 1684 as a home for retired soldiers and was used for that purpose for 250 years. The building was restored in 1984 and opened as the Irish Museum of Modern Art in May 1991. You'll appreciate the massive courtyard with its arcades, which run around three sides. There are many exhibits going on at once as well as the museum's permanent collection of internationally known artists on display, plus the work of local Irish artists.

IRISH MUSIC HALL OF FAME, 57 Middle Abbey Street, Dublin 1; phone: 1-878-3345; fax: 1-878-2225. Open daily from 10 A.M.–6 P.M. Admission fee. All tickets for shows can be ordered through Ticketmaster at 1-456-9569; Web site: *www.irishmusichof.com*

This is a new music experience. This center consists of the **Hall of Fame Tour, HQ,** and **The Jam Restaurant** and the **IMHF Store.** The tour takes almost two hours and documents Ireland's contribution to music. Using a headset, follow the history of music through soundtracks, visuals, and media. Memorabilia has been donated for exhibitions by some of the most famous Irish entertainers including U2, Van Morrison, The Chieftains, The Undertones, The Dubliners, Phil Coulter, Sinead O'Connor, Bob Geldof, B*Witched, Boyzone, Westlife, and many others. At the end of the tour there is a movie that celebrates the famous people in Irish music. **HQ** is a new multipurpose theater with only five hundred seats. They host top Irish and international acts. Waiter service is available during the concerts. A few of the performers who entertained recently are Glenn Tilbrook, Aly Bain and Phil Cunningham, and Dylan Moran. **The Jam Restaurant** serves Irish food and is open from 9 A.M. until after dinner.

IRISH WHISKEY MUSEUM: THE OLD JAMESON DISTILLERY, Smithfield Village, Dublin 7; phone: 1-872-5566. Wheelchair accessible. Admission fee. Open daily from 10 A.M.–6 P.M., and you must take a tour. Your admission fee includes a glass of Jameson's. The museum is dedicated to the history of Irish whiskey. There is a model of a distillery, which was made for the 1924 World Exhibition. Whiskey was produced here from 1791 until 1966 when the distillery was moved to County Cork.

JAMES JOYCE CENTRE, 35 North Great George's Street, Dublin 1; phone: 1-878-8547; fax: 1-878-8488; e-mail: *joycecen@iol.ie*

Open Monday to Saturday 9:30 A.M.–4:30 P.M., Sunday 12:30–5 P.M. Admission charge. There is a bookshop and café called the "Ulysses Experience," and an interesting audio-visual presentation of turn-of-the century Dublin. David Norris, an Irish senator and Joycean scholar, bought this beautiful 1784 Georgian mansion and fully restored it. The first-floor library is fascinating with its various Joyce editions and translations, works of other Irish writers, and information related to both Dublin and Ireland.

JAMES JOYCE MARTELLO TOWER, Sandycove, County Dublin; phone and fax 1-280-9265. Open April through October, Monday to Saturday 10 A.M.–1 P.M., 2 P.M.–5 P.M., Sunday 2–6 P.M., and November through March by appointment. Admission fee. Limited wheelchair access. Located on the coast road eight miles from Dublin by DART train.

The Martello Tower was built in the early nineteenth century because of a fear of an invasion from Napoleonic France. There is a combined ticket for the James Joyce Museum and the Dublin Writers Museum. James Joyce spent a week at the Martello Tower as a guest of his friend Oliver St. John Gogarty in 1904. Gogarthy rented the Tower while studying medicine. Joyce used his experience there in his first chapter of *Ulysses* and used Gogarthy as a model for the character Buck Mulligan. In 1962 the Tower became the **Joyce Museum,** which now displays Joyce's first edition books, photographs, waistcoat, embroidered by his grandmother, walking stick, cigar case, guitar, traveling trunk, and death mask.

MALAHIDE CASTLE AND FRY RAILWAY MUSEUM, Malahide. *See* chapter 12, "Day Trips"

MARITIME MUSEUM OF IRELAND, Dun Laoghaire. *See* chapter 12, "Day Trips"

MUSEUM OF CHILDHOOD, Rathmines, Dublin 6. *See* chapter 11, "Dublin for Children"

NATIONAL GALLERY OF IRELAND, Merrion Square West, Dublin 2; phone: 1-661-5133; fax: 1-661-5372; e-mail: *artgall@eircom.net*; Web site: *www.nationalgallery.ie*

Open Monday to Saturday 9:30 A.M. to 5:30 P.M., Thursday 9:35 A.M.–8:30 P.M., Sunday 12 P.M.–5 P.M. Free admission. This museum now incorporates the new Yeats Museum. Public areas are wheelchair accessible. Established in 1854 by an act of parliament and opened in 1864 with one hundred paintings, this is now one of the great museums of Europe. The collections include works from the fourteenth century through the twentieth century. There are Irish painters represented, and works by Degas, El Greco, Goya, Monet, Picasso, and many more.

NATIONAL HISTORY MUSEUM, Merrion Street, Dublin 2; phone: 1-677-7444; fax: 1-677-7828. Open Tuesday to Saturday 10 A.M.–5 P.M., Sunday 2 P.M.–5 P.M. Free admission. This museum is part of the National Museum of Ireland and also connects with the "Museumlink" bus. It is a wonderful zoological museum, which opened in 1857. Dubliner's call this museum "the dead zoo," but I find it very interesting especially if you have a child with you. The exhibits include the **Irish Room** with Irish elk, whales found stranded on Irish beaches, Irish wildlife, red deer, and other Irish animals and wildlife. There is also a **World Collection** with animals from around the world that are now extinct or quite rare.

NATIONAL MUSEUM OF IRELAND, KILDARE STREET, AND NATIONAL MUSEUM OF IRELAND, COLLINS BARRACKS, Note: There is a new bus service called "Museumlink" that connects these two museums. Both are well worth visiting.

This outstanding museum is now divided in two locations. The first and oldest is at **Kildare Street,** Dublin 2; phone: 1-677-7444; fax: 1-676-6116; e-mail: *nmi2@indigo.ie.* Limited wheelchair access. Open Tuesday to Saturday 10 A.M.–5 P.M., Sunday 2–5 P.M. Free admission except for the Treasury Exhibit.

The museum, which opened in 1890, is located next to Leinster House. The main exhibits show the history of Ireland from the Bronze Age (2000 B.C. to 700 B.C.) to the present. The other wonderful exhibit is the **Treasury Exhibit,** which displays the eighth-century **Tara Brooch,** the eighth-century **Ardagh Chalice** and the twelfth-century **Cross of Cong.** Also *An Thoir na Saoirse,* which means **The Road to Independence,** tells the political history of Ireland between 1900–1921. There is also a **Viking Exhibit** with a full size Viking skeleton and other artifacts discovered in Dublin. The exhibit **Or-Irelands Gold** displays a collection of prehistoric gold artifacts. The **Ancient Egypt** exhibit tells the history of Egyptian Archaeology.

The museum is now restoring ancient Viking silver artifacts that were recently found in a cave in County Kilkenny. They are considered to be one-of-a-kind silver coins and buttons, which date back a thousand years. A special exhibit of the museum, *Sheela-na-gigs,* stone carvings of women, requires the permission of the curator—apply in advance.

The new branch of the museum is at **Collins Barracks,** next to

Heuston Train Station on Benburb Street, Dublin 7; phone: 1-677-7444. Open Tuesday to Saturday 10 A.M.–5 P.M., Sunday 2 P.M.–5 P.M. This building was acquired by the National Museum in 1994. It is the oldest military barracks in Europe and the oldest continuously occupied barracks in the world. The museum exhibits decorative arts, political and military history, science and information on the Middle Ages. A permanent exhibit called **The Way We Wore** celebrates Irish clothing and jewelry over the last two hundred and fifty years. Exploring the lives of the tailors, weavers, shoemakers and others who worked in the textile industry, as well as the lives of the wearers, this is a remarkable sample of Irish culture. One of the highlights is a dress worn by the mother of the Irish patriot, Theobald Wolfe Tone, about 1775. The dress was altered and worn more than one hundred years later by a descendant of Mrs. Tone to celebrate the centenary of the 1798 Rebellion. A gold brooch commissioned for Queen Victoria's visit to Trinity College in 1849 is also on display.

NATIONAL WAX MUSEUM, Dublin. *See* chapter 11, "Dublin for Children."

NATIONAL PRINT MUSEUM, Garrison Chapel, Beggars Bush, Haddington Road, Dublin 4; phone: 1-660-3770; fax: 1-667-3545; e-mail: *npmuseum@iol.ie.* Open May through September Monday to Friday 10 A.M.–12:30 P.M. and 2:30 P.M.–5 P.M.; Saturday, Sunday, bank holidays noon–5 P.M., October to April Tuesday, Thursday, Saturday, and Sunday 2–5 P.M. All admissions include guided tour and audio-visual show. Admission charge. Coffee shop open daily.

This new museum opened in 1996 in a former soldier's chapel, and houses an extensive collection on the history of printing. On exhibit are cases of type used in the days of setting pages by hand, linotype machines, printing presses, old newspapers, and some of the early computers used for printing.

NUMBER 29, 29 Lower Fitzwilliam Street, Dublin 2; phone: 1-702-6165; e-mail: *numbertwentynine@mail.esb.ie*

Open Tuesday to Saturday 10 A.M.–5 P.M., Sunday 2–5 P.M., Admission charge, free for people under sixteen. If you want to see how middle-class Dubliners lived in the eighteenth and early nineteenth century this is the museum for you. It is located in a restored four-story townhouse with exhibits of carpets, decorations, curtains, dolls, toys, and furnishings. You can wander from the basement to the attic seeing all the things that made a home work.

OSCAR WILDE HOUSE, One Merrion Square, Dublin 2; phone: 1-662-0281; fax: 1-662-1896. Open for guided tours of the ground and first floors only, Monday, Wednesday, and Thursday from 10 A.M.–noon. The admission charge of IR2.00 goes toward the restoration of the rest of the house. Oscar Wilde's family lived in the house for twenty-three years, from 1855 to 1878. The ground and first floors have been restored and work is being done on the rest of the house. The house was built in 1762 and was one of the first houses built on Merrion Square.

Since 1994 the **American College Dublin** has occupied the house and is slowly restoring it to its former splendor. Information: Dean of Admissions, American College Dublin, 2 Merrion Square, Dublin 2; phone: 1-676-8939; fax: 1-676-8941; e-mail: *degree@amdc.ie*

The college offers degrees in Liberal Arts, International Business, International Tourism, Behavioral Science. All courses may be taken as full- or part-time studies. The school also offers adult and continuing education classes such as computer courses, wine appreciation, photography, film appreciation, and some language courses.

PEARSE MUSEUM, St. Edna's Park, Grange Road, Rathfarnham, Dublin 6; phone: 1-493-4208; fax: 1-493-6120. Admission free. Open daily 10 A.M. to 5:30 P.M., closed 1–2 P.M. Closes earlier winter months.

This museum is located on the grounds of St. Edna's Park in a school that Padraig (Patrick) Pearse ran from 1910 until he was executed for being a leader of Dublin's 1916 Easter Rising. Patrick's brother Willy ran the school with him, and he was also executed for being part of the Rising. The museum houses Pearse family documents and photographs. In the park are trails and a lake.

RHA GALLAGHER GALLERY, 15 Ely Place, Dublin 2; phone: 1-661-2558. Open Monday to Saturday 11 A.M.–5 P.M., Thursday 11 A.M.–9 P.M., Sunday 2 P.M.–5 P.M. Associated with the Royal Hibernian Academy, this gallery exhibits the work of modern Irish and international artists. There is no permanent collection, which makes this gallery very interesting.

SHAW BIRTHPLACE, 33 Synge Street, Dublin 8; phone: 1-475-0854; fax: 1-872-2231. Open May through October Monday to Saturday 10 A.M.–6 P.M., Sunday and public holidays 11:30 A.M.–6 P.M. Admission charge. One ticket admits you to both the Shaw Birthplace and the Dublin Writers Museum. There is a wonderful bookshop in the museum.

Nobel Prize–winning author George Bernard Shaw's home was open to the public in 1993. The house has been restored and it now looks as though the family still lives in this lovely Victorian home. You can see the room he lived in, the front parlor, and the drawing room where his mother had held her musical evenings. There is a plaque outside the house that says "Author of Many Plays."

CHURCHES

Christ Church Cathedral, Christchurch Place, Dublin 8; phone: 1-677-8099; e-mail: *cccdub @indigo.ie*; Web site: *www.cccdub-ie*. Open Monday to Saturday 10 A.M.–5 P.M., and Sundays between church services. Sitric, the Norse king of Dublin, and Donat, first bishop of Dublin, founded Christ Church in 1038. It is Dublin's oldest building. It was originally a wooden church, but it was rebuilt between 1173 and 1220 with stone. It remained that way until 1831 when it was rebuilt again in the Gothic style. Richard Fitz Gilbert de Clare, known as Strongbow, was the first Norman conqueror of Ireland and is buried in the Cathedral. The cathedral choir, which was founded in 1493, took part in the April 13, 1742, world premier of George Frederick Handel's *Messiah* in the old musick hall in Fishamble Street, Dublin. In 1999, the Cathedral added another seven bells and is now probably the largest ringing peal in the world. The Cathedral is linked by a bridge to the Synod House, where you can visit **Dublinia,** the exhibition relating the city's development from Strongbow to the sixteenth century.

St. Anne's Church, Dawson Street, Dublin 2; phone: 1-676-7727. Open daily. After much ado, and more than 150 years later, this church was completed in 1868. In 1723 Lord Newton put up a shelf near the altar to distribute bread to the poor. There are often lunchtime recitals held here. A few of the famous people who worshiped in this church were Oscar Wilde, Wolfe Tone, and Bram Stoker.

St. Audeon's Churches, Cornmarket, High Street, Dublin 8; phone: 1-677-8714. Free admission. This is the oldest and only surviving medieval parish church in Dublin and is also a **Protestant Church.** The Normans founded the church in the twelfth century. The tower, which dates from the twelfth century, and three of the six bells, which date from the fifteenth century make them the oldest in Ireland. The other **St. Audeon's Roman Catholic Church,** is located next door on High Street, and dates from 1846. It is open daily from 10 A.M.–4:30 P.M.; admission charge. Shown at the church is an audio-visual, *The Flame on the Hill,* which tells the story of Christianity in Ireland.

ST. FRANCIS XAVIER CHURCH, located on Upper Gardiner Street, this is a Catholic Church built in the early 1800s. It has a beautiful Italian high altar and exquisite ceiling.

ST. MARY'S ABBEY, Chapter House, Meetinghouse Lane, Dublin 1; phone: 1-872-1490. Open Wednesday and Sunday. Admission charge. Founded in 1139 by the Benedictine Order, it came under Cistercian rule eight years later. It is considered one of the greatest medieval abbeys in Dublin This was also one of the most important monasteries in Ireland until 1537, when Henry VIII dissolved it. Lord Fitzgerald renounced his allegiance to the king in this building, and was executed soon thereafter.

ST. MARY'S CHURCH, Mary Street, Dublin 1. This church was built in 1702, and at one time was considered one of Dublin's most fashionable churches, as can be seen by the events that occurred here. Arthur Guinness was married here in 1793, Theobald Wolfe Tone was baptized here, as was Sean O'Casey.

ST. MARY'S PRO CATHEDRAL, Marlborough Street, Dublin 1; phone: 1-874-5441. Open daily from 8 A.M.–6 P.M. This is Dublin's main Roman Catholic church. Although it is called a cathedral it has never been granted full cathedral status. Construction on the building began in 1815, when Archbishop Troy laid the foundation stone, and was completed in 1825. Daniel O'Connell attended the dedication of the church celebrated by Archbishop Murray. The exterior resembles Notre Dame de Lorette in Paris, the interior resembles St. Philippe du Roule Church in Paris. The choir still sings in Latin on Sundays at 11 A.M. mass.

ST. MICHAN'S CHURCH, Lower Church Street, Dublin 7; phone: 1-872-4154. This church was built on the site of a Danish church founded in 1096, and its square tower is believed to be from that time. The present St. Michan's Church dates from the seventeenth century. The organ of the church dates from 1724 and it is believed that Handel played the *Messiah* on it; the organ is still in the church. The vaults of St. Michan's are world-renowned because their dry atmosphere has preserved some corpses, which lie on view in open caskets.

ST. PATRICK'S CATHEDRAL, Patrick Street; phone: 1-453 9472; fax: 1-454-6374; e-mail: *stpcath@iol.ie*; Web site: *www.stpatrickscathedral.ie* Wheelchair accessible by arrangement prior to visit. Open Monday to Friday 9 A.M.–6 P.M., Saturday 9 A.M.–5 P.M., and Sunday 10 A.M.– 3 P.M. (6 P.M. March to October). St. Patrick's is the national cathedral of the Church of Ireland. The church was founded in 448 A.D. and is considered the oldest Christian site in Dublin. Supposedly St. Patrick baptized a local king there in 450 A.D. St. Patrick's Cathedral was dedicated on St. Patrick's Day in 1192. It partly burned down on April 6, 1362 but Thomas Minet, Archbishop of Dublin, rebuilt its burned-out section in 1370. He also added the steeple. In 1749 a spire was added. The church is the longest in Ireland, with a three-hundred-foot-long interior. The first university in Ireland was founded here in 1320 and closed by Henry VIII in 1539. There are many memorials in the Cathedral of Irish political figures, writers, musicians, soldiers, and presidents of Ireland. There is a memorial to Douglas Hyde, the first president of Ireland. Jonathan Swift was dean of the Cathedral from 1713–1745, and his grave and epitaph are located on the south side of the Cathedral. His companion, Stella Johnson, is buried next to him. Sir Benjamin Lee Guinness (of brewery fame) restored the Cathedral from 1854–1860. There is also a Choir School that is part of the Cathedral and it was founded in 1432. The choir took part in the first performance of Handel's *Messiah* in 1742. Today there are two choirs, one male and one female.

Christmas Eve: Every Christmas Eve the Cathedral hosts a gorgeous carols service, which is broadcast on national radio. It starts with a boy soprano singing "Hark in Royal David's City" and ends with the congregation singing "Hark! The Herald Angels Sing!" At the end of the service the Cathedral bells ring.

After seeing the Cathedral, visit **Marsh's Library,** *See* chapter 6, "Sights."

ST. WERBURGH'S CHURCH, Werburgh Street, off Christchurch Place, Dublin 8. This church dates from 1718, although the original church was built in the twelfth century. The church has been restored and is considered the most perfect Georgian church in Dublin. There are twenty-seven vaults beneath the church, one of which contains the remains of Lord Edward Fitzgerald who was a leader of the United

Irishmen. He died during the Rebellion of 1798. Mrs. Molly Malone, fishmonger, is also listed in the church records as having died in 1734.

WHITEFRIAR STREET CARMELITE CHURCH, Whitefriar Street, Dublin 2; phone: 1-475-8821. Open daily from 8:30 A.M.–6:30 P.M.

In 1836 Pope Gregory XVI gave the remains of the body of **St. Valentine** to this Church and it is enshrined in the altar. Also in this church is **Our Lady of Dublin,** the life-size oak fifteenth-century statue of the Virgin and Child.

ST. ALBERT'S WELL. Albert was born in Sicily and died in 1306 and was sainted. On August seventh (his feast day) a relic of the saint is dipped in water, and a prayer is said asking him to heal the mind and body of the sick. Located inside the Whitefriar Street Church.

8. Literary Dublin

Ireland has produced brilliant writers including four Nobel Prize–winners of literature. The first Irishman to win the Prize was **William Butler Yeats** in 1923. He was also one of the founders of the Abbey Theatre. **George Bernard Shaw,** author of *Pygmalion* among other works, won the prize in 1925. His birthplace in Dublin is now a museum. **Samuel Beckett** was also a native of Dublin. He won the Nobel Prize in 1969, and his most famous play was *Waiting for Godot.* Most recently **Seamus Heaney** won the Prize in 1995. Born in 1939 in Derry, Northern Ireland, his poetry has focused on the "Troubles."

Other great Irish writers include Oscar Wilde, Oliver Goldsmith, Sean O'Casey, Brendan Behan, Jonathan Swift, James Joyce, JM Synge, and Bram Stoker.

Today's Irish writers are equally well known both in Ireland and around the world. Roddy Doyle, Patrick Kavanagh, Dermot Bolger, Brendan Kennelly, and Maeve Binchy among others have wide international audiences.

Of all the Irish authors, James Joyce is perhaps the most well-known and celebrated in Dublin. Each year on June sixteenth **"Bloomsday"** is marked with numerous readings and performances from Joyce's masterpiece, *Ulysses.* Leopold Bloom is the main character in *Ulysses* and the events in the novel take place in Dublin on June 16, 1904. People who celebrate usually dress in the clothing worn at that time and visit the locations mentioned in the novel. *Joyce's Dublin, A Walking Guide to Ulysses* by Jack McCarthy is a good guide to the events and characters in the book with maps of the city for easy reference. **For information** contact the **James Joyce Museum,** Joyce Tower, Sandycove, County Dublin; Phone: 1-280-9265; e-mail: *joycetower@dublintourism.ie*

The James Joyce Center, 35 North Great Georges Street, Dublin 1;

phone: 1-878-8547; fax; 1-878-8488; e-mail: *joyceen@iol.ie*; Web site: *www.jamesjoyce.ie*

One of the wonderful tours that can be taken in Dublin is the **Literary Pub Crawl.** It operates year-round and can be booked by a hotel concierge, the Dublin Tourist Office, or by calling directly. Summer season, April through October nightly at 7:30 P.M., Sundays at noon and 7:30 P.M.; Winter season, November through April, Thursday through Sunday at 7:30 P.M., an extra one Sunday at noon. **Phone:** 1-670-5602; Fax: 1-670-5603. e-mail: *info@dublinpubcrawl.com*; Web site: *www.dublinpubcrawl.com.* You can also just show up at the starting point: upstairs at The Duke Pub at 8/9 Duke Street, Dublin 2. The tour takes approximately two and half-hours. Professional actors read from the works of Dublin writers as you visit the famous pubs frequented by those writers.

LEGENDS AND STORIES

Ireland is filled with stories, legends and folklore. It was customary for each village in Ireland to have a *Seanchai,* or local storyteller, who would recount tales passed down through generations. The tradition is kept alive today by a few traveling *Seanchai* who visit hotels and bars, usually in the west and southwest of Ireland. I still remember the stories I heard from one in Kenmare.

Books about fairies, strange animals, and of course leprechauns, make wonderful gifts for children. One of my favorite books is the beautifully illustrated *Lady Cottington's Pressed Fairy Book* by Terry Jones and illustrated by Brian Froud.

Following are just a few Irish legends.

> **The Banshee** is frightening because of her awful wail, signaling an approaching death.
>
> **The Blarney Stone** is said to be Ireland's lucky charm. It is a large block of limestone, which is located in a tower of Blarney Castle in County Cork and supposedly has magical powers. If you kiss the Blarney Stone you develop the famous Irish "gift of gab." The stone was placed there in 1446 and seems to have been working ever since.
>
> **Cuchulain** is a favorite of Irish children. This mythological hero is said to have singlehandedly fought off an invading army.
>
> **Irish Shamrock.** If you are lucky enough to find a shamrock, do not throw it away. This is not a four-leaf clover; this has three leaves and always brings good luck. St. Patrick used the shamrock to tell the story of the Holy Trinity. It is considered the national plant of Ireland.

Leprechauns. You can buy little Leprechauns all over Ireland in every souvenir shop. There are many stories about leprechauns, known to wear green outfits, sit under trees, repair fairies' shoes, and keep a pot of gold at the end of the rainbow.

Pooka is a fun-filled fairy that likes to enjoy himself, but will also help with the work.

The Children of Lir is a famous legend about the four children of Lir who were condemned to spend four hundred years as swans by their evil stepmother. (*See* chapter 6, "Staying Busy."). It is illegal to kill swans in Ireland because of this story. *The Children of Lir* by Sheila MacGill-Callahan and illustrated by Gennady Spirin is a beautiful picture book of the story.

BOOK STORES

There are many wonderful bookshops, which I have not mentioned for lack of space. If you love books, keep looking. Bookshops are everyplace in Dublin and Ireland. There are small, independent bookshops along with the chain stores. I recommend an afternoon of buying or browsing. You can find Irish literature in Dublin that cannot be found at home. There is no tax on books, so it is one less VAT worry.

BOOKS UPSTAIRS, 36 College Green; phone: 1-679-6687. Located opposite Trinity College. They have a huge selection of Irish literature and drama, which is what you want to buy in Ireland. Forget about the American titles.

CATHACH BOOKS, 10 Duke Street; phone: 1-671-8676; fax: 1-671-5120; e-mail: *cathach@rarebooks.ie*; Web site: *www.rarebooks.ie*. Open Monday to Saturday 9:30 A.M.–6 P.M. This is an antiquarian bookshop, dealing in rare books of Irish interest. They specialize in books written by and about James Joyce, Samuel Beckett, W.B. Yeats, Oscar Wilde, and Seamus Heaney. I love this shop with its first editions, signed copies, secondhand and rare books, maps, and prints. This is a wonderful shop for buying those special occasion gifts. I did a lot of Christmas shopping here. They will ship books all over the world at reasonable prices. They also have a book search service.

DE BÚRCA RARE BOOKS, "Cloonagashel," 27 Priory Drive, Blackrock, County Dublin; phone: 1-288-2159; fax: 1-283-4080; e-mail: *deburca@indigo.com*; Web site: *http://indigo.ie/~deburca/*

This antiquarian bookseller specializes in books relating to Ireland, and volumes on Irish history, genealogy, topography, biography, and literature fill the shelves. They will mail a catalog or any book throughout the world and do book searches for hard-to-find items.

DUBLIN BOOKSHOP, 24 Grafton Street; phone: 1-677-5568. This is an excellent family-owned shop with Irish books plus the usual novels. There is also a good children's section.

EASON & SON, 40 O'Connell Street, Dublin 1; Phone: 1-873-3811; Web site: *www.eason.ie*; e-mail: *info@eason.ie*
This is a major chain store selling Irish and all other types of books, stationery, magazines, calendars and art supplies. There are many branches throughout the city.

FRED HANNA'S, 27–29 Nassau Street, Dublin 2; phone: 1-873-3811; e-mail: *info@eason.ie*; Web site: *www.hannas.ie*
The Hanna family had owned this excellent bookshop since 1910, and now it's part of Eason's. They sell Irish fiction, literature, history and poetry, limited editions, secondhand Irish books, and children's books.

HODGES FIGGIS, 56–58 Dawson Street, Dublin 2; phone: 1-677-4754; fax: 1-677-3402; e-mail: *irish@hodgesfiggis.ie*; Web site: *www.hodgesfiggis. com*
With over a million books on three floors, the oldest bookshop in Ireland is also one of the most comprehensive. A café is on the first floor.

KENNYS BOOKSHOP, High Street, Galway, Ireland; phone: 091 562739; Fax: 091 568544; e-mail: *desi@kennys.ie*; Web site: *www.kennys.ie*
Not just an Irish bookshop, it is a worldwide shop due to its "Kennys Irish Book Parcel Plan." Give Kennys a budget, reading interest, author preference, and how often you would like to receive a parcel and they do the rest. If you are not happy with a book, send it back for a refund or replacement. It's an easy way to keep up with what's new in Irish books.

WATERSTONE'S, 7 Dawson Street, Dublin 2; phone: 1-679-1415. Web site: *www.waterstones.com*
This shop is part of a British chain of bookshops. Hodges Figgis is almost directly across the street from Waterstone's, and they are both busy and a book lover's paradise. They have a large area of Irish books plus popular new books by international authors. They have a won-

derful children's section and book readings that are well worth attending.

WINDING STAIR, 40 Lower Ormond Quay Lower; phone: 1-873-3292. This shop features rare and many secondhand books and it's a great place for browsing. The café overlooks the River Liffey.

LIBRARIES

CHESTER BEATTY LIBRARY AND GALLERY OF ORIENTAL ART, *see* chapter 6, "Sights"

MARSH'S LIBRARY, *see* chapter 6, "Sights"

NATIONAL LIBRARY OF IRELAND, *see* chapter 6, "Sights"

NATIONAL PHOTOGRAPHIC ARCHIVE, *see* chapter 6, "Sights"

> *May good luck be with you*
> *Wherever you go,*
> *And your blessings outnumber*
> *The shamrocks that grow.*
> ♣ —IRISH BLESSING ♣

9. Shopping in Dublin

Banks are open Monday to Friday 10 A.M.–4 P.M. and 5 P.M. on Thursday. There are also ATMs located throughout the city.

Shops are usually open Monday to Friday from 9:30 A.M. and close at 5:30 P.M., Saturday until 6 P.M. Thursday evening many shops stay open until 8 P.M. in Dublin. Since Sunday closings have changed in Ireland many shops now open on Sunday from noon–4 P.M. Supermarkets have late evenings, but check all of this out if you plan on shopping at odd hours. Bookshops usually stay open later than most shops in the city and are also open on Sundays. As the Christmas holidays approach shops usually have later closing times and those that do not open on Sundays will do so for the holiday season.

SHOPPING

See section on VAT in Introduction section.

Remember that if you live outside the European Union you are entitled to VAT, Value Added Tax, Refund. If you wish to receive information on the VAT before leaving home contact: Global Refund, Spiddal Industrial Estate, Spiddal, Co. Galway, Ireland. Phone from the U.S.: 011-353-91-553258; fax 011-353-91-553403; e-mail: *cbgal@iol.ie*

Dublin Airport office: 1-844-5351
Shannon Airport Office: 61 472-454

To find out how much you can bring home duty-free, and what you can buy, go to *www.customs.gov/travel/travel.htm*, click on "Know Before You Go"

May the roof above us never fall in, and may we
Friends gathered below never fall out.

♣ —IRISH BLESSING ♣

A good Web site for Aran sweaters, claddagh rings, Irish genealogy books and all things Irish is *www.shopshamrock.com*

CLOTHING SIZES

Women's Dresses

UK	8	10	12	14	16	18
EUROPE	36	38	40	42	44	46
U.S.	6	8	10	12	14	16

Women's Shoes

UK	4	5	6	7	8
EUROPE	36	37	38	39	40
U.S.	5	6	7	8	9

Men's Suits

UK	36	38	40	42	44	46
EUROPE	46	48	50	52	54	56
U.S.	36	38	40	42	44	46

Men's Shoes

UK	6	7	8	9	10	11
EUROPE	39½	41	42	43	44½	46
U.S.	7	8	9	10	11	12

Men's Shirts

UK	14½	15	15½	16	16½	17
EUROPE	37	38	39	40	41	42
U.S.	14½	15	15½	16	16½	17

THE MAIN SHOPPING STREETS

Dublin has many shopping areas, but the main ones are found on Grafton Street, Henry Street, Wicklow Street, Powerscourt Townhouse, Dawson Street, Nassau Street, and Suffolk Street. These streets are all within walking distance of one another.

DEPARTMENT STORES

ARNOTTS, 12 Henry Street, Dublin 1; phone: 1-805-0400. Open Monday to Saturday 9 A.M.–6:30 P.M., Thursdays 9:30 A.M.–9 P.M., Sunday noon–6 P.M. This is an old Dublin shop recently renovated and updated with a large range of items from expensive to cheap.

BROWN THOMAS, Grafton Street, Dublin 2; phone: 1-605-6666. Open, Monday to Saturday 9 A.M.–6 P.M., Thursday till 8 P.M., Sunday noon–6 P.M. This is the most posh of Dublin's department stores with famous designer clothing, perfumes, and cosmetics. They also have a beautiful department for Waterford crystal, Irish gift items, and houseware items.

BOTTOM DRAWER, third floor; phone: 1-605-6696. This is a special department within the store that sells products made by a handful of ladies who carry on the tradition of handmade Irish lace and linen. Along with your handmade Donegal tablecloth you will receive a handwritten note naming the person who was the embroiderer. Nuns based in County Cork have also been producing Corabbey linens for over one hundred fifty years. The department also sells embroidered towels.

CLERY'S, O'Connell Street; phone: 1-878-6000. There are four floors full of clothing, home appliances, and gift items.

DEBENHAMS, Jervis Shopping Centre, Dublin 1; phone: 1-878-1222. Debenhams is an import from Britain. The store is located in a shopping mall that opened in 1996. The mall has at least forty shops of which this is the largest. It has everything you might look for in a department store such as clothing, shoes, hats, lingerie, makeup, etc.

DUNNES STORES, St. Stephen's Green, Center Henry Street, Ilac Shopping Center, Mary Street. Dunne's is Ireland's largest chain of stores for household goods, clothing, and grocery items at reasonable prices.

EASON'S, 40 O'Connell Street; phone: 1-873-3811; or Ilac Shopping Center, Mary Street; phone: 1-872-1322. They are known for books, magazines, stationery, records, CDs, and anything musical.

MARKS AND SPENCER, Grafton Street; phone: 1-679-7855; Mary Street, phone: 1-872-8833. These are great shops direct from the UK with a wide variety of reasonably priced clothing and wonderful groceries.

WEIR AND SONS, corner of Grafton and Wicklow Streets; phone: 1-677-9678. This is a gorgeous shop chocked full of beautiful jewelry, silver, leather goods, watches, small gift items such as Waterford crystal, and other gift items.

WHAT TO BUY AND WHERE

Antiques

The best-known antique dealers are located around Francis Street, Patrick Street, Dawson Street, and the north quays off O'Connell Street. I would suggest always calling ahead if you know where you want to go because antique dealers seem to be very leisurely about store hours. If you just want to wander then you can take your chances about finding the shops open.

ALEXANDER ANTIQUES, 16 Molesworth Street, near Dawson Street. Phone: 1-679-1548.

ANTHONY ANTIQUES, 7 Molesworth Street. Phone: 1-677-7222.

BUTLER ANTIQUES, 14 Bachelor's Walk, along the north quays. Phone: 1-873-0296.

GORDON NICHOL ANTIQUES, 67–68 Francis Street. Phone: 1-454-3322.

JOHN FARRINGTON, 32 Drury Street, near Grafton Street. Specializing in antique jewelry, watches, frames and other small items. Phone: 1-679-1899.

O'SULLIVAN ANTIQUES, 43–44 Francis Street. Sells mainly Irish Victorian and Georgian furniture. Phone: 1-454-1143.

China

China, including the famous Irish china **Belleek,** is sold in many department stores, small shops, and Weir and Sons in Dublin. You can also call or go on-line directly to Belleek for all of their items plus discounts. They will also ship worldwide. Toll-free phone: 888-874-2494; toll-free fax: 888-874-1793; e-mail: *gifts@belleekshop.com*; Web site: *www.belleekshop.com*

Claddagh Rings and Necklaces

Claddagh rings and necklaces, in gold or silver, are very popular items and are available in most gift, jewelry, airport, and craft shops. Designed with a heart and crown held by two hands, the claddagh represents love, loyalty, and friendship. It's important to know how to wear the rings. If the bottom of the heart is facing your wrist then your heart belongs to another; if the bottom of the heart is facing out you are still available.

Crystal

There are quite a few companies that produce beautiful crystal in Ireland and it is on display everyplace. Waterford and Tipperary and Galway crystal are most popular and are probably the most expensive, with Waterford the priciest. You can buy Waterford gift items such as a small ring holder, makeup brush, letter opener, and small candy dishes at very reasonable prices, plus you get the VAT refund, which is always a bonus. These companies all put out small crystal villages and small crystal animals, Cinderella's slippers, candlesnuffers, cheese knives, and salad sets.

The Louise Kennedy Collection of Tipperary Crystal

Louise Kennedy is an Irish fashion designer who was commissioned by Tipperary Crystal to design a collection for them. They are beautiful works of arts and can be seen and bought at Louise Kennedy, 56 Merrion Square, Dublin 2; phone: 1-662-0056, toll-free from U.S.: 800-414-6825; toll-free fax: 800-414-6826; e-mail: *tippcrys@iol.ie*; Web site: *www.tipperary-crystal.com*

Donegal Tweeds

The Donegal Shop, 201 St. Stephen's Green Centre, 2nd floor, Grafton Street, Dublin 2; phone and fax: 1-475-4621; e-mail: *info@donegalshop.ie*; Web site: *www.donegalshop.ie*. This shop specializes in beautiful Donegal tweed jackets, tweed hats, scarves, capes, Irish linen, pottery, and cashmere sweaters.

Irish Linen and Lace

Not all linen and lace is handmade anymore, but it is still beautiful. Tablecloths that are hand-embroidered with matching napkins are usually quite expensive. You can also buy linen placemats with napkins. Handkerchiefs are a wonderful, small gift for you or for others. They come personalized with initials, and in different sizes for men, women, and children, lace-trimmed, and in a wide range of prices. Other small lace or linen gift items are tissue holders, sachet holders, bibs, blouses, and baby dresses.

THE DUNSANY HOME COLLECTION, Dunsany Castle, County Meath; phone: 46-26202; fax: 46-25823; Web site: *www.dunsany,com/dhc.htm.* Open daily. This boutique is located in the eight-hundred-year-old Dunsany Castle twenty miles north of Dublin. This is a trip well worth taking if you love beautiful things. There are beautiful table and bed linens, bedspreads, and gorgeous porcelain and table settings. Gorgeous damask cloths, Irish linen placemats, napkins, French stoneware, and Belgian glassware are also for sale. Even if you don't buy anything it is a treat to see what is on display in these lovely surroundings.

Men's Clothing

KENNEDY AND MCSHARRY, 39 Nassau Street, Dublin 2; phone: 1-677-8770. They specialize in Irish and international clothing such as Donegal tweeds, Aran wools, and men's suits.

KEVIN AND HOWLIN, 31 Nassau Street, Dublin 2; phone: 1-677-0257. They sell handmade tweed, cashmere, and mohair jackets, suits, and hats. You can also purchase fabrics here to take to your own tailor.

LOUIS COPELAND AND SONS, 39 Capel Street, Dublin 1; phone: 1-872-1600. This is the top men's shop in Dublin.

Weaving

ALICE RODEN, 2 Brookville, 89 Monkstown Road, Monkstown, Dublin; Phone: 1-230-2347. Monkstown is located in between Blackrock and Dun Laoghaire; e-mail: *aliceroden@ireland.com*

Alice Roden sells from and has her workshop at her home. You can drop in to visit her and see her beautiful upholstery fabric, wool throws, and other things that she weaves and has been weaving in her workshop for the last thirty years. She would prefer if you could call a day in advance for an appointment, but if not she will happily stop what she is doing to show you around. Alice Roden says she uses color and texture in her designs and that's what makes them so interesting. The colors are yellows, pinks, blues, browns, and greens and her textures come from silks, linens, and wool, sometimes woven together, sometimes not. This is definitely worth the short trip to Monkstown to see Alice Roden at work, and treat yourself to something beautiful.

Women's Clothing

Naturally, all of the department stores have excellent women's clothing, but sometimes I prefer a small shop. I will list a few of our favorites and perhaps you can add your own "finds."

CLEO, 18 Kildare Street, Dublin 2; phone: 1-676-1421. I love this little shop, which also has a shop in Kenmare. I bought beautiful pewter pins here, but it is their women's clothes and sweaters that makes Cleo famous. In this lovely shop you can find crochet shawls, socks, Aran sweaters, handwoven jackets, belts, children's knitwear, linen shirts, wool capes, and coats.

CLOTHES PEG, 3 Sutton Cross Shopping Centre, Sutton Cross, Dublin 13; phone: 1-832-1130; fax: 1-832-1442. The owner of this shop, Kay Lennox, is very helpful and has a good eye.

LOUISE KENNEDY, 56 Merrion Square, Dublin 2; phone: 1-662-0056 (listed under Crystal too), sells her own designer women's clothes and accessories in her beautiful townhouse.

Woolens

AVOCA HANDWEAVERS, 11–13 Suffolk Street, located near the Dublin tourist office; phone 1-286-7466; e-mail: *info@avoca.ie*; Web site: *www.avoca.ie*. Wheelchair accessible. Each of the Avoca shops sells a wide range of clothing including Aran sweaters, Irish tweeds, and Irish foodstuffs. They also sell pottery and glass, stationery, posters, and souvenir items. There is also a café.

AVOCA HANDWEAVERS, Kilmacanogue, Bray, County Wicklow. If you have a car and want to take a ride this is a nice trip.
This shop is a half hour drive from Dublin. Open daily 9 A.M.–6 P.M. Kilmacanoque (pronounced kill-mechanic) is near Powerscourt

and the two places could make a nice day trip. There is a cafeteria-style restaurant with hot and cold food and drinks, and an outdoor patio for good weather dining.

Avoca Handweavers, The Old Mill, County Wicklow. Open daily. This Avoca shop is an hour's drive from Dublin and you need a car to get there.

The oldest surviving hand-weaving company in Ireland, it dates from 1723. They weave tweeds and knitwear such as scarves and caps and gloves. You can also watch the weavers at work and buy their products in the outlet store. There is also a very nice restaurant with indoor and outdoor seating.

Blarney Woollen Mills, 21–23 Nassau Street (Metal Bridge Corner at Ha'Penny Bridge), Dublin 2; open daily Monday to Saturday 9 A.M.–6 P.M., Sunday 11 A.M.–6 P.M., Thursday until 8 P.M.; phone: 1-671-0068; fax 1-671-0156; e-mail: *blarney@blarney.ie*; Web site: *www.blarney.ie*

Aran woolens are sold all over Ireland and for good reason. I used to look for only handmade woolen Aran items, but now you can buy less expensive machine-made Aran items, and some are also made of silk and wool and synthetics. They come in children's and adult sizes. The store also sells postcards, gift items, Waterford crystal, Belleek china, Irish linen, and Irish crafts.

Dublin Woolen Mills, beside the Ha'Penny Bridge, 41 Lower Ormond Quay, Dublin 1; phone: 1-677-5014. This large wool shop sells beautiful sweaters for the entire family plus skirts, kilts, hats, gloves, scarves, and Irish souvenirs.

Monaghan's, 15–17 Grafton Street, Grafton Arcade; phone: 1-677-0823. Located at the beginning of the arcade. They specialize in gorgeous cashmere sweaters.

Major Crafts Shopping Centers

The Powerscourt Townhouse Shopping Center, located between South William Street and Clarendon Street west of Grafton Street, Dublin 2; phone: 1-679-4144. You can't miss it. Built in 1981, this complex was created out of an eighteenth-century townhouse and courtyard. Open daily from 9 A.M. to 6 P.M. Monday–Saturday, and 7 P.M. on Thursday. There are free lunchtime concerts. This is a four-story shopping complex with more than sixty boutiques, galleries, wine bars, and restaurants. The shops sell everything from antiques, crafts, jewelry, leather goods, clothing, cheese, candy, and everything else in between.

TOWER DESIGN CENTER, Pearse Street at Grand Canal Quay, Dublin 2; phone: 1-677-5655. Open Monday to Friday 9 A.M.–5:30 P.M. There is a restaurant here for a light lunch. This center was opened in 1983 after extensive renovation to an 1862 sugar refinery. They specialize in crafts from pottery, stationery, ceramics, gold jewelry, Celtic jewelry, and much more. You can also watch many of the craftspeople at work.

DESIGNYARD, 12 East Essex Street, Temple Bar, Dublin 2; phone: 1-677-8453. This was a Victorian warehouse redesigned and converted into a design center. It is a nonprofit center for Irish and European furniture, jewelry, glass, ceramics, lighting and textiles. Everything here is for sale.

Malls

Unfortunately Dublin and its suburbs now have over forty malls and shopping centers, just like any city. Try to avoid them. They have the same tacky shops that can be found anyplace. It is much more fun and interesting to shop and eat in the local villages or the souvenir shops right in the center of Dublin.

Markets

MOTHER REDCAP'S MARKET, 40–48 Back Lane, Dublin 8; phone: 1-453-8306. Open Friday, Saturday, and Sunday 10 A.M.–5:30 P.M. This is an enclosed market in the heart of Old Dublin filled with stalls selling used books, antiques, silver, crafts, coins, tapes, furniture, and Ryefield Food stall selling wonderful cheeses, jams, homebaked breads and cakes.

BLACKROCK MARKET, 19A Main Street, Blackrock, Dublin, is easily accessible by DART train to Blackrock Station. Open Saturday 11 A.M.–5:30 P.M., Sunday noon–5:30 P.M. and bank holidays noon–5:30 P.M. There are more than fifty stalls selling items from crafts to antiques, food, and clothing.

TEMPLE BAR BOOK MARKET, Saturdays 11 A.M.—5 P.M. This market sells old and new books. It is fun just to wander and browse.

Records

CLADDAGH RECORDS, 2 Cecilia Street, Temple Bar; phone: 1-677-0262; fax: 1-679-3664; e-mail; *claddagh@crl.ie.* They specialize in traditional Irish music, and will take orders and mail them worldwide.

VIRGIN MEGASTORE, 14 Aston Quay; phone: 677-7361. Anything and everything you can possibly want or think of is here.

WALTONS: 2 North Frederick Street; phone: 1-874-7805 or 69–70 South Great George's Street; phone: 1-475-0661; specializes in traditional Irish music, records, and instruments.

10. Leisure Activities

ACTIVITIES IN AND AROUND DUBLIN

Off-season Ireland is one of the most wonderful locations I can think of. The weather is mild all year round so almost all activities can be pursued whenever you visit. Golf is a twelve-month sport as is fishing, horse racing, and hiking. It's often easier to obtain a reservation during the off-season, but try to plan ahead as much as possible. Remember that it does rain in Ireland, so do bring proper attire (and shoes) for outdoor sports.

ADVENTURE

ADVENTURE ACTIVITIES DUBLIN, 5 Tritonville Avenue, Sandymount, Dublin 4; phone: 1-668-8047, e-mail: *eileent@tinet.ie.* All activities offered by this company are within a thirty-minute trip from the city center. Transportation and instructors are available for all levels of activities. Canoeing and kayaking are available in Sandycove Bay, only eight miles from Dublin. All equipment such as wetsuits, life preservers, and helmets are supplied. This company also has hiking in Dublin and the Wicklow Mountains and rock clmbing in the Dalkey Quarry.

BEACHES

Don't plan your trip to Ireland with swimming in mind, but there are some beautiful "strands" or beaches to walk along and admire. Beaches within a fifteen-mile radius of Dublin are mainly on the north side and on the DART, train, or bus lines: Dollymount, Howth, Sutton,

Portmarnock, Donabate, Malahide, and Skerries. Sandycove and Killiney beaches are on the south side.

BOATING

Boating in Ireland is becoming more and more popular. You can rent a boat for an hour or for days on the Grand Canal, linking Dublin to the Rivers Shannon and Barrow, and have loads of fun. Information is available through any Irish Tourist Office. The River Barrow offers cruising on one of Europe's most navigable waterways. There are thirty-two locks on the river. The other alternative is to boat on the Shannon, Ireland's longest river. Along the shores are castles, abbeys, and beautiful scenery. There are also areas along the routes for water skiing, windsurfing, canoeing, jet skiing, fishing areas, and bird watching. Small villages and pubs offer places to dock for the evening.

Barge, River, and Canal Trips

There are many companies that provide excellent trips through the rivers and canals in Ireland. I have listed a few reliable companies that I know and trust to run good trips. Many companies represent the Shannon Princess, but they also represent other cruisers. There are small boats and large ones, and all different price ranges. Check out these companies in addition to the Irish Tourist Office, which can supply other company names. Some companies are located in Ireland and others in the United States.

THE SHANNON PRINCESS is a twelve-passenger barge offering six night trips on the River Shannon. The barge is 105-feet long and has a lounge, bar, dining room, sun deck, and seven cabins all with in-room baths. The barge stops at little villages, sights, and naturally pubs. There are also golf cruises, which include tee times at the famous Lahinch, Galway Bay, Glasson, and other courses.

Boat Companies

THE BARGE LADY, Ellen Sack, 101 West Grand Avenue, Suite 200, Chicago, Illinois 60610. Phone toll-free: 800-880-0071; e-mail: *ellen www.bargelady.com*; Web site: *www.bargelady.com*

The Barge Lady represents the *Shannon Princess* and the *Bona Spes.*

The *Bona Spes* is an eight-passenger boat that cruises the River Shannon. It can be an entire boat charter or individual per person accommodations. It is an informal boat and it makes local stops along the river. You can also arrange for golf at Slieve Russel, Athlone, Glasson, Galway Bay, and Birr. Both are excellent choices as is this company.

CROWN BLUE LINE, phone: 888-355-9491; e-mail: *crownbluelineus@att. net*; Web site: *www.crown-blueline.com.* This company has self-skippered cabin cruisers with weekly rentals.

EMERALD STAR LINE, 47 Dawson Street, Dublin 2; phone: 1-679-8166; fax: 1-679-8165

EUROPEAN WATERWAYS, phone: 800-546-4777; Web site: *www. ewaterways.com.* This company also uses the *Shannon Princess* and cruises from Athlone to Killaloe along the Shannon River. A group can charter the entire barge for a week, and stop to play golf at the top courses.

LE BOAT, 10 S. Franklin Turnpike, Suite 204B, Ramsey, NJ 07446; phone: 201-560-1941, Toll Free in U.S. and Canada 800-992-0291; fax: 201-560-1945; e-mail: *debbie@leboat.com*; Web Site: *www.leboat.com*; toll-free for Yacht Charters: 877-453-2628. This company has an entire Ireland brochure and ten boats that they represent plus the *Shannon Princess*. Some sail on the Shannon, others can include two lakes. They provide many extras such as airport pickup, bicycles, one-way sailing, free parking at all starting points, and much more. There are also golf weeks where you can sail and play golf each day.

SHANNON CASTLE LINE, Williamstown Harbor, Whitegate, County Clare; phone: 61-927-042; Web site: *www.shannoncastleline.com*

BICYCLE TRIPS AND RENTALS

There are many companies that have bicycle trips or you can rent a bicycle on your own; buy a good map and off you go. It is easy to bike ride around Dublin since there are no steep hills, but there is a lot of traffic, horn honking, and taxis. Be sure to lock your bicycle if you leave it unattended.

BICYCLE RENTALS: Rentals usually cost approximately IR 35-40 per week plus a deposit. The tourist office can supply a complete list of rental companies. Here are just a few: **Joe Daly,** Lower Main Street,

Dundrum; phone: 1-298-1485; **C. Harding,** 30 Bachelor's Walk; phone: 1-873-2455; **McDonald's,** 38 Wexford Street; phone: 1-475-2586; and **Track Cycles,** 8 Botanic Road, Glasnavin, Dublin 9; phone: 1-873-2445.

Where the tongue slips, it speaks the truth.

♣ —IRISH PROVERB ♣

Bicycle Trips

BACKROADS, 801 Cedar Street, Berkeley, CA 94710-1800; phone 800-GO-ACTIVE; 510-527-1555; fax 510-527-1444; Web site: *www. backroads.com*

This is an outstanding company with excellent guides and hotels or inns. The bike trip is expensive, but well worth it. You must be in good condition since the current Cork and Kerry trip requires a minimum of sixteen miles per day of riding. The tour includes most meals, but transportation to and from the meeting point, bike rentals, and single supplement are not included.

BUTTERFIELD AND ROBINSON, 70 Bond Street, Toronto, Ontario, Canada M5B 1X3; phone 416-864-1354; fax 416-864-0541; e-mail: *info@butterfield.com*; Web site: *www.butterfield.com*

This year the Ireland Bike Tour is Biking through Connemara and the Aran Islands. This is the West Coast of Ireland, and the tour starts and ends in Galway. B&R is a top-of-the-line company so the tour is expensive, but if you can do it you won't be sorry.

DUBLIN BIKE TOURS, the Harding Hotel, Fishamble Street, Dublin 2; phone: 1-679-0899; e-mail: *dublinbiketours@connect.ie*

This company conducts a variety of tours daily from April 1 until October 31. There are two 3-hour tours. One departs at 10 A.M. and the other at 2 P.M. both with local guides provided. The tour is conducted through the quieter streets of Dublin so you can avoid the busy traffic. There is a snack stop at a historical location. If you don't have a bicycle you can rent one.

BIRD WATCHING

Ireland has over sixty bird sanctuaries. Just bring your binoculars and write or call for information on trips and the seasons and locations to view the birds.

WILDLIFE SERVICE, OFFICE OF PUBLIC WORKS, 51 St. Stephen's Green, Dublin 2; phone: 1-661-3111

IRISH WILD BIRD CONSERVANCY, Rutledge House, 8 Longford Place, Monkstown, Dublin; phone: 1-280-4322

THE BOOTERSTOWN MARSH AND BIRD SANCTUARY, Booterstown, Dublin 4

BULL ISLAND INTERPRETATIVE CENTER on Dublin's northside is a national nature reserve with many wading birds.

Located within County Dublin a short car or DART train ride away is the largest wildlife preserve in the area. Here you can see kingfishers, herons, and many rare birds. Ireland has over one hundred twenty-five species of wild birds.

SANDYMOUNT STRAND, located on Dublin's southside is another place to see a large number of birds especially during the summer months.

BUS TOURS IN THE CITY CENTER AND BEYOND

BOYNE VALLEY TOURS, Phone: 46-25239; toll-free: 850-241-555; fax: 046-25588; e-mail: *stnhouse@indigo.ie*

This tour begins at 8 A.M. in Dublin at one of many pickup points and returns to Dublin at 8 P.M. The tour includes beautiful sightseeing in the Boyne Valley, the Hill of Tara, Dunsany, Newgrange, Knowth and Dowth, plus more. Lunch and dinner are also included. Discounts are available for prebooking, seniors, and groups.

BUS EIREANN, Phone: 1-830-2222; e-mail: *info@buseireann.ie*; Web site: *www.buseireann.ie.* Tours can be booked at the Bus Eireann Desk, Tourist Centre, Suffolk Street, Dublin 2; Dublin Bus Office, 59 Upper O'Connell Street, Dublin 1; hotel concierge; phone orders with a credit card 1-872-5022. There are various pick-up points in the city, which you can decide upon when you buy your ticket. All of the tours mentioned here are one-day tours.

Bus Eireann has operated bus tours from Dublin for over sixty years. They run tours on- and off-season with different schedules and rates. Some tours run by Bus Eireann are Glendalough and Wicklow Panorama, Newgrange and the Boyne Valley, Kilkenny City and Nore

Valley Drive, Ballykissangel and Wicklow, Powerscourt Gardens, River Barrow Luncheon Cruise and Waterford Crystal, and the last day tour is the Mountains of Mourne.

DUBLIN BUS TOURS, 59 Upper O'Connell Street, Dublin 1; phone: 1-873-4222. Tours depart from the Dublin Bus Office, but hotel pickup is available. Arrange with your hotel concierge. Operates daily from 8:30 A.M. You can take the **Grand Dublin City Tour** that lasts three hours or the **Dublin City Hop-On Hop-Off Tour** of ten major Dublin points of interest, the three-hour **Coast and Castle Tour,** the **Dublin Ghost Bus Tour,** or the **South Coast Tour.**

GUIDE FRIDAY BUS TOURS/GRAY LINE SIGHTSEEING TOURS, phone: 1-676-5377. Children under five tour free with adult. Hop-On Hop-Off Bus tours of the city of Dublin plus half- and full-day tours outside of Dublin. They operate open-top double-decker buses. Tour highlights include the National Art Gallery, Dublin Castle, Trinity College, the Guinness Brewery, the GPO, the president of Ireland's residence, Phoenix Park, Dublin Zoo, and much more.

Half-day tours include Malahide Castle and North Dublin including the village of Howth. Another half-day tour is to Glendalough in Wicklow. A beautiful half-day tour is to Powerscourt House and the village of Enniskerry. For a full-day tour you might include a trip south to Glendalough, Wicklow Mountains, Sandycove, Dun Laoghaire, Dalkey, and Killiney. Extended tours include two days to the Ring of Kerry, one day to Killarney, and other interesting trips.

IRISH CITY TOURS, Keatings Park, Rathcoole, Dublin; phone: 1-458-0054; fax: 1-458-0808. Tickets are available from the driver for this Hop-On Hop-Off tour of Dublin. The tour lasts approximately ninety minutes if you stay on the entire tour, and can be picked up at any of the fourteen stops the bus makes. There is a tour that departs every twenty minutes from 9:30 A.M. to 4:30 P.M. The first pick-up point is 12 Upper O'Connell Street. Some of the other stops and highlights include Trinity College, Grafton Street, National Gallery, Leinster House, Fitzwilliam Square, St. Stephen's Green, Temple Bar, Dublin Castle, Christ Church Cathedral, St. Patrick's Cathedral, Guinness Brewery, and Phoenix Park.

MARY GIBBONS & DAUGHTER TOURS, Contact Dublin Tourist Office, 1-460-4464, Fax: 1-460-4426; e-mail: *marygibbonstours@tinet.ie*

The excellent full and half-day tours can be reserved through the

Irish Tourist Board or you. Daily half-day start at one of several pickup points at 9 A.M. and end at Trinity College at 12:15 P.M. The tour includes Phoenix Park, Dublin Castle, Christ Church Cathedral, the General Post Office, O'Connell Street, St. Patrick's Cathedral, and the National Museum and library. Other longer half-day tours are of Glendalough and Powerscourt or the Boyne Valley.

OVER THE TOP AND INTO THE WEST, Phone: 1-838-6128 or 088-259-3467; e-mail: *info@irishbustours.com*; Web site: *www.irishbustours. com.* Winter schedule: weekends only. All tours start from the Dublin Tourist office at Suffolk Street, Dublin 2 daily at 9:30 A.M. and return at 5:30 P.M. Maximum number of passengers in each tour is fourteen.

The tour travels over the Dublin Mountains to Sally Gap in the Wicklow Mountains. Visit the sights where *Braveheart* and *Ballykissangel* were filmed. Then on to lakes, waterfalls, Glendalough, lunch, a walk and back to Dublin. There are weekend tours from Dublin to Connemara in County Galway and the Burren in County Clare.

VIKING SPLASH TOUR, phone: 1-855-3000; Web site: *www. vikingsplashtours.com*

This is a combined tour on land and sea. The tour lasts 1 hour and 15 minutes, Tuesday to Saturday and departs every half hour. The tour departs from the garden side of St. Patrick's Cathedral. First there is a short tour by bus of Dublin and then a tour by boat of the Grand Canal Basin.

WILD WICKLOW TOURS, Aran Tours Ltd.; phone: 1-280-1899; mobile 87-274-4727; e-mail: *wildcoachtours.com*; Web site: *www.wildcoachtours.com*

Daily March through November and every Saturday and Sunday all year round. There is pickup starting at 8:50 A.M. at the Shelbourne Hotel in Dublin and continuing to other stops. When you make your reservation request a pickup near your hotel. The tour returns you to your pickup point starting at 5 P.M.

Advance reservations are required. This is a full day "off the beaten track" tour in a twenty-six-seat Mercedes bus. The day includes Dun Laoghaire Harbour, Sandycove's James Joyce Tower, Killiney Bay, Avoca Handweaver's shop for coffee and shopping, Glendalough, lunch in Laragh in a traditional Irish pub, and finally the mountains and lakes for gorgeous views, and then back to Dublin via the villages of Glencree and Enniskerry.

May the hinges of our friendship never grow rusty.
♣ —IRISH PROVERB ♣

CAMPING

The Irish Tourist Board has a complete brochure listing all campsites. Camping is the least expensive way to stay in Ireland and still see everything. Facilities have improved greatly for campers and for those who rent trailers, known as caravans. Ask for **Caravan and Camping Ireland** at the Tourist Board.

CARRIAGE TOURS

DUBLIN HORSE-DRAWN CARRIAGE TOURS, St. Stephen's Green, Dublin 2; phone: 1-453-8888. Usually it is first-come, first-served, but you can call in advance. Carriages usually hold from two to five people. Available from April through October, day and night depending on the weather. Prices depend on the number of passengers and the length of the tour so speak with the carriage driver and negotiate. The driver is usually full of information and will take you on a Georgian Tour or Old City tour.

COOKING SCHOOLS

BALLYMALOE COOKERY SCHOOL, Ballymaloe Cookery School, Shanagarry, Midleton, County Cork, Ireland; phone (from U.S.): 011-353 (0) 21-4646-785; fax: 011-353-(0)21-464-6909; e-mail: *info@ cookingisfun.ie*; Web site: *www.cookingisfun.ie*

This school was opened in 1983 and is open all year. It is located in a village near the sea in the South of Ireland and it is one hour from the Cork Airport, which is a forty-five-minute flight from Dublin Airport or a four-hour drive from Dublin. Pickup is provided for airport or train station arrivals. There are one- to five-day hands-on courses and twelve-week certificate courses. There are also a variety of options such as a one-day Christmas cooking demonstration and a weekend Entertaining course. Courses also include seafood and vegetarian dishes. Rates in 2000 were: one-day courses are IR135, weekend courses are IR295, and five-day courses are IR520. Accommodation is extra. Fishing and golf is available nearby. It is important to check the rates since they are subject to change and also depend on which of the many excellent courses you choose. Also at Ballymaloe are Wine Courses, Gardening Courses, Painting, Writing Skills, Photography, Restaurant Management, and much more.

HILLIARD & OLANDER, LTD., 608 Second Avenue South, Minneapolis, MN 55402; phone: 612-333-1440, toll-free in the U.S. 800-

229-8407; fax. 612-333-3554; e-mail: *diane@hilliardolander.com*. This fifteen-year-old company specializes in European cooking and travel experiences. The year 2000 Ireland trip included staying at country houses and enjoying country gardens, homes, and kitchens.

BALTIMORE INTERNATIONAL COLLEGE, 17 Commerce Street, Baltimore, MD 21202; phone toll-free: 800-624-9926, 410-752-4710; fax: 410-752-3730; Web site: *www.bic.edu.* Ireland's campus is in County Cavan, fifty miles outside Dublin. Courses are held all year round. Students may also participate in golf, tennis, fishing, and boating. This is a private college established in 1987 offering an associate degree in Professional Cooking. The school is also open to non-professionals.

DIVING

IRISH UNDERWATER COUNCIL, 78A Patrick Street, Dun Laoghaire; phone: 1-284-4601. For all information on SCUBA diving in Dublin and Ireland.

OCEANTEC, 10–11 Marine Terrace, Dun Laoghaire; phone: 1-280-1083. Located in Dun Laoghaire, this school offers lessons, rents equipment, arranges for local dives, and can arrange diving vacations.

EQUESTRIAN VACATIONS

(*See* "Horse Racing" in this section)

FISHING

Ireland is well known for its fishing; some tourists come here exclusively to fish. The fishing season is January 1 to September 30. Fishing is available in the greater Dublin area and in many areas around Ireland. The Irish Tourist Board, Bord Failte, has a great deal of information on fishing plus an excellent brochure, *Angling in Ireland*. Another good source of information is the *Dublin Freshwater Angling Guide* available through The Dublin Initiative, Balnagowan, Mobhi Boreen, Glasnevin, Dublin 9; phone: 1-837-9209.

You must have a permit for fishing and a government license for salmon and sea trout fishing. Permits are obtainable from fishing-tackle shops. You can also get equipment, bait, and all the help you might need from the shopkeeper. Good areas for sea fishing are Howth, Dun Loaghaire, and Greystones. The River Liffey has salmon and trout fishing. Ireland has lakes, ponds, streams, and creeks all full of fish such as perch, rudd, pike, salmon, sea trout, and brown trout.

The village of Howth has a club located right on the pier. **Howth Sea Angling Club,** 15A West Pier, Howth, County Dublin.

> *May your troubles be less*
> *And your blessings be more.*
> *And nothing but happiness*
> *Come through your door.*
>
> ♣ —IRISH BLESSING ♣

GAELIC GAMES

The Gaelic Athletic Association (GAA), Croke Park, Jones Road, Dublin 3; phone: 1-836-3222. Gaelic Football and Hurling are fast, exciting games. Hurling is played with something that looks like a hockey stick and is called a "hurley." Gaelic football is different from soccer and U.S. football. There are games held in the park stadium but if you want to see a final match call for a ticket while reading this book. They are very difficult to get. The All-Ireland finals are held each September and it is almost impossible to get tickets, but pre-final game tickets are usually available.

GARDENING COURSES

BALLYMALOE, Shanagarry, Midelton, County Cork; phone from the U.S. 11-353-(0)-21-4646-785; fax: 011-353-(0)-21-4646-909. Courses are conducted from March through early October. They run from half day, one day, one and a half days, or five days, and range in price from 50 Irish Pounds (punts) for a half-day course to 750 Irish pounds for the five-day course plus accommodations if required. Course choices include Window Box and Hanging Baskets, Grow Your Own Herbs, Organic Gardening, Seed Saving, and Garden Design.

GARDEN TOURS

EXPO GARDEN TOURS, 33 Fox Crossing, Litchfield, CT 06759; phone: 860-567-0322, 800-448-2685; fax: 860-567-0381; e-mail: *info@expogardentours.com*

This company runs garden tours throughout the country. There is a new brochure issued each year with a complete itinerary including fees for accomodation and travel. An example is the "Hidden Gardens of Ireland" tour. Fly into Dublin with the group or on your own, and the first three of the nine nights in Ireland are spent in Dublin visiting the gardens of Mr. and Mrs. Guinness of brewery fame, and other private gardens. Continue on to County Wicklow and its famous Powerscourt Gardens. Then to Cork, Killarney, and home from Shannon.

Note: This tour was discontinued for the year 2001, but they plan to continue it again in 2002.

PRIVATE GARDEN TOUR, 45 Sandford Road, Ranelagh, Dublin 6; phone/fax: 1-497-1308. This is a private home and garden located ten minutes by bus from the city center or a leisurely half hour walk. The gardens are open to visitors at certain hours. The gardener is Helen Dillon who is a garden designer and has designed gardens for many beautiful homes in Ireland. Open from 2–6 P.M. in March, July, and August and Sundays in April, May, June, and September.

GARDENS TO VISIT

ARDGILLAN VICTORIAN GARDEN, Balbriggan, County Dublin; phone: 1-849-2212. Open all year from 10 A.M.–5 P.M. Rose gardens, herb and vegetable gardens and unusual fruits. While there visit the Victorian style house and tea room.

GARDEN OF REMEMBERANCE, Parnell Square East, Dublin 1. Open daily 9:30 A.M.–8 P.M. Dedicated to the memory of those who died for Irish freedom.

HOWTH CASTLE RHODODENDRONS, Contact the Deer Park Hotel, 1-832-2624.

IVEAGH GARDENS, Clonmel Street, Dublin 2; phone: 1-661-3111. Beautifully restored gardens open daily from Monday to Saturday at 8 A.M.

JAPANESE GARDENS, Tully, County Kildare. Open daily 9:30 A.M.– 6 P.M. *See* Chapter 12, "Day Trips."

MALAHIDE CASTLE GARDENS, phone: 1-872-7777. Open May through September daily 2–5 P.M. Known as the Talbot Botanic Gardens, the gardens have over five thousand types of plants covering 22 acres. *See* Chapter 12, "Day Trips."

NATIONAL BOTANIC GARDENS, Glasnevin, County Dublin; phone: 1-837-7596. Open daily. *See* chapter 12 "Day Trips."

NEWBRIDGE DEMESNE, Donabate, County Dublin; phone: 1-843-6064. Open all year. Walled gardens located at Newbridge House. *See* chapter 12 "Day Trips."

POWERSCOURT GARDENS, Enniskerry, County Wicklow. *See* chapter 12 "Day Trips."

ST. STEPHEN'S GREEN, Dublin 2. Open Monday to Saturday from 8 A.M. This is a beautiful twenty-two-acre Victorian park in the city center.

WAR MEMORIAL GARDENS, Islandbridge, Dublin 8. Open daily. This garden is dedicated to the soldiers who died in World War I.

GLIDING AND HANG-GLIDING

For general information on gliding in the Dublin area contact the following organization:

DUBLIN GLIDING CLUB, phone: 45-897-681.

GOLF

GOLFING UNION OF IRELAND, 81 Eglinton Road, Dublin 4; phone: 1-269-4111. This is Ireland's golfing association, and they can supply information on all courses and the calendar of golf events throughout the year. (This includes the thirty-two counties of the Island of Ireland.)

There are 355 golf courses in Ireland so you have many options. Ireland also has three of the top twelve courses in the world. Some courses are links and others parkland, some have carts or caddies available and others you walk and pull a cart. Besides having some of the best golf courses they have excellent golf tours and companies that handle them. If you are traveling independently you can fax your hotel and request tee times to be secured for you, or you can also call the club on your own and schedule tee times. Or you can plan your trip with a company that will arrange for the best courses and tee times for you. Do not wait to arrive in Ireland to try to get a tee time. It will be difficult.

Golfing Ireland: Reservations call center, phone: 66-979-2022; fax: 66-979-2035; e-mail: *golf@iol.ie*; Web site: *www.golfing-ireland.com.*

This is a tee time reservation service established by the Irish Tourist Board and participating golf clubs. They are also associated with tour operators and will plan an entire golf holiday and represent over 25 of the top courses and clubs.

To Keep in Mind When Planning a Golf Vacation

IT MAY RAIN There is no such thing as a rain check. In one day it is possible to see rain, sun, wind, and sleet. If you plan on playing more than one round of golf, come prepared. Bring a sweater, waterproof shoes, and raingear. Ireland can have all four seasons in one day.

SUNDAY BAGS If you plan to play more than one round and are traveling with your own clubs, bring a light bag. Caddies and carts are not always available. On some courses you might have to carry your own bag, or hire a pull cart.

PRIVATE CLUBS AND PAY AND PLAY COURSES **Private clubs** in Ireland do not let visitors play if you just show up unannounced. You can try booking in advance and in most cases you can secure a time, but members have priority. Some clubs permit visitors only on certain days and during certain hours. Other clubs cater to visitors, but still should be reserved before arrival. **Pay and Play** are public courses that welcome all players, but still should be reserved in advance so you are not disappointed.

> I called to reserve a tee time for my husband at a famous club. I identified myself as "Mrs. Lehman." The golf pro said, "Would that be for Tom Lehman?" (One of golfing's greatest). I had to admit the truth, the Pro laughed, but unfortunately the course could not accommodate him for the time we were in Dublin. Maybe next time!

Golf Tour Companies

The following companies will organize independent itineraries and, if necessary, car rentals, driver service, hotels, tee times at the best courses in addition to courses that are not quite so popular and well known, but are excellent. If you do not want to travel with your own clubs, many clubs rent them and you just need to bring shoes. Some clubs require a Handicap Certificate and Letter of Introduction from a home club, whereas others are happy to book outsiders. It is your responsibility to have these available for some courses, and be sure to ask these companies about everything that is required.

ADVENTURES IN GOLF, Ken Hamill, Director, 11 Northeastern Blvd., Suite 360, Nashua, NH 03062; phone 1-603-882-8367; fax 603-595-6514; e-mail: *aig@hamilltravelsvcs.mv.com*

ATLANTIC GOLF, 237 Post Road West, Westport, CT 06880; phone 203-454-1086; fax 203-454-8840, toll-free: 800-542-6224; e-mail: *AtlanticGolf@AtlanticGolf.com*; Web site: *www.AtlanticGolf.com*
This excellent company provides customized as well as preplanned tours. They also have special off-season golf tours at very reasonable rates. If you want to plan for the Ryder Cup to be held in Ireland in 2005, plan now. A few of the many courses that are available through this company are: Ballybunion Old, Lahinch, Waterville, Tralee, Connemara, and Royal Portrush.

CARR GOLF TRAVEL, Three-time British Amateur Champion and Walker Cup player, Joe Carr, bases this firm in Ireland. Dublin office: Carr Golf and Corporate Travel, 30 Upper Abbey Street, Dublin 1, Ireland; phone: in the U.S. 800-882-2656, 011-353-1-873-4244; fax: 011-353-1-873-4091; e-mail: *carrgolf@indigo.ie*; Web site: *www.carrgolf.com* and *www.golfingireland.com*

ITC GOLF TOURS, 4134 Atlantic Avenue, Suite 205, Long Beach, CA 90807; phone: 562-595-6905, toll-free: 800-257-4981; fax: 562-424-6683; e-mail: *itcgolf@juno.com*
This company will arrange group or custom tours in Ireland as well as in many other countries. They also have many price ranges, from deluxe to tourist class accommodations. This company also has golf tours to Northern Ireland. The tours all have Dublin extensions so you can have the opportunity to play the famous Portmarnock or Royal Dublin course.

JAMESON: THE GOLFERS GUIDE TO IRELAND. This is an outstanding publication, which you can receive free from the Irish Tourist Board. It lists all of the courses and tour companies. You'll have to make the necessary reservations.

JERRY QUINLAN'S CELTIC GOLF, 1129 Route 9 South, P.O. Box 608, Cape May Court House, NJ 08210; phone: 800-535-6148, 609-465-

0600; fax: 609-465-0670; e-mail: *celticgolf@aol.com*; Web site: *www.jq celticgolf.com.*

This company offers escorted golf tours to Ireland's Northwest, Southwest, Dublin as well as special event tours such as couples only, father and son tours, and tournaments. Links courses, gourmet tour with golf, and tours that include the British Open plus Ireland golf.

PERRY GOLF, 8302 Dunwoody Place, Suite 305, Atlanta, GA 30350-3317; phone: 800-344-5257, 770-641-9696; fax: 770-641-9798; e-mail: *perrygolf@golftravel.com*; Web site: *www.golf.com/travel/PerryGolf/*

GOLFING IRELAND, 18 Parnell Square, Dublin 1; phone: 1-872-6711; fax: 1-872-6632; e-mail: *golf@iol.ie*; Web site: *www.golfing-ireland. com*

Their publication can be obtained free of charge from the Irish Tourist Board or by contacting them. It lists clubs near Dublin and other areas, rates, days that visitors are allowed, reservation service for tee times, and national golf events.

ROUND BALL GOLF TOURS, P.O. Box 16286, Pittsburgh, PA 15242. Phone: 1-800-238-7170. They offer customized packages from B&B's to Castle hotels. Courses played include Ballybunion, Lahinch, Royal County Down, Royal Portrush, Portmarnock, and more.

A Few of the Fifty Courses Within an Hour's Drive of Dublin

South of Dublin

DRUIDS GLEN, Gleann na Drioite: Newtownmountkennedy, County Wicklow; phone: 1-287-3600; fax: 01-287-3699; e-mail: *info@druidsglen.ie*; Web site: *www.druidsglen.ie*

This is an 18-hole, par 71 course. It is a gorgeous parkland course, which opened in 1995. The club is located thirty minutes from Dublin in County Wicklow. There are caddies, carts, a practice area, golf shop, and restaurant. To play here you must be a member of another club and reserve ahead of time. At the time of this writing the green fees per person, per round, is 90 Irish pounds.

THE K CLUB, Kildare Country Club, Straffan, County Kildare; phone: 1-601-7200; fax: 1-601-7299; e-mail: *hotel@kclub.ie*; Web site: *www.kclub.ie*

Green fees at time of writing: 130 Irish pounds per person, per round. Bring a handicap certificate from your home club.

Located seventeen miles west of Dublin, it is an 18-hole, par 72 parkland course designed by Arnold Palmer. It will host the 2005 Ryder Cup Tournament. Non-members can play daily except Monday and Friday for a very steep fee. The up side is the course is gorgeous and difficult. It is a major challenge for a fine player. There are caddies, caddy carts, club rental, and pro shop, restaurant, and shoe rental and practice area.

POWERSCOURT GOLF CLUB, Enniskerry, County Wicklow; phone: 1-204-6033; fax: 1-276-1303; e-mail: *golfclub@powerscourt.ie*; Web site: *www.powerscourt.ie/golfclub.* Open daily.

This is a par 72 championship parkland course with views of the sea and Sugar Loaf Mountain and lower green fees before 10 A.M. Golf clubs, carts, or golf trolleys are available for hire for driving or pulling. There is a clubhouse with a bar, restaurant, Pro shop, and a practice range. There is also a small apartment complex; advance reservations required.

ROUNDWOOD GOLF CLUB, Newtownmountkennedy, County Wicklow; phone: 1-281-8488; fax: 1-284-3642. Located on the Roundwood Glendalough Road in a beautiful part of County Wicklow with views of mountains, lakes, and the sea. Open daily. Pull carts and snack bar available. Everyone is welcome at this reasonably priced course.

North of Dublin

CORBALLIS GOLF LINKS, Donabate, County Dublin; phone: 1-843-6583; fax: 1-822-6668; Web site: *www.golfdublin.com*; e-mail: *corballis@golfdublin.com*

Located thirty minutes north of Dublin, this is Ireland's only public links course, and it is open all year. It has been described as a "little gem." Visitors are always welcome to this 18 hole, par 65 course, which charges very reasonable greens fees. You can rent clubs; caddies are available; and there's a very nice restaurant next door.

DEER PARK HOTEL AND GOLF COURSES, Howth, County Dublin; phone: 1-832-2624; fax: 1-839-2405; e-mail: *sales@deerpark.iol.ie*; Web site: *www.deerpark-hotel.ie*

Located nine miles from Dublin on the grounds of the Howth Castle overlooking the Irish Sea, there is a hotel plus four parkland courses on the grounds. There are 18- and 9-hole courses on the grounds with very reasonable greens fees. There are no restrictions for guest players. Club rentals are available.

ISLAND GOLF CLUB, Corballis, Donabate, County Dublin; phone: 1-843-6104. Located fifteen miles from Dublin, this is a links course that could only be reached by boat until 1960. This is an 18-hole, par 71 course. Non-members can play there on Monday, Tuesday, and Friday. There is a practice area and restaurant.

PORTMARNOCK GOLF CLUB, Portmarnock, County Dublin; phone: 1-846-2794/846-2968; fax: 1-846-2601; e-mail: *secretary@portmarnock-golfclub.ie*; Web site: *www.portmarnockgoldclub.ie* Founded in 1894, Portmarnock is considered one of the greatest links golf courses in the world. It is surrounded by water on three sides. Visitors can play here by prior arrangement only on certain days and hours.

PORTMARNOCK HOTEL AND GOLF LINKS, Portmarnock, County Dublin, phone: 1-846-0611; toll free from the U.S.: 800-457-4000; fax: 1-846-2442; e-mail: *reservations@portmarnock.com*; Web site: *www.portmarnock.com*
Portmarnock Hotel and Gold Links is located at the former home of the Jameson family. It was converted into a deluxe hotel in 1996.

ROYAL DUBLIN GOLF CLUB, Dollymount, Clontarf, County Dublin; phone: 1-833-6346. Located only four miles from Dublin on Bull Island, which is also a bird sanctuary, this is a links club with an 18 hole, par 72 course. Non-members can play on Monday, Tuesday, Thursday, and Friday. There is a practice area, caddies, caddy carts, and a restaurant.

ST. MARGARET'S GOLF AND COUNTRY CLUB, St. Margaret's, County Dublin; phone: 1-864-0400; fax: 1-864-0289. This beautiful parkland course opened in 1992. It has 18 holes and is par 72. Guests can play daily. There is a practice area, caddies, caddy carts, club rentals, a bar and restaurant.

SWORDS OPEN GOLF COURSE, Balheary Avenue, Swords, County Dublin; phone: 1-840-9819. This is a very inexpensive, 18-hole club to play and it is open daily for outsiders. In 2000 their fees were 9 IR pounds during the week and 12 IR pounds on weekends.

GREYHOUND RACING

Racing is held year-round at the **Shelbourne Park Greyhound Stadium,** Shelbourne Park, Dublin 4; phone: 1-668-3502 and **Harold's Cross Stadium,** 151 Harold's Cross Road, Dublin 6; phone: 1-497-1081. For the complete yearly schedule of races contact: Bord na gCon, which is the Greyhound Board at Shelbourne Park, 1-668-3502. Races usually start at 8 P.M. and are over by 10 P.M. There is betting, bars, and restaurants at these facilities.

HEALTH CLUBS

Many hotels now have health clubs and swimming pools. If your hotel does not have a health club, you can easily find one in Dublin. Check the local phone book.

JACKIE SCALLY STUDIOS, 41–42 Clarendon Street, Dublin 2; phone: 1-677-0040. Located behind the Westbury Hotel. Open Monday to Friday 6:30 A.M.—9:30 P.M., Saturday 9:30 A.M.–6 P.M., Sunday 10:30 A.M.–5 P.M. They have cardiovascular and weight training, and accept visitors for a day at off-peak hours.

WORLD GYM, 8–9 Talbot Street, Dublin 1; phone: 1-874-6099. Open Monday to Friday 10 A.M.–10 P.M., Saturday 10 A.M.–4 P.M., Sunday 10 A.M.–2 P.M. This club has free weights, bikes, a steam bath and solarium. They accept per-day guests at any time.

Wisdom makes a poor man a king.
♣ —IRISH PROVERB ♣

HORSE RACING

If you love horses you have come to the right place. Ireland breeds beautiful horses and they race well and often. There are currently twenty-seven racecourses in Ireland, all of which have an upbeat atmosphere. More courses are under construction. They are informal and children are welcome. There are Festival meetings as well as just race days. Festival meetings usually include evening and day races, and the town of the meet has other activities such as processions, music, theater, and fun. The Galway races in the fall coincide with the opening of the oyster season. The major festivals are: Fairyhouse Easter Festival in April, Punchestown Spring Festival in April, Killarney Spring Festival in May and again in July, Curragh Derby Festival in June, Galway Summer Festival in July and again in September, Tramore Festival in August, The Rose of Tralee Festival in August, Listowel Festival in September, and two Christmas Festivals, one at Leopardstown and one in Limerick. As you can see, off-season racing is very popular. If you are interested write to the racing authority at the address below. Festival dates change yearly.

For information before leaving home: contact the **Irish Horseracing Authority,** Leopardstown Racecourse, Foxrock, Dublin 18, Ireland; phone: 011-353-1-289-2888; fax: 011-353-1-289-2019; e-mail: *info@irishracing.iha.ie*; Web site: *www.iha.ie/iharace*

If you write or e-mail, you will receive the annual **Irish Racing Calendar,** which will supply you with all of the information necessary for the entire year of racing. The calendar includes all races, and they are run someplace in Ireland every month, off-season and on. The calendar also includes major races, festival meetings, and general information such as race time, admission prices for adults, senior citizens, students, and children under fourteen.

There are two very interesting books that can be obtained from the Irish Horseracing Authority. I love *Travelling the Turf in Ireland.* It has beautiful color pictures of horses, plus all the race dates of the flat and hurdle races, a map of where the courses are located, and a description of the major courses, how to get there, and what is available when you arrive. You'll also get information or restaurants, hotels, places of interest, and transportation. The other book is the *Irish Field Directory,* which includes information on pony clubs, riding centers, hunting, stallions, studs, riders, and trainers. Have fun, but be sure to save some money for a good dinner, a pub, or some music.

The highlight of the year is the show organized by the **Royal Dublin Society** (**RDS**) held each year during the first week of August from Wednesday to Sunday. It is known as the **Kerrygold Horse Show.** For exact dates and events call the RDS Events Department. Phone: 1-668-0866; fax: 1-660-4014; e-mail: *info@rds.ie*; Web site: *www.rds.ie*

In 1999 I attended the 127th annual show and Irish President Mrs. Mary McAleese presented the winner of the famous Aga Kahn Nations Cup race with the trophy. That event is always held on Friday and is always sold out. Buy your tickets early if you wish to attend. Other events during the week include the best horses in the country in show jumping, bands, ponies, the antique fair held in the main building, children's shows, restaurants, Ladies' Day held on Thursday with the Best Dressed Lady receiving a prize too. It is a wonderful event. If you love horses try to attend at least one event during the week.

BEACH RACING: This is only a one evening event each year and is held on the beach at Laytown, 23 miles from Dublin in County Meath. It is usually held in June and is the only beach race held in the country. Call 41-984-2111.

> *Have sense, patience, and self-restraint, and no mischief will come.*
>
> ♣ —IRISH PROVERB ♣

Important Race Courses

THE CURRAGH is the premier flat course in Ireland. It is located in County Kildare, twenty-seven miles southwest of Dublin. On race days there are special buses from Dublin. The Irish Derby is held here on the last weekend in June. Phone 45-441205.

FAIRYHOUSE was the first official steeplechase course in Ireland and is located twelve miles northwest of Dublin in County Meath.

LEOPARDSTOWN is only six miles south of Dublin and is very popular due to low admission fees and facilities. Also located at Leopardstown is the **ICON,** the home of Bailey's Irish Cream; phone: 1-289-1000; Web site: *www.baileys.com*

Open daily except Christmas and Good Friday. Admission charge. Bailey's has developed an entertainment, shopping, and eating center at the racetrack. There is a twelve-minute 3-D video about Ireland past and present, and a complimentary glass of Baileys at the end of the video. There are two shops, the Kilkenny shop and the Bailey's shop and many restaurants and pubs.

PUNCHESTOWN is located twenty miles south of Dublin in County Kildare. The National Hunt festival is held here in April and is considered one of the biggest meetings of the year.

There are many other courses, but I have mentioned just a few of many highlights. If you are interested in racing contact the Horseracing Authority at the above address.

Riding and Equestrian Vacations

There are many stables throughout Dublin and Ireland—call the Tourist Office, look in the Yellow Pages of the phone directory, or ask the hotel desk clerk. Horseback riding is a very popular activity.

A Few Local Stables for an Hour's Ride

CARRICKMINES EQUESTRIAN CENTRE, Glenamuck Road, Foxrock, Dublin 18; phone: 1-295-5990

THE PADDOCKS RIDING CENTRE, Woodside Road, Sandyford, County Dublin; phone: 1-295-4278. There are various family possibilities at this center. There are adult and children's lessons, pony camps for children, woods and mountain trails, and cross country rides, a clubhouse, canteen, and shower rooms.

SPRUCE LODGE EQUESTRIAN CENTRE, Kilternan, County Dublin; phone: 1-295-2109

Riding and Training Vacations

BALLYROGAN EQUESTRIAN TRAINING CENTRE, Redcross, County Wicklow; phone: 404-47464 and 404-47208; fax: 404-47300; e-mail: *info@ballyrogan.com*; Web site: *www.ballyrogan.com/ballyrogan*

Located one hour from Dublin in an Irish Georgian estate between the sea and the hills. Riders from fourteen years and up are accepted and trained in dressage, show jumping, American hunting, or improving what you already know. Only six students are accepted at a time so there is a lot of individual training. Simple and comfortable accommodations are available at the center. Within the area are golf courses, fishing, hiking, and language courses.

CROSS COUNTRY INTERNATIONAL, P.O. Box 1170, Millbrook, NY 12545; phone (toll-free in the U.S.): 800-828-8768; fax 845-677-6077; e-mail: *xcintl@aol.com*; Web Site: *www.equestrianvacations.com*

This excellent company offers trips and camps for children and adults in every aspect of riding and training. Both novice and seasoned riders are welcome. Their courses include **horse training, riding camps** for adults and young people, **trail riding, hunt seat training, cross-country training, polo training, fox hunting** or a deluxe week at the **Mount Juliet Hotel for riding, fishing, shooting, hiking, tennis** and

golf. Many of the above courses and camps are held throughout the year. Since the weather is mild in Ireland riding is a year-round sport. Some of the tours are conducted from April through October, others run all year. Most of the trips are for one week, and include guest-houses or bed and breakfast stays, meals, private bath with hot showers, and luggage transport to each destination. The 2001 brochure includes: trail riding tours to Killarney and the Ring of Kerry, Ireland's Kinnitty Castle Trail Ride, Galway and Clare Trail Ride, and Wicklow's Inn to Inn Ride. Send for the brochure. If you love horses you will have a hard time deciding where and what to do, so much is offered. Some of the destinations also offer golf and other activities. Non-riders are welcome on all of these trips.

Trail Riding

CROSS COUNTRY INTERNATIONAL also has a one-week Wicklow Trail Riding tour, an excellent tour held in County Dublin that is only an hour from the city of Dublin, so it is easy to get to and offers the opportunity to have a city and riding vacation. You can fly into Dublin and be met at the airport and transported to the hotel for the riding trip. Rates start at $1345.00 per person, double occupancy for six nights; single supplement is $36.00 per night. This tour is available April through October.

IRISH STEP DANCING LESSONS

There are at least eighty registered and certified Irish dancing teachers in the Dublin area. If you want to reserve lessons prior to leaving home you can contact **Irish Dancing Association of America,** 10608 Lockwood Avenue, Oak Lawn, Illinois, 60453; phone: 708-636-8241. They will recommend a school in Dublin or anyplace in Ireland. There are beginners courses held at most schools that last for ninety minutes to two hours long. The prices vary from school to school, but they are all quite reasonable, starting as low as $5.00 per session.

MARATHONS

MARATHON TOURS, Phone: 617-242-7845; fax: 617-242-7686; e-mail: *marathon@shore.net*; Web site: *www.marathontour.com.* This company is located in Charleston, Massachusetts, and they specialize in organizing trips to cities that hold marathons, Dublin included. They will also tell you the proper attire for the city you are running in; it does vary.

Also check with the Dublin Marathon Office, P.O. Box 1287, Dublin 2, County Dublin, attention Carol McCabe; phone: 1-623-2159.

POLO

Polo matches are played right in Phoenix Park in Dublin's west side. Matches are held on Saturday and Sunday afternoon and Wednesday evening from May to mid-September. There is no charge for attending this fast-moving match. For details contact the **All Ireland Polo Club,** Phoenix Park, Dublin 8; phone: 1-677-6248.

RAIL TOURS

RAILTOURS IRELAND, 58 Lower Gardiner Street, Dublin 1; phone: 1-856-0045; fax: 1-856-0035; e-mail: *railtour@iol.ie*; Web site: *www. railtours.ie*

Reservations are required. Trips run daily from 9 A.M. There are no departures on Sundays or bank holidays. Children under sixteen pay half price. These tours are an excellent way to see the beautiful countryside without the hassle of driving. Tours are reasonably priced starting at 20 IR pounds and are available to Northern Ireland as well as the Republic of Ireland. Some tours offer either full-day sightseeing or the option to stay overnight and return to Dublin the next day. One of the trips offered is "The Ring of Kerry," a one-day trip departing at 7:30 A.M. from Dublin's Heuston Station or the option of staying overnight in Killarney and returning the following day. Another trip with the overnight option is "Connemara and Galway Bay." A few of the one-day tours offered are the "Cork and Killarney Experience," and the "Waterford, Kilkenny and East Coast." If you wish a day in Northern Ireland try the "Hills of Donegal and the Causeway Coast." One of the half-day tours trips is to Ballykissangel.

RUGBY

IRISH RUGBY FOOTBALL UNION, Lansdowne Road Stadium; phone: 1-668-4601. Matches are held during the winter and spring. Local matches are played every weekend.

A foot at rest meets nothing.
♣ —IRISH PROVERB ♣

SAILING

Information: **Irish Sailing Association,** 3 Park Road, Dun Laoghaire; phone: 1-280-0239. Open daily from 9:30 A.M.–5 P.M. Since Ireland is surrounded by water there are many opportunities for sailing. In the Dublin area Howth, Malahide, and Dun Laoghaire are excellent choices, but there are other sailing areas. These schools offer classes on everything connected with boats and water for adults and children. There are courses for windsurfing, sailing, power boating, rowing, canoeing, navigation, survival, first aid, and probably anything else you want to know about the water and safety.

FINGAL SAILING SCHOOL, Upper Strand, Malahide, County Dublin; phone: 1-845-1979

HOWTH MARINA, phone: 1-839-2777

IRISH NATIONAL SAILING SCHOOL, Dun Laoghaire; phone: 1-284-4195

MALAHIDE MARINA VILLAGE, phone: 1-845-4129

SOCCER

Football Association of Ireland, 80 Merrion Square South, Dublin 2; phone: 1-676-6864. The Lansdowne Stadium is where the international matches are held. Check the *Irish Times* for schedules.

SUMMER SCHOOL

UNIVERSITY COLLEGE DUBLIN, UCD INTERNATIONAL SUMMER SCHOOL, Newman House, 86 St. Stephen's Green, Dublin 2; phone: 1-475-2004; fax: 1-706-7211; e-mail: *summer.school@ucd.ie*; Web site: *www.ucd.ie/summerschool*

Summer school is held in July and is usually full with high school students from Spain, Italy, Portugal, and Ireland. Accommodations are on campus or with local families. Courses include art, history, politics, folklore, music, drama, theater visits, musical events, and poetry readings.

Also in July at University College Dublin are other summer school courses:

JAMES JOYCE SUMMER SCHOOL, write to: James Joyce Summer School, University College Dublin, Belfield, Dublin 4; phone: 1-706-8480; fax: 1-706-1174; e-mail: *helen.e.gallagher@ucd.ie*; Web site: *www.artsworld.ie/joyce_school/*

ENGLISH LANGUAGE COURSES FOR FOREIGNERS, write to: Applied Language Centre, Daedalus Building, UCD, Dublin 4; phone: 1-706-7900; fax: 1-706-1188; e-mail: *alc@ucd.ie*

TENNIS

Dublin has many outdoor tennis courts in places such as **Herbert Park** and **Bushy Park** on the south side and **St. Anne's Park** on the north side. There is a 2 IR pound fee per hour, no reservations needed. Show up with your racquet and play.

TRACING YOUR ROOTS

Anyone who loves Ireland and has any Irish blood in them will want to trace their roots. Gather as much information about your ancestors as possible before you arrive in Ireland. Knowing their birthplace, occupation, and religion will speed up the process. Once you arrive in Ireland there are many ways to go about finding those roots. You can use an agency or do the research on your own at the library. The following names and addresses will get you started:

GENEALOGICAL OFFICE, 2 Kildare Street, Dublin 2; phone: 1-661-8811. This office has meetings by appointment only, and they charge a small fee for their research. A one-hour meeting is approximately 25 Irish pounds.

There is also a unique museum on the premises, **The Heraldic Museum,** with free admission. Phone: 1-603-0311; fax: 1-662-1062. Open Monday to Friday 10 A.M.–4:30 P.M.. The museum exhibits shields, banners, coins, paintings, and stamps. The office of the chief herald of Ireland is located in the museum. For a fee he will start your search into your roots.

HIBERNIAN RESEARCH COMPANY, P.O. Box 3097, Dublin 6, Ireland; phone: 1-496-6522; fax: 1-497-3011. This is probably the best agency to use if you don't want to do the work yourself. They employ full-time professional genealogists.

THE NATIONAL ARCHIVES, Bishop Street, Dublin 8; phone: 1-407-2300; fax: 1-407-2333; Web site: *www.nationalarchives.ie.* Open Monday to Friday 10 A.M.–5 P.M.

Some important information was lost during the fire of 1920, but luckily much was saved, including the Griffith's Primary Valuation of Ireland 1848–63, which recorded those who owned or occupied land or property in Ireland at that time. Also saved was the national census of 1901–11. Now there is also a microfilm library of the Church of Ireland Parish Registers. You can get much information here and there is no fee.

THE NATIONAL LIBRARY, Kildare Street, Dublin 2; phone: 1-603-0200; Web site: *www.heanet.ie/natlib. See* Chapter 6, "Staying Busy."

The library has a collection of pre-1880 Catholic records of baptisms, births, marriages and newspapers, histories, and an index file that is very helpful.

THE OFFICE OF THE REGISTRAR GENERAL, 8–11 Lombard Street East, Dublin 2; phone: 1-635-4000; Web site: *www.groireland.ie*
Open Monday to Friday 9:30 A.M.–4:30 P.M. There is a fee of approximately 12 pounds for a general search, and a smaller fee for a birth, death, or marriage certificate. Marriages of non-Catholics were recorded from 1845 on. Catholic marriages were recorded from 1864 on.

THE REGISTRY OF DEEDS, Henrietta Street, Kings Inn, Dublin 1; phone: 1-670-7500; Web site: *www.irlgov.ie/landreg*
Open Monday to Friday 10 A.M.–4:30 P.M.. There is a fee of approximately 10 pounds per day to do your own research, but they will help you to use the index. The records here include land information from 1708 on, plus information on wills, mortgages, and property.

Other Web Sites for Finding Your Family Roots

IRISH ANCESTORS, *www.irish-times.com*

FAMILY TREE MAKER'S GENEALOGY SITE, *www.familytreemaker. com/index.html*

CYNDI'S LIST OF GENEALOGY SITES ON THE INTERNET, *www. cyndislist.com/ireland.htm*

THE ASSOCIATION OF PROFESSIONAL GENEALOGISTS IN IRE-LAND (APGI), *www.indigo.ie/~apgi/*

WALKING TOURS

Walking tours or independent walks are a wonderful way to see and explore at your own pace. I have included both local Irish companies for one-day walks, independent walks, and large American companies for a week or more of walking. Some people like to walk with local guides and other tours allow you to do your own thing such as sleep late, walk fast, stop for a rest, shop in small village. Or you can be programmed at all times. Be sure to pick a tour on your own level. The most important thing is to have a good pair of broken-in walking boots and socks that fit and do not rumple in your shoes. Don't try to walk with sneakers; they will not do for a long walk. You might want to buy a wonderful Irish walking stick as a souvenir.

The tours included here are of different price ranges. Do your homework well, so you are not upset when you arrive at a B&B when you expect a castle or have dinner in a castle and need a jacket when you planned on a pub. Read carefully and have fun.

All of the tours can begin and end in Dublin even though they walk in other parts of the country. Dublin is only a short train, bus, or car ride away from these tours.

ABERCROMBIE & KENT INTERNATIONAL, 1420 Kensington Road, Oak Brook, IL 60523-2140; Phone: (toll-free in U.S.) 800-323-7308; fax: 630-954-3324; Web site: *www.abercrombiekent.com*

A&K currently has one "Walking in Ireland" tour for six nights at an easy level. The trip starts and ends in Shannon. This walking tour is in the West Coast and includes the Burren and Connemara.

BACKROADS, 801 Cedar Street, Berkeley, CA 94710-1800; phone: 800-GO-ACTIVE, 510-527-1555; fax: 510-527-1444; Web Site: *www. backroads.com*

A six-day tour starting and ending in Cork. The price includes most meals, but you're on your own for transportation to starting cities. Single supplement is extra. This trip requires a minimum of four to six miles of walking per day.

BUTTERFIELD AND ROBINSON, 70 Bond Street, Toronto, Ontario, Canada M5B 1X3; phone: 416-864-1354, 800-678-1147; e-mail: *info@butterfield.com*; Web site: *www.butterfield.com*

B&R is one of the more expensive companies and for good reason. Everything about it is deluxe. This year's walking tour starts and ends in Galway. The tour is walking through Connemara and the Aran Islands. This is one of the easier B&R walking tours, and it is in a gorgeous part of the world.

COUNTRY WALKERS, P.O. Box 180, Waterbury, Vermont 05676-0180; phone: 800-464-9255, 802-244-1387; fax: 802 244-5661; e-mail: *info@countrywalkers.com*; Web site: *www.countrywalkers.com*

This is an excellent company with various walking tours each year. For example, the 2001 trips are Connemara and the Burren, which is the West Coast of Ireland. The trip starts and ends at Shannon Airport and includes walks along the Cliffs of Moher and Connemara National Park. The second trip is called "The Magical Southwest," which also starts and ends at Shannon Airport. It includes the Dingle Peninsula and Bantry Bay among other spots.

CROSS COUNTRY INTERNATIONAL, P.O. Box 1170, Millbrook, NY 12545; Phone: 1800-828-8768; fax: 914-677-6077; e-mail: *xcintl@aol.com*; Web site: *www.walking vacation.com/*

This company offers seven excellent reasonably priced tours in Ireland including the Ulster Walk through Northern Ireland. All tours can start or end with a few days in Dublin. Their tours are: The Heart of Ireland Tour, Beara Peninsula Tour, Burren and Connemara Walk, Dingle Peninsula Walk, Ring of Kerry Walk, and more.

> *Wherever you go*
> *and whatever you do,*
> *May the luck of*
> *the Irish be*
> *there with you.*
> ♣ —IRISH BLESSING ♣

THE WAYFARERS, 172 Bellevue Avenue, Newport, RI 02840; phone: 401-849-5087, toll-free: 800-249-4620; fax: 401-849-5878; e-mail: *wayfarer@thewayfarers.com*; Web site: *www.thewayfarers.com*

In 2001 their Irish trip was from Sunday to Saturday walking the Ring of Kerry. The pick up and drop off are the Killarney Rail Station, which is only a three-hour ride to Dublin.

WICKLOW WAY WALK The Wicklow Way Walk is an eighty-five-mile walk, which crosses the Wicklow Mountains through very rugged and beautiful landscape. You need rain gear, heavy walking boots and socks, and a windbreaker. It is best to go with a tour or group unless you are an expert hiker. There are B&Bs to stop at along the way, but bring sandwiches and drinks for the day. Get a map from the Wicklow Tourist Office or the Dublin Tourist Office. It takes about a week to complete this walk, but it can be done in short sections too.

Dublin is a small city so it is fun to walk around on your own. If you like company and guidance join a local tour. A very good book for independent walkers is *Walking Dublin* by Pat Liddy, published by Passport Books. It contains twenty-four walks in and around Dublin. The Dublin Tourist Office has a free booklet, *Walking Ireland,* that includes walks along the canals and the famous Wicklow Way. The Tourist Office also has a self-guided tour and map called *Walks through Europe, Dublin.* This is in map form and when you open it there are four walking tours with instructions on how to use the map and a separate description of each walk and a short description of each sight.

LOCAL DUBLIN WALKING TOURS, All of the tours included here have a small fee for joining.

If you like to follow a map and walk alone, stop at the Dublin Tourist Office on Suffolk Street for their excellent maps and follow the trails that are signposted in the city. **Audio Walking Tour of Dublin:** 7–9 Aston Quay; phone: 1-670-5266; e-mail: *resnet@tinet.ie*

This company gives you the pre-recorded headset and off you go. You can rent the audio set for half or full day.

DISCOVER DUBLIN TOURS, 20 Lower Stephen Street, Dublin 2; Phone: 01-478-0193. Reservations required. This company specializes in literary and musical walking tours.

DUBLIN FOOTSTEPS, phone: 1-496-0641. This tour originates at Bewley's Oriental Café on Grafton Street. Tours incorporate Medieval

Dublin, Georgian Dublin, and Literary Dublin.

HILL OF HOWTH, This is a beautiful six and a half mile walk, which takes between three to four hours depending on your speed and what you stop to see along the way. You can reach Howth on the DART from Dublin. The walk includes sea views, hills, the coast, and Howth harbor. After you walk stop in one of the many restaurants in Howth for lunch or a cup of tea. *See* chapter 12, "Day Trips" for Howth restaurants.

HISTORICAL WALKING TOURS OF DUBLIN, departs from the front gate of Trinity College; Phone: 1-878-0227; fax: 1-878-3787; e-mail: *tours@historicalinsights.ie*; Web site: *www.historicalinsights.ie*
    Reservations are not required. Conducted May through September Monday to Sunday 11 A.M., and 3 P.M. with an extra hour at noon Saturday and Sunday, October to April Friday, Saturday, and Sunday noon. Trinity College History graduate students who know their stuff guide the tours. The tour includes famous landmarks such as medieval walls, Viking remains, Christ Church, St. Patrick's Cathedral, Dublin Castle, City Hall, plus Irish history, the Potato Famine of 1845–49, the 1916 Rising, the War of Independence, partition, and the current situation with the peace process.

IRISH MUSIC PUB CRAWL, departs from the Oliver St. John Gogarty Pub, Temple Bar, Dublin 2; phone: 1-478-0193. Conducted daily May–October 7:30 P.M., November, December, January 15 to April, Friday and Saturday 7:30 P.M. If you love to sing or hear traditional Irish music this is your tour. You will even receive a songbook so you can join in the fun.

JAMESON LITERARY PUB CRAWL, Winner of the "Living Dublin Award" meets at the Duke Pub on Duke Street; phone: 1-670-5602. Conducted daily at 7:30 P.M. and Sunday at noon. I love this tour that takes you where the great Irish authors such as Beckett, Behan, Joyce, Shaw, and others also walked. The tour stops at pubs frequented by the writers, and local actors perform and read from their literary works.

OLD DUBLIN TOURS, Phone: 1-454-3423. This tour departs daily from the main gate of Christ Church Cathedral and covers medieval Dublin.

SLI NA SLAINTE, Irish Heart Foundation, 4 Clyde Road, Ballsbridge, Dublin 4; phone: 1-668-5001; fax: 1-668-5896; e-mail: *info@irishheart-foundation.ie*
    This walk was developed by the Irish Heart Foundation to promote walking for pleasure and good health. This is a free walk, which can start and end at any of the signs posted along its route. There are

routes both north and south of the city and are very easy to follow. *Sli na Slainte* translates to "Path to Health."

TEMPLE BAR WALKING TOURS, Phone: 1-672-5096. Tour departs daily at noon and 2 P.M. outside the ESB Building on Fleet Street.

TOUR OF REVOLUTIONARY DUBLIN FROM 1916–1923, Footsoldiers, 38 Lower Leeson Street, Dublin 2; phone: 1-662-9976. Reservations are not required. Departs 2:30 P.M. Monday to Friday, Saturday and Sunday at 2 P.M. This is a fascinating tour of the history of the 1916 Easter Rising, the War of Independence, and the Irish Civil War, and where these events occurred.

1916 REBELLION WALKING TOURS, 7 Upper Fitzwilliam Street, Dublin 2; phone: 1-676-2493. Tour operates from May 15 to August 31. Meet at the International Bar, 23 Wicklow Street, Dublin 2 at 11:30 A.M. Tuesday–Saturday. A guide will walk you to all the important sites of the 1916 Easter Rising. At the end of the tour all members receive a free copy of the Proclamation of the Republic of Ireland.

TRINITY COLLEGE TOURS, *See* Chapter 6, "Sights"

WINDSURFING

If you love windsurfing head for **Surfdock Center,** Grand Canal Dock Road, Ringsend, Dublin 4; Phone: 1-668-3945; fax: 1-668-1215. They give courses on windsurfing and rent equipment. They have a surfing shop with wetsuits and boards, all of which can be hired by the hour or longer.

11. Dublin for Children

CHILDREN'S ACTIVITIES

If you are traveling with children you have nothing to worry about. I have found Dublin to be very child-friendly at sights and restaurants. There are many activities to keep children happy and active, just remember not to overdo. Family bus passes are available for use for up to two adults and four children under the age of sixteen; for a small additional fee the DART and Suburban Rail can be included in the pass. The pass can be purchased in advance of your sightseeing from the Dublin Bus Office on O'Connell Street or other ticket agencies in the city, or from a hotel concierge.

ANIMAL FARM, Reynoldstown Naul; phone: 1-841-2615 or 1-841-1202. Located eighteen miles north of Dublin. Call for directions. This is a great opportunity for city children to see a working organic farm. Children may feed the farm animals on the guided tours.

ARK CHILDREN'S CULTURAL CENTER, 11A Eustace Street, Temple Bar, Dublin 2; phone: 1-670-7788; fax: 1-670-7758; Web site: *www.ark.ie*. Open: Tuesday to Friday 9:30 A.M.–4 P.M., Saturday 10 A.M.– 4 P.M., closed Sunday and Monday. The Ark is an arts center, theater, gallery, and workshop for children ages four to fourteen. The prices range from approximately $5.00 to $ 10.00 per day.

BEACHES: Portmarnock If you are staying in Dublin it is a fifteen-minute trip north to the beach by car. The sandy beach is clean and there is even a small fair and donkey rides. On Sundays there is harness racing nearby. Children are permitted to go to the races and even bet. On the south side the main beach is at **Killiney;** it's two miles long. This beach is easily reached by DART train from Dublin.

DUBLINIA, St. Michael's Hill, Christ Church, Place Dublin 8; phone: 1-679-4611. Open daily April to September 10 A.M.–5 P.M., October to March Monday to Saturday 11 A.M.–4 P.M., Sunday and bank holidays 10 A.M.–4:30 P.M. Admission fee. Dublinia is the story of Medieval Dublin from 1170–1540. There is an audio guide in five languages, and an audio-visual presentation of medieval Dublin. This excellent and accurate tour includes an illuminated medieval maze that tells the story of Ireland from the arrival of Strongbow and his knights in the twelfth century to Henry the VIII and the closing of the monasteries in the sixteenth century. There is also an exhibit of life in medieval Dublin.

DUBLIN'S VIKING ADVENTURE, Essex Street West, Temple Bar, Dublin 2; phone: 1-679-6040; fax: 1-679-6033. Open daily Monday to Saturday 10 A.M.–4:30 P.M., Sunday and public holidays 11:30 A.M.–5:30 P.M. Admission fee. Wheelchair accessible. This exhibit is a live interactive experience of life in Viking Dublin. You can tour the streets of the Viking village of "Dyflin" and talk to the local people and see them at work. You can see the houses they lived in and the clothes they wore. The Viking Adventure also includes a collection of artifacts discovered through excavations in Dublin. People of every age will enjoy this adventure.

There is also a **Viking Feast** held on Thursday, Friday, and Saturday at 7:30 P.M. Reservations are a must and can be made at the above phone number. Reservations are available for groups on other evenings. There is a live performance by the Viking cast, which includes traditional music.

DUBLIN ZOO, Phoenix Park, Dublin 7; phone: 1-677-1425; fax: 1-677-1660; e-mail: *info@dublinzoo.ie*; Web site: *www.dublinzoo.ie*

Open, summer season: Monday to Saturday 9:30 A.M.–6 P.M., Sunday 10:30 A.M.-6 P.M., off-season Monday to Friday 9:30 A.M.–4 P.M., Saturday 9:30 A.M.–5 P.M., Sunday 10:30 A.M.–5 P.M. Admission: there are different fees for different ages and family groups. Children under 3 are admitted free. Strollers are available for a small fee. Wheelchair accessible. There are picnic areas, gardens, a petting zoo, a small train ride, and pony rides. There is also a Discovery Center including the world's biggest egg. If you get hungry there is the Café Bar, a fast food restaurant, a lakeside café open during the summer, and many snack shops. If the "kids" get tired of seeing the animals there is also an excellent play area. The zoo has over seven hundred animals including snow leopards, lions, elephants, penguins, and monkeys. There are rare and endangered species on view too. Children can help feed some of the animals and the feeding times are listed at the entrance so you can plan your trip accordingly. If you visit during the winter and want to help feed the animals be sure to call ahead to check feeding times. Usually it is on weekends only.

Something new has been added in 2000: "The African Plains" is a thirty-three-acre area with paddocks for large African animals such as rhinoceroses, hippopotamuses, giraffes, and antelopes.

FORT LUCAN, Phone: 1-628-0166. Located in County Dublin off Strawberry Beds Road in Westmanstown in Lucan. It is important to call ahead before making this trip since opening times depend on the weather. Outdoor adventures and great fun if you are between the ages of two and fourteen. There is an Ariel runway, slides, swings, kart track, suspension bridge, a maze, a small child's play area, restaurant and tearoom.

FRY MODEL RAILWAY, Malahide Castle, Malahide, County Dublin; phone: 1-846-3779, Fax: 1-846-2537. *See* chapter 12, "Day Trips"; e-mail: *fryrailway@dublintourism.ie* Open all year, but call ahead for opening times. Admission charge.

HEY DOODLE DOODLE, 14 Crown Alley, Temple Bar, Dublin 2; phone: 1-672-7382; Web site: *www.heydoodledoodle.com*

This is an activitiy for a child or family if you have time to leave your project to be glazed and fired in a kiln. You can choose from a ceramic mug, bowl, plate, animal, and many other objects, paint it, and then leave it. It can usually be picked up the following day.

ICE SKATING: **Dublin Ice Rink,** Dolphin's Barn, South Circular Road; phone 1-453-4153 **Silver Skate Ice Rink,** North Circular Road, Dublin 7; phone: 1-830-4405

MUSEUM OF CHILDHOOD, 20 Palmerston Park, Rathmines, Dublin 6; phone: 1-497-3223. Open July and August, Wednesday and Sunday 2–5:30 P.M., rest of the year Sunday only 2–5:30 P.M. Admission charge. A lovely small museum, which houses a collection of dolls from 1730–1940. They also have doll carriages, doll houses, rocking horses, doll-house furniture, and a few other toys.

NATURAL HISTORY MUSEUM, Merrion Street, Dublin 2, phone: 1-677-7444. Open: Tuesday–Saturday 10 A.M.–5 P.M., Sunday 2–5 P.M. Free admission. This museum houses an outstanding collection of the wildlife of Ireland plus mammals, birds, fish, and fowl from Asia and Africa. There are also exhibits of skeletons of prehistoric animals.

NATIONAL SEA LIFE CENTRE, Strand Road, Bray, County Wicklow; phone: 1-286-6939. Open daily from 10 A.M. This center is easily reached by a thirty-minute DART train ride from Dublin or by car. See further description under Bray in chapter 12, "Day Trips."

NATIONAL WAX MUSEUM, Granby Row, off Parnell Square, Dublin 1; phone: 1-872-6340. Open Monday to Saturday 10 A.M.–5:30 P.M., Sunday noon to 5:30 P.M. Admission charge.

   Includes life-size figures of Irish literary, political, and historical personalities. There are also Irish and international sports and entertainment figures, children's fairytale figures, and a replica of Leonardo da Vinci's *Last Supper.* The Chamber of Horrors is not for the faint-hearted, and it can be avoided. There is a separate entrance, which I would take if I were with young children.

NEWBRIDGE HOUSE AND TRADITIONAL FARM, Donabate. *See* chapter 12, "Day Trips."

LAMBERT PUPPET THEATRE AND MUSEUM, Clifton Lane, Monkstown; Phone: 1-280-0974. Performances are held on Saturdays, but you can visit the museum on all other days.

LIBRARIES AND BOOK SHOPS

Libraries (free) and book shops, not so free if you buy, are excellent ways to spend some time with children. Dublin, being a literary haven, has many libraries and bookshops and all are worth visiting. *See* chapter 8, "Literary Dublin" for bookshops. For libraries contact Dublin's Central Library, ILAC Center, Henry Street, Dublin 1; phone: 1-873-4333.

MARLAY PARK, *See* chapter 6, "Sights."

PREMIER INDOOR KARTING, Unit 1A, Kylemore Industrial Estate, Killeen Road, Dublin 10; phone: 1-626-1444. This is a very expensive activity, but "kids" of all ages seem to love it. You get strapped into a kart and off you go around the track.

Summer Activities

If you are traveling with a child and need some time alone without spending a fortune for babysitters, or the kids are hot and tired and want an activity with other children, here are some good day-time activities for free or a small fee. There are other activities at museums and libraries, and the Tourist Office will have the complete list.

CENTRAL LIBRARY, IIAC Center, Henry Street, Dublin 1; phone: 1-873-4333. Free storytelling and creative writing programs are offered during the summer.

DUBLIN PARKS TENNIS LEAGUE, phone: 1-833-8711. Lessons are offered for children aged six to seventeen.

HUGH LANE MUNICIPAL GALLERY OF MODERN ART, Charlemont House, Parnell Square North, Dublin 1; phone: 1-874-1903. Hands-on workshops on Wednesday afternoons for ages six to eleven based on gallery exhibits.

NATIONAL GALLERY OF IRELAND, Children's Summer Club Education Department, Merrion Square West, Dublin 2; phone: 1-661-5133, ext. 164; fax: 1-661-0099; Web site: *www.nationalgallery.ie*
They offer drop-in art classes for children aged four to twelve in July, and a two-week teenagers class.

TENNIS IRELAND, phone: 1-668-1841; Web site: *www.tennisireland.ie*
This organization plans tournaments and also directs parents to camps and other programs.

RIDING CAMP, Cross Country International Equestrian Vacations, P.O. Box 1170, Millbrook, NY 12545; phone: 800-828-8768; fax: 845-677-6077; e-mail: *xcintl@aol.com* Located twelve miles from Dublin at the Calliaghstown Riding Centre in County Wicklow, the summer Young People's camp held during July and August includes transfers to and from the Dublin Airport, seven nights with a local Irish family, all meals, three hours of riding per day, lectures in horse care, horses, tack, and tax.

> *May you be in heaven half an hour*
> *before the Devil knows you are dead.*
> ♣ —IRISH TOAST ♣

12. Day Trips

Once you've seen Dublin, there are many smaller cities and villages to explore in the Irish countryside. And don't forget Northern Ireland as a possible destination, either. Belfast is only ninety minutes by train from Dublin.

Following are day trips within a three-hour radius of Dublin. Beyond three hours each way you should consider staying for more than a day.

The older the fiddle the sweeter the tune.

♣ —IRISH PROVERB ♣

SOUTH OF DUBLIN

The area south of Dublin has many interesting towns and villages. In half an hour you can be at the foothills of the Dublin Mountains. There are parks, recreational activities, sports, golf, racing, and water sports, biking, and fishing, plus castles, historic villages, and seaside resorts.

BRAY

Located fourteen miles south of Dublin and five miles east of Enniskerry.

Bray is a Victorian town easily reached by car, bus, or DART train. Bray has sandy beaches plus some interesting sights. James Joyce lived in Bray from 1888 to 1891.

Sights

BRAY ESPLANADE is a mile and a half walk along the sea and very pleasant on a nice summer evening.

NATIONAL AQUARIUM, The Esplanade, phone: 1-286-4688. Admission fee. The aquarium has over seven hundred different species on view. It is great fun, especially for children.

NATIONAL SEA LIFE CENTER, Strand Road, Bray; phone: 1-286-6939. Open daily. Children under fourteen must be accompanied by an adult. A new exhibit was introduced in 1999 called "Kingdom of the Seahorse." There is multi-level viewing of fish and there is also a touchpool, which enables people under supervision to pick up and handle many kinds of marine life such as crabs and starfish. Web site: *www.sealife.co.uk*

BRAY HEAD, This walk requires very good stamina. Located south of the Esplanade above the Irish Sea Bray Head boasts wonderful views. If the hike up Bray Head is too strenuous try the **Cliff Walk,** which is also quite a long walk, but not as difficult. Both walks require good walking shoes, good stamina, and a few hours.

BRAY HERITAGE CENTRE, Located in the Town Hall, the center has exhibits of Bray's history including photographs. Open Monday, Friday, and Saturday from 10 A.M.–5 P.M.

KILRUDDERY HOUSE AND GARDENS, open May, June, and September daily from 1 P.M.–5 P.M.; phone: 1-286-7128. Each year in early June Kilruddery House hosts the **Festival of Music in Great Irish Houses.** First Floor, Blackrock Post Office, Blackrock, County Dublin; phone: 1-278-1528; fax: 1-278-1529.

This chamber music festival was established over thirty years ago and brings musicians from around the world to play in some of Ireland's great houses.

Restaurants

TREE OF IDLENESS, Seafront, Bray, County Wicklow; phone: 1-286-3498; fax: 1-282-8183. Open Tuesday to Sunday 7:30–11 P.M., Sunday 7:30–10 P.M., closed Monday, the last week in August, and first week of September. Not wheelchair accessible. **Dinner only. Expensive.** This is an excellent (best in Bray) Greek-Cypriot restaurant located on the waterfront in an old Victorian house. One specialty is roast lamb stuffed with feta cheese and olives. They also have Irish beef and a variety of very good house wines plus Greek wines.

POPPIES COUNTRY COOKING, 1 Trafalgar Square, Greystones; phone: 1-287-4227. No credit cards. **Inexpensive.** Located in Greystones, also a seaside resort a few miles south of Bray on the coast. This is the second Poppies, the first is in Enniskerry. The food here as in the original is simple and delicious. On a nice summer day you can eat outdoors.

BLACKROCK

See chapter 9, "Shopping in Dublin, Markets,"

BOOTERSTOWN

See chapter 10, "Leisure Activities."

DALKEY

Dalkey is located eight miles south of Dublin and one mile from Sandycove. It has been designated a Heritage Town by the Irish Tourist Board. The best way to get to Dalkey is on the DART train and from the station walk into town.

Castle Street is Dalkey's main street and it is lined with houses, shops, the Exchange Bookshop selling new and secondhand books, restaurants, and the remains of a castle, which has been converted into the Heritage Center. Nobel Prize winner George Bernard Shaw lived on Dalkey Hill. The name of his home is **Torca Cottage.** James Joyce taught at the local school. Two modern-day authors still live in Dalkey, they are Hugh Leonard, and Maeve Binchy and her husband, Gorden Snell, who writes children's books and grows prize-winning roses. From the harbor in Dalkey you can take a fifteen-minute boat ride to the uninhabited **Dalkey Island.** Dalkey Island was originally inhabited in 3500 B.C. by Stone Age settlers. Dalkey Island has a Martello Tower and some wild goats and birds and **St. Begnet's Church and Holy Well,** located on the island. It is supposed to cure rheumatism.

Sights

DALKEY CASTLE AND HERITAGE CENTER, Castle Street, Dalkey, County Dublin; phone: 1-285-8366; fax: 1-284-3141, e-mail: *diht@ indigo.ie*; Web site: *www.Dalkey.homepage.ie*. Open March to October, Monday to Friday 9:30 A.M.–5 P.M., Saturday, Sunday, and public holidays 11 A.M.–5 P.M., November to February Saturday, Sunday, and public holidays 11 A.M.–5 P.M.

DALKEY QUARRY provided the stones used for building the Dun Laoghaire piers.

Restaurants

GUINEA PIG, 17 Railway Road, Dalkey, County Dublin; phone: 1-285-9055; fax: 1-285-8427; Web site: *www.dalkeyhomepage.ie*
Reservations advised. Open Monday to Saturday 5:30 P.M.–11 P.M., Sunday 5–9:30 P.M. There are prix fixe and special value menus served each evening so if you are interested check ahead. **Dinner only. Expensive.** This is basically a seafood restaurant, but they do have excellent lamb and pork dishes. Fish specialties include fillet of sole with mussel sauce. I love the Irish country décor. They also have an early-bird dinner.

SORRENTO PUB, Sorrento Road, Dalkey, County Dublin. **Moderate.** This is a typical Irish pub open for lunch and dinner serving very good, wholesome pub food such as Irish stew covered with mashed potatoes. They also have a good selection of wines and beers.

P. D.'s WOODHOUSE, 1 Coliemore Road, Dalkey Center; phone: 1-284-9399. Open Tuesday to Saturday noon–2:30 P.M. and 6–11 P.M. There are two dinner seatings. Reservations recommended. **Moderate.** An Irish restaurant with some Mediterranean flavor. There is Irish salmon, white sole, chicken, hamburgers, and even an early-bird menu.

DUN LAOGHAIRE

TOURIST OFFICE, Carlisle Terminal, phone: 1-284-4768. The first thing to know is how to pronounce *Dun Laoghaire*. It is pronounced *Dun Leary*. It is named after Laoghaire, a fifth-century Irish king who built a fort here. Nothing remains of the fort (dun) because it was destroyed when the train line was built. In 1821 the name was changed to Kingstown in honor of King George IV's visit, but in 1920 after the

Irish Rebellion the name was changed back to Dun Laoghaire. This is a small town only eight miles from the city of Dublin and with only one main street, **Upper** and **Lower George's Street,** which is parallel to the coast and has many shops and restaurants.

It is a stop on the DART, but its importance is its **ferry port.** From its port passengers can go by sea to Holyhead in north Wales and continue by train on to England and Scotland. You can be a walk-on passenger, go by tour bus, or in your own car. It is also a busy seaport for freight service. There is a busy and beautiful pleasure boating center with the members-only Royal Irish, National, and Royal St. George Yacht Clubs. They were all founded over one hundred years ago.

Dun Laoghaire has two piers, the East and West Piers, each one and a half miles long. Each pier ends with a lighthouse, which was built in the 1850s. The harbor was built between 1817 and 1859. The East pier has a bandstand where musicians perform during the summer.

Sights

THE NATIONAL MARITIME MUSEUM is located in a former Mariners' Church built in 1823 for seamen in Dun Laoghaire. Haigh Terrace, phone: 1-280-0969. Open May through September Tuesday to Sunday 1–5 P.M. Admission charge.

On display is a French longboat that was captured in Bantry Bay, County Cork, in 1796. The museum's collections include maritime models, documents, photographs, pictures, charts, maps, flags, stamps, and postcards. One model is the *Great Eastern,* which was a steam-powered ship that laid the first transatlantic telegraph cable.

Restaurants

BRASSERIE NA MARA, 1 Harbour Road, Dun Laoghaire; phone: 1-280-6767. Closed Sundays. Reservations required. **Expensive.**

This restaurant is part of the DART station and worth a trip. The Gaelic words "na mara" mean of the sea and their fish is just excellent.

MORELS BISTRO, 18 Glasthule Road; phone: 1-230-0210. Not wheelchair accessible. Open daily except for lunch on Monday, Wednesday, and Saturday. **Moderate.** They serve delicious fresh fish dishes including a seared salmon that I highly recommend. Also served in this fine restaurant are delicious roast duck, beef, and pasta dishes. They have a good wine list and fair prices. **Eagle House** is a pub located on the first floor of Morels and they serve food from that restaurant. Phone:

1-280-4740. Open for lunch daily, dinner Monday to Friday 5:30–9
P.M., all day Saturday, and Sunday 12:30–7 P.M.

SANDYCOVE

Located one mile south of Dun Laoghaire along the sea, the reason to visit Sandycove is to see the **James Joyce Martello Tower.**
Phone: 1-280-9265. Fax: 1-872-2231. Open April through October,
Monday to Saturday 10 A.M.–1 P.M., 2–5 P.M., Sunday and public holidays 2–6 P.M., November to March by appointment only. Admission
charge. *See* chapter 7, "Museums and Churches."

Sights

Forty Foot Pool is located near the Sandycove Martello Tower. This
was an all-male, open-air, nude bathing pool, but is now a coed
bathing suit pool. In *Ulysses* one of the characters, Buck Mulligan,
goes to the pool for a morning swim. The pool is not named for its
size. It is named for the 40th Regiment of Foot that used to be sta-
tioned there.

Restaurants

Fitzgeralds of Sandycove, The Joycean Pub, Albert House, 11
Sandycove Road; phone: 1-280-4469. Open for lunch Monday to Friday. Inexpensive.

Caviston's, 59 Glasthule Road, Sandycove; phone: 1-280-9120; fax:
1-284-4054. Not wheelchair accessible. Open daily for lunch with the last
seating at 3:15 P.M. Closed Saturday. **Moderate.** e-mail: *caviston@indigo.ie*;
Web site: *www.cavistons.com*
Located next to their wonderful delicatessen where if you have an
apartment you will definitely want to shop. The well-priced restaurant
serves wonderfully fresh fish such as sardines, monkfish, smoked and
grilled salmon, mullet, and lobsters among other dishes. The wines
are also good and fairly priced.

KILLINEY

Pronounced "kill eye nee" is located just over three miles north of
Bray and nine miles south of Dublin overlooking Dublin Bay, and is
also a stop on the DART line. There is a beach over two miles long

with good swimming and great views. For a view of the bay try walking up the hill in **Killiney Park.**

Sights

THE OBELISK Located on the top of Killiney Hill and built in 1742, the views and walks are gorgeous.

AYESHA CASTLE Located below the village is this Victorian castle built in 1840. It was originally called Victoria Castle in honor of the queen. It was gutted by fire in 1924 and purchased by Sir Thomas Power in 1928, who restored and renamed it. The castle is now owned by a famous Irish singer, who has spent a fortune to secure her privacy. Please respect her wishes.

Restaurants

FITZPATRICK CASTLE DUBLIN HOTEL, Killiney, County Dublin; phone: 1-284-0700; fax: 1-285-0207, e-mail: *info@fitzpatricks.com*

THE COURT HOTEL, Killiney Bay, County Dublin; phone: 1-285-1622; fax: 1-285-2085. Stop here for tea or a drink in the conservatory overlooking the bay.

COUNTY WICKLOW

County Wicklow is located twelve miles south of Dublin and called the "Garden of Ireland." If you are driving, go south from Dublin toward Killiney, past Dun Laoghaire, toward Vico Road for exquisite views of Killiney Bay and Dublin Bay. Continue on to Bray (a stop on the DART) and have lunch at Vevay Inn at 21 Vevay Road. Then continue on to Glendalough. On the way back to Dublin you can stop in the small, beautiful village of **Enniskerry** for tea at Poppies, which is located in the little village square.

TOURIST OFFICE, Fitzwilliam Square, Wicklow. Phone: 404-69117. Open all year. If you do not want to drive this on your own there are interesting tours, one of which is **Off the Beaten Path** from Dublin to the Wicklow area. The tourist office in Dublin sells tickets for this tour. Another tour to the Wicklow area is **Wild Wicklow Tour.** Phone 1-280-1899; mobile: 87-274-4727. E-mail: *info@wildcoachtours.com*; Web site: *www.wildcoachtours.com*

Tours operate every day from March to November and Saturday and Sunday all year. There are various pickup points starting at 8:50 A.M. at the Shelbourne Hotel in Dublin. The tour includes a coastal drive through Dun Laoghaire, Sandycove, Killiney Bay. Stop at Avoca for coffee and shopping, Glendalough for a tour, lunch in the village of Laragh, then continue on to Sally Gap and the beautiful mountains and lakes and on the way back through Glencree and Enniskerry.

Other tours are conducted by **Bus Eireann,** phone: 1-830-2222 and **Guide Friday Bus Tours,** Phone: 1-676-5377.

Sights

AVONDALE HOUSE, Rathdrum, County Wickow, phone: 404-46111. Admission charge, Open daily May through September 10 A.M.–6 P.M., October through April 11 A.M.–5 P.M. Avondale is the restored home of the nationalist leader Charles Stuart Parnell (1846–1891). The house was built in 1779, and is now a museum in his memory.

RUSSBOROUGH HOUSE, located two miles south of Blessington in County Wicklow. Phone: 45-865239. Open April and October, Sunday and bank holidays 10:30 A.M.–5:30 P.M., May and September Monday to Saturday 10:30 A.M.–4:30 P.M., Sunday 10:30 A.M.–5:30 P.M., June through August daily 10:30 A.M.–5:30 P.M., closed November to Easter. Built in 1741. This is one of the most beautiful Palladian mansions in Ireland. It houses the **Beit Art Collection,** which includes the works of Rubens, Frans Hals, Gainsborough, Goya and many more great European masters. Part of this private collection has been donated to the National Gallery of Ireland. The house is surrounded by gorgeous gardens and visitors are welcome to wander the area.

WICKLOW'S HISTORIC GAOL, Kilmantin Hill, Wicklow Town, Wicklow; phone: 404-61499; fax: 404-61612. Open daily March through October 10 A.M.–6 P.M.; e-mail: *wccgaol@eircom.ie*; Web site: *www.wicklow.ie/gaol*

Wicklow's Historic Gaol (jail) opened in 1702 and was used until 1924. It reopened as a museum in 1998 after a major restoration project. The jail is located next to the courthouse and Market Square. The exhibitions tell the story of jail life during the eighteenth and nineteenth centuries. You see the history of the 1798 Rebellion, the Famine, and the transportation of convicts to Australia. The convict ship *Hercules* was reconstructed and you can now go on the ship to see what life was like.

Restaurant

OLD RECTORY COUNTRY HOUSE, Wicklow Town; phone: 404-67048; fax: 404-69181. Moderately priced. Located off the main road from Dublin to Wicklow Town in a lovingly restored country house that was once a nineteenth-century rectory. Try the delicious salads made with all local fresh greens and in season, decorated with edible flowers.

Arklow

Arklow is a little fishing town founded by the Vikings in the ninth century and noted for its boat building. The *Gypsy Moth III* that Sir Francis Chichester sailed around the world in 1967 was built here. Arklow is also a resort with beaches, boating, and golf.

Sights

ARKLOW MARITIME MUSEUM, St. Mary's Road, phone: 402-032868. The museum has exhibits of Ireland's maritime history since the 1850s.

Ashford

MOUNT USHER GARDENS, Ashford, on the Dublin–Wicklow Road; phone: 404-40116. Open March through November daily 10:30 A.M.–6 P.M. These beautiful gardens are located on the banks of the River Vartry. The gardens were laid out in 1868 and contain rare trees, shrubs, seventy varieties of eucalyptus and flowers from all over the world. There are suspension bridges over waterways, a craft shop, and tea-room.

Glendalough

The easiest way to reach Glendalough is by car, but if you are not driving try to get on a bus tour. It is an easy ride and well worth it. The area is beautiful, located in the heart of the Wicklow Mountains near two lakes, and it is one of the country's most important historical sites. **ST. KEVIN'S BUS** departs daily from St. Stephen's Green at 11:30 A.M. It returns from Glendalough Monday to Saturday at 4:15 P.M., Sunday at 5:30 P.M. Phone: 1-281-8119. Check with the local bus companies or the Irish Tourist Board for other bus tours to the area. **BUS**

EIREANN has daily tours to Glendalough and Wicklow from April to October, and Wednesday, Saturday, and Sunday from January through March. The trip leaves Busaras at 10:30 A.M. and returns at 5:45 P.M. during the summer and 4 P.M. during the winter. The tour bus can also be picked up at 11 A.M. from the Dun Laoghaire Tourist Office.

TOURIST OFFICE, Glendalough; phone: 404-45325/45352. Open daily from 9:30 A.M. to 6 P.M. during the summer and 4:30 P.M. from November to February. The center has a model of what the monastery looked like in its heyday, a video, postcards, and souvenir books. Glendalough is located thirty miles south of Dublin.

Sights

GLENDALOUGH MONASTERY was founded by St. Kevin in the sixth century, and it continued to be an important monastery until the mid-seventeenth century. Today there are just a few remains of the ancient building. Supposedly St. Kevin, who died in 618, came to Glendalough to avoid the advances of a beautiful woman. Some of the building's early remains are accessible only by boat and are on the south side of the Upper Lake. This includes the reconstructed **Templena-Skellig** and **St. Kevin's Bed,** reached only by a steep climb. Also of interest are the Round Tower, which is quite well preserved—a roofless cathedral of St. Peter and St. Paul—and St. Kevin's Church. There are other churches and ruins of a prehistoric fort, gravestones, and crosses.

Monuments you can see in the **Lower Valley: The Gateway** to the monastic city of Glendalough, now considered one of the most important sights; **The Round Tower,** which served as a place of refuge in times of attack and also as a bell tower; **The Cathedral,** which is the largest building at Glendalough. Near the Cathedral is an early cross of granite and is known as **St. Kevin's Cross.** There are also many walks, which start at the Tourist Center. Also on display at the center are antiquities found in the area.

WICKLOW MOUNTAINS NATIONAL PARK, Glendalough; phone: 404-45425. Open daily year-round, weekends only April to September, 10 A.M.–6 P.M. This park includes two nature reserves, the Glendalough Valley and the Upper Lake and the Glendalough Wood Nature Reserves.

Restaurants

ROUNDWOOD INN, Roundwood, County Wicklow; phone: 1-281-8107. Bar meals: Monday to Saturday 12:30–9:30 P.M., Sunday 12:30–2 P.M., 4–9:30 P.M.; restaurant: lunch Tuesday to Sunday, dinner Tuesday to Saturday. Closed Good Friday and Christmas day. I love this inn for lunch or dinner. The bar lunches are excellent, and dinner is more formal with reservations usually required. They serve soups, shellfish, trout and a wonderful Irish stew.

GLENDALOUGH HOTEL, Glendalough; phone: 404-45135; fax: 404-45142. Closed January. Overlooking the monastery and the mountains, the restaurant in this nineteenth-century hotel serves a simple Irish menu, which is moderately priced. The hotel pub is the only one in the area.

Enniskerry

Sights

POWERSCOURT GARDENS AND WATERFALL, Enniskerry, County Wicklow. Powerscourt is located twelve miles southeast of Dublin near the small village of Enniskerry. Phone: 1-204-6000; Web site: *www.powerscourt.com*

Gardens open daily from 9:30 A.M.–5:30 P.M.; waterfall, three miles from the garden, is open daily 9:30 A.M.–7 P.M., winter months 10:30 A.M. to dusk. Garden center open all year. Powerscourt is wheelchair accessible in the Garden Center only. Easily reached by tour bus, DART train to Bray, then bus to Enniskerry, then walk (about twenty minutes), or bus from Dublin. **Powerscourt Terrace Café,** phone: 1-204-6070. You can have a very nice lunch here or a scone and a cup of coffee. It is self-serve and inexpensive to moderate, depending on what you eat.

Powerscourt and its waterfalls are a major attraction and for good reason. They are both spectacular. The River Dargle **waterfalls** are the highest in Ireland and Britain. You can get to the waterfalls on foot or by car. Just be prepared for a long walk (about four miles). Located in the middle of the Wicklow Mountains, the Powerscourt House and Gardens are gorgeous. The gardens were laid out in the seventeenth century and have been constantly cared for and improved. The house burned down in 1974, but has since been rebuilt complete with shops, indoor and outdoor restaurant, garden center, picnic area and playground. Walk through the entrance hall and out to the back gardens for a spectacular view with the Great Sugar Loaf Mountain in the background. Continue down the steps and follow the wide path to the Japanese gardens, American gardens, a pet cemetery, lakes, fountains and statues.

POWERSCOURT GOLF CLUB, *See* chapter 10, "Leisure Activities"

Restaurant

POPPIES RESTAURANT, The Square, Enniskerry; phone: 1-282-8869; on the way home from Powerscourt or County Wicklow. Open daily until 6 P.M. weekdays, 7 P.M. on weekends. This small country restaurant/teashop is a nice stop for an inexpensive and delicious lunch of quiche, salad, shepherd's pie, and fresh baked desserts.

NORTH OF DUBLIN

The area of North County Dublin, extending from the River Liffey in Dublin to Balbriggan, is known as **Fingal.** The name "Fingal" is an old name that was re-adopted in 1994 after years of that area being called "North County Dublin." The North County has many golf courses, villages along the sea, fishing villages, and interesting sights.

BALBRIGGAN

Balbriggan is the most northern town in the North County Dublin area. Its Irish name is *Baile Brigin,* which means "the town of small hills." Although there are beaches and a harbor the highlight of the town is **Ardgillan Castle.** *See* "Skerries" in this chapter.

CLONTARF

This coastal village northeast of Dublin is a major fishing village and seaside resort. The Battle of Clontarf, where the High King Brian Boru defeated the Vikings in 1014, occurred here. There is a castle in Clontarf, Ireland, built by the Normans in 1179, which is now a hotel. (*See* hotel section, chapter 2). The original castle was one of the first within the English Pale.

MARINO CASINO

Malahide Road, Marino, Dublin 3; phone: 1-833-1618, admission charge. Open: daily June through September 9:30 A.M.–6 P.M., May and October 10 A.M.–5 P.M., November, February, March, April, Sunday and Wednesday noon to 4 P.M. This is not a house of gambling, rather it is a beautiful Palladian-style summerhouse built for Lord Charlemont in the 1760s. It was fully restored in 1984. Four stone lions guard the house. Urns on the roof cleverly conceal the chimneys, and columns conceal the water drains. The highlights inside are four very ornate state-rooms, with beautiful inlaid floors and decorated plaster ceilings. Other rooms are decorated with antique furniture and silk hangings.

DONABATE

Donabate is twelve miles north of Dublin and close to Malahide. If you wish to visit both sights there is a joint ticket for admission to the Newbridge House of Donabate and the Malahide Castle in Malahide. Donabate and Malahide are ten minutes away from each other by train. From Dublin take the DART to Malahide and the train to Donabate. From the train station in Donabate it is a twenty-minute walk or taxi ride to Newbridge House. **Newbridge House,** phone: 1-843-6534. Open April to September Tuesday to Friday 10 A.M.–5 P.M., Saturday 11 A.M.–6 P.M., Sunday and public holidays 2–6 P.M., closed Mondays. October to March Saturday, Sunday, and public holidays 2–5 P.M. Admission charge. Coffee shop. Newbridge House was built in 1737 for Charles Cobbe, the Archbishop of Dublin. In 1985 the state bought the house from the Cobbe family along with the furnishings and paintings. The purchase included 350 acres of beautiful grounds. There is original furniture, kitchen utensils, a dairy, a blacksmith's forge, and carpenter's shop. Also on the grounds are an aviary and a dollhouse/museum. The dollhouse has twenty-five furnished rooms. There is also a farm with sheep, poultry, and farm animals. A must-see in the house is **The Great Drawing Room,** considered to be one of the most beautiful Georgian rooms in Ireland. In 1965 Newbridge House was used as a location for the film *The Spy Who Came in from the Cold.* Donabate also has sandy beaches, caves, and a Martello Tower next to the Dunes Hotel. The tower was built in 1830. There are also a few golf courses in Donabate. As you can see, Donabate can be a full-day trip or can be combined with other areas.

WILD FOWL RESERVES, ROGERSTOWN, DONABATE, Rogerstown is located between Portrane and Donabate. There are huge areas of wetlands, rivers, the sea, and meadows. In this area are a variety of sea birds and wildlife.

Restaurant

THE DUNES HOTEL ON THE BEACH, Donabate, County Dublin; phone: 1-843-6153; fax: 1-843-6111. Open all year except December 25. Breakfast is served until noon, and there's a bar menu for lunch and early dinner (until 6:30 P.M.) at this perfectly located hotel and restaurant on the beach ten minutes from the airport and thirty minutes from the city center.

> *May you have the hindsight to know where you've been*
> *And the foresight to know where you're going*
> *And the insight to know when you're going too far.*
>
> ♣ —IRISH TOAST ♣

HOWTH

Howth (sounds like "both")can be reached by car or DART. The name *Howth* comes from the Viking word "hoved" or "hofud," meaning a headland or promontory. The Vikings set up Howth as a port over 1,000 years ago, having conquered the local Celtic inhabitants in 897. The present harbor was built between 1807 and 1809 and was the main harbor for boats to Holyhead, Wales, until 1833. Howth Head in County Dublin to Slyne Head in Galway are used to measure the width of Ireland. Howth is a beautiful seaside village with a wonderful harbor full of sailing and fishing boats. If you have a rental apartment in Dublin you can come here and buy your fresh fish right off the boats.

THE FOOTSTEPS OF KING GEORGE IV 12 Aug 1821 ARE RECORDED IN STONE BY STONEMASON ROBERT CAMPBELL 16 PACES IN THIS DIRECTION →

In 1914 Erskine Childers landed in Howth with his yacht *Asgard* full of ammunition and guns to supply the Irish Volunteers. The National Museum of Ireland has a display of photographs of this event. The yacht can be seen in the courtyard of the Kilmainham Goal. There is talk of it being moved to The National Museum, so if you wish to see the yacht it is advisable to find out where it is currently located. King George IV visited Howth in 1821 and his footprint where he stepped ashore is on the West Pier.

Sights

ST. MARY STAR OF THE SEA, generally known as "the Old Abbey," located near the town center, is in ruins. In 1038 the Viking king, Sitric Mac Aulaffe, high king of Dublin gave the land to the local

people to build the Abbey. The abbey is one of the few remaining
Gothic buildings in Dublin. The tomb of Christopher St. Lawrence
(Lord Howth) located at the abbey dates from 1470. If you wish to en-
ter the abbey you need to get the key from the caretaker.

IRELAND'S EYE is an island one and a half miles offshore by boat
from Howth and is now a bird sanctuary. Take a picnic lunch and enjoy the views. Boats leave from Howth harbor's East Pier during the
summer. They are operated by Frank Doyle and Sons; phone: 1-831-
4200. There is a sixth-century church, now in ruins, and a Martello
Tower on the island.

> **Martello Towers**
> There were thirty-four Martello Towers built around the coast of Ireland. In and around the
> Dublin area they can be found in Sandycove, Dalkey Island, Killiney, Bray, Howth, Sutton and
> Portmarnock, and Ireland's Eye. The design was copied from a tower at Cape Mortella in Corsica.

Howth also has a **beach** if by some chance you are lucky enough to
be in Ireland during a heat wave. Don't plan on it, though, and if you
don't have room in your luggage for a swimsuit, that's fine too.

HOWTH CASTLE AND GARDENS, Open April through June, 8 A.M.
to sunset. Admission is free to the gardens. The castle is closed to the
public. There is a gorgeous rhododendron garden here that was
planted in 1875, and now has over two thousand varieties of plants.
The flowers are in bloom and full color in May and June.

HOWTH JAZZ FESTIVAL, Held annually during the Easter Bank Holiday. Open all day. Admission to the different events varies in price.
This is one of the major jazz festivals and is always crowded. The pubs
and hotels are overflowing with bands, people, and fun, and as the
Irish say *craic*. If you plan to drive, leave for Howth early in the day.
There is not a lot of parking and it is a small town. The best way to
travel to Howth is by DART train, and then walk into town. For information on what's going on and when, call or write to the Irish Tourist
Office.

HOWTH OCTOBER BANK HOLIDAY EVENT, Live and Unplugged.
Phone: 1-873-3199 or the Irish Tourist Board for information.

NATIONAL TRANSPORT MUSEUM, Open from Easter to September
daily from 10 A.M.–6 P.M., weekends the rest of the year. The exhibits in-

clude horse-drawn carriages, fire-fighting equipment, the Hill of Howth tram, which served Howth until forty years ago, and early motorcars.

Restaurants

There are many restaurants and cafés along the seafront.

ABBEY TAVERN, Abbey Street; phone: 1-839-0307; fax: 1-839-0284. Reservations required. Open 10:30 A.M.–11:30 P.M., closed December 25 and Good Friday. **Moderate.** There are three parts to this sixteenth-century tavern. There is a bar, a restaurant, and a wonderful place to hear traditional Irish music. The restaurant serves seafood such as scallops, salmon, and prawns plus duck and other meat dishes.

DEE GEE'S WINE AND STEAK BAR, Harbour Road; phone: 1-839-2641. **Moderate.** Open daily 12:30 P.M.–2 P.M., 6–10 P.M. Located opposite the DART station. You can't go wrong here if you want an informal lunch, dinner, snack, or a cup of tea. Sit indoors or outdoors, depending on the weather.

KING SITRIC RESTAURANT AND ACCOMMODATION, East Pier, Howth, Phone: 1-32-5235/1-832-6729, Fax: 1-839-2442. E-mail: *info@kingsitric.ie*
Reservations required. Open for lunch and dinner Monday to Saturday all year. **Expensive.** Dinner menu includes à la carte or prix fixe menus. This restaurant and hotel are wonderfully located overlooking Balscadden Bay at the beginning of the East Pier. While having dinner here we saw the *QE2* come around the bend right in front of the restaurant. King Sitric serves excellent local fish such as filet of sole with lobster mousse, monkfish, Howth fish ragout, Dublin prawns, plus steak, poultry, and excellent desserts. The eight-room hotel overlooking the sea is attached to the restaurant. All the bedrooms are named for a lighthouse and all have beautiful views with every amenity.

MALAHIDE

Malahide is on the coast, eight miles from Dublin, and north of Howth. Howth and Malahide can be seen in one day, especially if you are driving. The main attraction in Malahide is the Castle. Phone: 1-846-2184. Open from April to October, Monday to Friday 10 A.M.–5 P.M., and Saturday 11 A.M.–6 P.M., Sunday 11:30 A.M.–6 P.M., November to March, Monday to Friday 10 A.M.–5 P.M., Saturday and Sunday 2–5 P.M. Admission charge.

Built in 1185 by Richard Talbot, and occupied by the Talbot family until 1973 when the last of the Talbots died, the castle was then sold to the Dublin County Council. It was restored and opened to the public. **Malahide Castle** looks like what a castle should look like. If you are traveling with children this is a must. There are turrets, towers, and beautiful grounds with more than five thousand varieties of plants and flowers. There is a beautifully preserved medieval hall. **The National Portrait Collection** is now housed there. Many portraits are on loan from the National Gallery. There are also rooms filled with eighteenth-century furniture.

TARA'S PALACE DOLL HOUSE, located in the Dolls Museum in the Courtyard of Malahide Castle; phone: 1-846-3779; fax: 1-846-3723; admission charge, which supports children's charities in Ireland. Open all year, closed daily from 1–2 P.M. It took ten years to build Tara's Palace, with each room individually furnished with exquisite miniature furniture, miniature glass and porcelain. There are also displays of dolls, toys, and other eighteenth- and nineteenth-century dollhouses. It's a must for anyone who loves dolls and their houses.

On the grounds of the castle is the **Fry Model Railway Museum,** phone: 1-846-3779; fax: 1-846-3723; e-mail: *fryrailway@dublintourism.ie*

Open all year usually the same hours as the castle, but it is good to check ahead if you are making the trip to see the trains. The museum has rare models of the Irish railway system from the beginning of train travel until the present. There are more than three hundred model trains. There is also a working miniature railway system. Cyril Fry, who was a railway engineer, built many of the trains. There are also displays of bridges, buses, barges, and boats.

Restaurants

BON APPETIT, 9 Jame's, Malahide; phone: 1-845-0314. Open daily for lunch and dinner except for Saturday, when no lunch is served. Closed on Sunday. Jacket and tie for dinner. **Expensive.** The menu includes Dublin Bay prawns with pine nuts, filet of sole stuffed with prawns and turbot, duck, and many other excellent choices.

DUFFY'S BAR AND LOUNGE, Main Street; phone: 1-845-0735. Open for lunch only, you can get pub food snacks all day, traditional music on Thursday nights only. Open at night as a pub, and TV for sporting events.

OSCAR TAYLOR'S, Island View Hotel, Coast Road, Malahide; phone: 1-845-0099; fax: 1-845-1498; e-mail: *info@islandviewhotel.ie*
Open Monday to Friday for dinner, Saturday from 3 P.M. through dinner, Sunday noon–11:30 P.M. **Moderate.** The highlight here is the view, which overlooks the Malahide Estuary and Lambay Island. The food is good, too, serving Irish fish and dishes.

SIAM THAI RESTAURANT, Gas Lane, Malahide; phone: 1-845-4698. Open Monday to Saturday. Closed Sunday. Tasty chicken satay, spicy fresh prawns, spring rolls, and delicious "beggars purses" stuffed with seafood.

SMYTH'S, New Street, Malahide; phone: 1-845-0960 or 1-845-3485; fax: 1-845-3128. Lunch served daily from noon. This pub is over one hundred years old and has been owned by only three families during this time. The current owners, the Smyth family, bought the pub in 1979.

PORTMARNOCK

Located eight miles from Dublin, Portmarnock has a popular beach and two golf courses, one world-famous. *See* chapter 10, "Leisure Activities."

GLASNEVIN

Sights

NATIONAL BOTANIC GARDENS, Botanic Road, Glasnevin, Dublin 9; phone: 1-837-4388; fax: 1-836-0080. Open daily April through October, daily 9 A.M.–6 P.M., Sunday 11 A.M.–6 P.M., November through March 10 A.M.–4:30 P.M., Sunday 11 A.M.–4:30 P.M. Free admission. Located a short bus ride away from the center of Dublin, the Botanic Gardens were established by the Royal Dublin Society in 1795, but is now run by the National Heritage Service. There are over twenty thousand varieties of plants and trees; the tallest is a California Redwood. There are also greenhouses with tropical plants, rock gardens, a pond, a palm house, a complex for ferns, and much more.

GLASNEVIN CEMETERY, Finglas Road, Glasnevin; phone: 1-830-1133. Admission free. This is also known as **Prospect Cemetery** or **The**

Irish National Cemetery. It backs up to the gardens, but they do not connect. Open daily from 9:30 A.M.–5 P.M. Free guided tour held on Wednesday and Fridays at 2:30 from the main entrance. Visit the graves and memorials of many well-known Irish men and women. Daniel O'Connell, Michael Collins, Eamon de Valera, Charles Stewart Parnell, Christy Brown, and Brendan Behan are among those buried here.

LUSK

See "Skerries" below

SKERRIES

Skerries, an hour from Dublin, is one of the largest seaside resorts on the northeast coast. There are wide streets, historic buildings, and safe beaches. The skyline of Skerries is dominated by a windmill, which has recently been restored. Supposedly St. Patrick arrived in Ireland via Red Island, which is now connected to the mainland. There is a boat trip to nearby St. Patrick's Island where there is a ruined church that had a synod held in 1148. There is a "healthy" cliff walk from Skerries to the Bay of Loughshinny.

Sights

SKERRIES MILLS, phone: 1-849-5208; fax: 1-849-5213; e-mail: *skerriesmills@indigo.ie*

Open daily except for December 20 through January 1. Admission charge. A tea-room and craft shop are available at the center.

Skerries Mills is an Industrial Heritage Center as well as a town park. Here you can see the workings of a watermill, five-sail windmill, four-sail windmill, a millpond, and wetlands. The watermill and windmills have been restored and tours are available to learn about the workings of the mills.

On the way to Skerries from Dublin you pass the **Lusk Church,** which is now a part of the **Lusk Heritage Center;** phone: 1-843-7683. The center is open on Wednesday and Sunday only from 2–5 P.M. from mid-June to mid-September. (Please call ahead if you plan to visit.) There is an admission charge. Lusk is a medieval village with a round tower built in the tenth century as well as a medieval tower, which houses artifacts from various churches in North County Dublin.

ARDGILLAN CASTLE, Balbriggan, Fingal; phone: 1-849-2212; fax: 1-849-2786. Open Tuesday to Sunday 11 A.M.–6 P.M. Closed January. Free admission. There is wheelchair access to ground floor of the castle only.

This is a large country manor house with a walled garden and Victorian conservatory. Located north of Malahide **between Balbriggan and Skerries.** The house was built in 1738 and one family lived in it until 1962. The ground floor is furnished with Georgian and Victorian furniture and includes the morning room, dining room, library, and drawing room. The kitchen is in the basement and can be visited, too. The first floor is an exhibition area.

Restaurants

RED BANK RESTAURANT, 7 Church Street, Skerries; phone: 1-849-1005; fax: 1-849-1598; e-mail: *redbank@iol.ie*
Redbank also has a guesthouse next to the restaurant.

This restaurant serves Sunday lunch and dinner Tuesday to Saturday. **Moderate.** This is an excellent fish restaurant and well worth the stop.

WINDMILL LOUNGE AND RESTAURANT, 17 New Street; phone: 1-849-1215. Open daily for lunch, dinner Monday to Saturday from 6 P.M., Sunday 5 P.M. Bar food served daily from 12:30 P.M.–6 P.M. at very reasonable prices, live music on the weekends. A large menu of fish, meat, vegetarian food, and just about anything else you might want.

THE WATERFRONT, Harbour Road, Skerries; phone: 1-849-1964. Open daily for lunch and dinner, closed Mondays. Moderately priced serving fresh fish.

SWORDS

The village of Swords is less than an hour from Dublin and near Malahide. It is now the administrative center for Fingal. The Archbishop of Dublin built a palace here in the twelfth century, which is open daily from 9:30 A.M. until dusk and there is no admission charge.

A round tower is all that remains of an ancient monastery built between 1400 and 1700. It is located on grounds owned by the Church of Ireland.

Restaurant

THE OLD SCHOOLHOUSE, Church Road Coolbanagher, Swords; phone: 1-840-2846. Lunch is served Monday to Friday and Dinner Monday to Saturday. **Moderate.**

THE BOYNE RIVER VALLEY

The Boyne Valley is north of Dublin, but is not part of the Fingal area of North County Dublin. The Boyne Valley is full of the history of Ireland's past. The Battle of Boyne was fought here in July 1690. King William III (William of Orange) defeated the exiled King James II for the English Crown. This changed the history of Ireland forever. At the border of County Louth and County Meath is a sign that marks where the battle took place. There are also markers showing where the armies camped and where the river was crossed.

TOURIST INFORMATION OFFICES, Dundalk Tourist Office, Jocelyn Street, County Louth; phone: 42-933-5484-35484. **Open all year** for information on Counties Meath and Louth.

SEASONAL TOURIST OFFICES, Newgrange Tourist Office, phone: 41-988-0305. Open from Easter to October; Drogheda Tourist Office; phone: 41-983-7070. Open from June to September.

The Boyne River Valley is located only thirty miles north of Dublin in County Meath.

BUS TOURS, If you prefer not to drive I suggest a bus tour to this historic area. All tours can be booked through the Dublin Tourist Office on Suffolk Street.

BOYNE VALLEY TOURS, run by the Station House Hotel and Restaurant, Phone: 46-25239; e-mail: *stnhouse@indigo.ie*; Web site: *www.boynevalleytoursltd.com*

Departs Dublin between 8 A.M. and 9 A.M. depending on pickup point and returns to Dublin at 8 P.M. For information, price, and reservations call the Dublin Tourist Center on Suffolk Street or ask your hotel concierge. Price includes light lunch, dinner at the Station House Restaurant, and bus tour. Entrance fees to sites are not included. Tour includes visits to Hill of Tara, Dunsany, lunch at Kilmessan, Newgrange, Dowth and Nowth, Trim, and dinner.

Bus Eireann, phone: 1-830-2222, operates full-day tours to the Boyne Valley and Newgrange departing at 10 A.M. and returning at 5:45 P.M.

Guide Friday Bus Tours, phone: 1-676-5377. This company operates half-day tours to the Boyne Valley and Newgrange departing at either 10 A.M. or 2:30 P.M.

Mary Gibbons & Daughter Tours, contact Dublin Tourist Office; phone: 1-460-4464; fax: 1-460-4426; e-mail: *marygibbonstours@tinet.ie*
   The tour of Newgrange in the Boyne Valley is five hours round-trip from Dublin and is held on Monday, Wednesday, and Friday. Pick-up is at the Tourist Centre on Suffolk Street or some hotels. If you prefer a full-day tour there is a city tour combined with the Newgrange tour.
   Note: Access to the Newgrange historic site is by guided tour only. There is a steep underground staircase plus narrow passageways, so do not attempt the Newgrange part of any tour unless you feel able.

COUNTY LOUTH

County Louth, located north of Meath, is the smallest county in Ireland. There is not as much to see in County Louth as in County Meath, but it is still worth the stop if time permits. If you wish to take an interesting walk through the town of Drogheda, you can buy the guide book *Drogheda Tourist Trail,* and follow the marked "Tourist Trail" through the town.

Drogheda

Founded by the Danes in 911, Drogheda (pronounced draw-hee-da) is a medieval town and was a Viking trading center. Drogheda was a prosperous town and one of the only four walled towns in Ireland. In 1649 Oliver Cromwell invaded the town and killed its two thousand inhabitants. Today it is a thriving port and industrial town.

Dundalk

Dundalk is the main town of County Louth and dates from the seventh century. The area is associated with **Cuchulainn,** pronounced *coo hullen,* considered a folk hero to the Irish people. He is purported to have single-handedly defeated the armies of Ulster in battle.

Sights

MELLIFONT ABBEY, near Collon, northwest of Drogheda; phone: 41-26459. Admission fee. Open May to November 10 A.M.–5 P.M., summer months, 9:30 A.M.–6:30 P.M.

Founded in 1142, this was Ireland's first Cistercian monastery, and was established by St. Malachy of Armagh. What remains today is part of the square gatehouse, ruins of a cloister, an octagonal lavabo from about 1200, and a thirteenth-century chapter house.

MILLMOUNT MUSEUM, Duleek Street, Drogheda; phone: 041-983-3097. Admission fee. Open May to September, Tuesday to Sunday 2–6 P.M., October to April, Wednesday and Saturday and Sunday 3–5 P.M. This museum is located in the courtyard of a twelfth-century fort, which later became an army barracks. One of the exhibits is the history of Drogheda and the Boyne Valley. Also on display are painted banners of the old trade guilds, a Bronze Age oracle, and medieval tiles. There is also a geological exhibit of stones from all of the counties of Ireland plus Europe. Other exhibits include kitchen items, spinning wheels, shipbuilding and ironworks.

MONASTERBOICE, near Collon, northwest of Drogheda in County Louth. Open daily. No phone or admission fee. Chosen as a monastic site by St. Buite, Monasterboice dates back to the sixth century. The main sight to see here is the **Muiredach Cross,** which is a seventeen-foot-tall cross traced back to 922. The cross is carved with scenes of Eve tempting Adam, Cain murdering Abel, and the Adoration of the Magi. One side of the cross is a scene of the Crucifixion and the other is of the Last Judgment. Also located at Monasterboice is a 108-foot tenth-century round tower, two early gravesites, and an early Irish sundial.

Restaurants

BUTTERGATE, located next to the Millmount Museum; phone: 041-34759. **Moderate.** The restaurant serves food all day, but specializes in traditional Irish dishes for both lunch and dinner.

BOYNE VALLEY HOTEL AND COUNTRY CLUB, Dublin Road, Drogheda; phone: 41-983-7737; fax: 41-983-9188. Stop here for lunch at the Cellar Restaurant, specializing in fresh fish. Price for a three-course lunch including tax, but not wine or tip, ranges from 15–20 IEP.

> *May the road rise to meet you.*
> *May the wind be always at your back.*
> *May the sun shine warm upon your face; the rains*
> *   fall soft upon your fields*
> *And, until we meet again,*
> *May God hold you in the palm of His hand.*
>
> ♣ —IRISH BLESSING ♣

COUNTY MEATH

The main town in County Meath is Navan. Nearby is Kells, known for the Book of Kells, the illustrated manuscript on display at Trinity College in Dublin. A copy of the Book of Kells is on display at the Church of Ireland in Kells.

Sights

THE HILL OF TARA, Navan, County Meath; phone: 46-25903. Open daily May to mid-June 10 A.M.–5 P.M., mid-June to mid-September 9 A.M.–6:30 P.M., September and October 10 A.M.–5 P.M. Check opening times for the rest of the year.

The Hill of Tara is one of Ireland's most important historic sites. It towers three hundred feet above the countryside and is known as the seat of the early High Kings of Ireland, which lasted until the eleventh century. Every three years a national assembly known as a *feis* was held here to pass laws and settle disputes. The Hill of Tara was an important religious and political center in early Christian times. The last king to live there was Malachy II who died in 1022. Ireland's patron saint, St. Patrick, preached here in the fifth century and used the three-leaved shamrock to illustrate the doctrine of the Trinity. To best understand the importance of this area there is an audio-visual show called "Tara, Meeting Place of Heroes," which is shown continuously in the visitor center.

SLANE HILL In 433 St. Patrick proclaimed the arrival of Christianity by lighting the Paschal fire at Slane Hill north of Slane town. From the top of the hill there is a beautiful view of the Boyne Valley.

NEWGRANGE, Phone: 41-988-0300. Open June to mid-September daily from 9 A.M.–7 P.M., mid-March to May and mid-September to October 9:30 A.M. to 5:30 P.M., November to mid-March Tuesday to Sunday 9:30 A.M. to 5 P.M. Admission charge.

Access to Newgrange is via Bru na Boinne (Palace of the Boyne) at the Boyne Valley Visitor's Center.

Newgrange is one of the prehistoric and archaeological wonders of the world. This burial mound and tomb was built more than 5,000 years ago, before the pyramids of Egypt and Stonehenge. The mound is 36 feet high and 260 feet in diameter and was built with over 200,000 tons of stone. Each stone, carved in various geometric symbols, fits together seamlessly, creating a watertight seal. Once a year at the winter solstice at 8:58 A.M. as the sun rises, sunlight enters the inner chamber for about 17 minutes.

DOWTH AND KNOWTH Near Slane and one mile from Newgrange are these prehistoric sites that are still being excavated. Combined tickets for Newgrange and Knowth can be purchased at the Newgrange Visitor's Centre. Dowth is still closed to the public. Knowth has a large central mound and seventeen smaller ones. The earliest carved stones and tombs date from 3000 B.C. Knowth is believed to have been the burial site of the high kings of Ireland. This site has the largest collection of passage tomb art ever discovered in the Western world. There are at least seventeen small passage graves and the carvings are unique with spiral and line carvings plus zigzags and parallel lines.

NEWGRANGE FARM, Slane, County Meath; phone: 41-24119. Open April through September, daily from 10 A.M.–5 P.M. Admission charge. This is a 330-acre farm run by the Redhouse family. They run an hour and a half tour of the farm that grows corn, wheat, oats, and barley, along with vegetables. You can also participate in farm activities such as feeding ducks, petting a pony, playing with a pig, bottle-feeding baby lambs or goats. You might like to help groom a calf or watch a chick hatch in the incubator. There are horse stables and a working forge. See spinning of wool and then perhaps stop at the coffee shop in the old coach house. Don't rush this tour especially, if you are with children. On Sundays at 3 P.M. there is a Derby race with the farm sheep participating in the run. The **Newgrange Farm Coffee Shop,** is self-service and open when the farm is open. **Inexpensive,** no credit cards. Located on the grounds of the farm, the Redhouse family prepares soups, sandwiches, cakes, pies, and delicious scones daily using ingredients grown on their farm or locally.

TRIM

Visitors Center, Mill Street, phone: 046-36633. Open May through September, Wednesday to Sunday 9:30 A.M.–5 P.M., October to April by appointment only. The center has an excellent audio-visual display called "The Power and the Glory," which tells the history of medieval Trim.

Located on the Boyne River with some of the best medieval ruins in Ireland. Most of Trim's residents were killed when Oliver Cromwell captured the town in 1649.

Sights

BECTIVE ABBEY You can see the remains of one of the largest Cisterian monasteries in Ireland, which was founded in 1147. It is located in a field on the west bank of the River Knightsbrook.

TRIM CASTLE Built in 1181, Trim Castle, also called King John's Castle, is one of the largest medieval castles in Europe. The film *Braveheart* was filmed there. The ruins include the **Keep,** which was built between 1220 and 1225. It has seventy-foot-high turrets and towers. Drawbridges protect the **Dublin Gate.** The upper floor is where Richard II kept Henry IV prisoner until he escaped and captured the throne of England.

TOWN GATE has a medieval stone floor and arches. **Sheep Gate** is where tolls were collected from people bringing their sheep to sell at the sheep fairs.

ROYAL MINT is another ruin that shows the great importance of Trim during the Middle Ages.

YELLOW STEEPLE Built in 1368, the Yellow Steeple overlooks Trim from a ridge opposite the castle. In 1649 much of the steeple was destroyed so that Oliver Cromwell would not capture it, and today only the east wall still stands.

The Pale
    During the Middle Ages the Irish who did not live in Louth, Meath, Dublin, Kilkenny, Tipperary, Waterford and Wexford were considered "beyond the Pale." By the end of the 15th century the Pale shrunk to the counties of Louth, Meath, Dublin, and Kildare.

Restaurants

STATION HOUSE HOTEL AND RESTAURANT, Kilmessan, County Meath; phone: 46-25239 or 1850-241-555; e-mail: *stnhouse@indigo.ie*; Web site: *www.thestationhousehotel.com*

Moderate. The hotel is located fourteen miles from Newgrange, one and a half miles from the Hill of Tara, and seven miles from Trim, Navan, and Dunshaughlin. This is a small family-run hotel and restaurant with all the amenities if you wish to stay in this area for more than a day. It is also pet friendly.

NEWGRANGE HOTEL, Bridge Street, Navan, County Meath; phone: 46-74100; fax: 46-73977. This first-class hotel is well located for an overnight stay—thirty minutes from Dublin and close to all the Boyne Valley sights or just for a rest and lunch or dinner after sightseeing on a day trip. There are two restaurants, a pub, and a lounge.

WEST OF DUBLIN
COUNTY KILDARE

County Kildare is an easy and interesting day trip. It is less than an hour by car from Dublin. There is train and bus service to Kildare, but as always a car is more direct. If there are any races going on while you are in Ireland I suggest you attend. Racing is a big part of Irish life for young and old. Everyone bets and it's an exciting, fun day. County Kildare is known as horse country because of its many stud farms and racetracks. Kildare is the home of the **Curragh Racetrack** (phone: 045-441205) where the Irish Derby is held. **Punchestown** (phone: 045-897704) and **Naas** (045-897391) racetracks are also in Kildare although they are smaller than the Curragh. *See* chapter 10, "Leisure Activities" for more information on horse racing.

There are also beautiful parkland golf clubs in County Kildare. They can be reserved for a fee. Bring your own shoes, but clubs can be rented. As always check and reserve ahead.

TOURIST OFFICE, Town Square, Kildare; phone: 045-522696; open June through mid-September.

CASTLETOWN HOUSE, Celbridge, County Kildare; phone: 1-628-8252.

As of this writing, the house is closed for renovations. The grounds are open but the house, one of Ireland's great Palladian Mansions, is the real attraction. Call for information.

Golf

KILDARE COUNTRY CLUB, known as the "K" Club, Straffan, County Kildare; phone: 1-601-7200. Fee: approximately $200.00 per person, per day. This is a very famous, very beautiful par 72 course, which has hosted the European Open for the last few years and is scheduled to host the Ryder Cup in 2005. There is a pro-shop, restaurant for indoor or outdoor lunch, and carts, known as "buggies" if you need one. The **Kildare Hotel and Country Club;** e-mail: *hotel@kclub.ie*; Web site: *www.kclub.ie* This is a very expensive, very beautiful, five-star hotel and resort on the same grounds. It is ideal for a golf vacation. It is located twenty miles west of Dublin.

KILKEA CASTLE GOLF CLUB, Castledermot, County Kildare; Phone: 503-45555. Fee: approximately $35.00 per person, per day. **Kilkea Castle:** Phone: 503-45156 or 503-45100; fax: 503-45187. Located on the same grounds as the golf club, but owned by different people. If you wish to play golf you must call the club separately. This beautiful Castle is thought to be the oldest inhabited castle in Ireland dating back to 1180.

CURRAGH GOLF CLUB, Curragh, County Kildare; phone: 45-441238. Fee: approximately $35.00 per person, per day.

Horseback Riding

DONACOMPER RIDING SCHOOL, Celbridge, County Kildare; phone: 1-628-8221. Hourly riding fee.

KILL INTERNATIONAL EQUESTRIAN CENTRE, Kill, County Kildare, phone: 45-877208. Hourly riding fee.

IRISH NATION STUD AND JAPANESE GARDENS AND ST. FIACHRA'S GARDEN, located off the N7 Dublin/Cork Road, Tully, Kildare, County Kildare; phone: 45-521617/522963; fax: 45-522964; e-mail: *stud@irish-national-stud.ie*; Web site: *www.irish-national-stud.ie* Open February 12 to November 12 daily 9:30 A.M.–6 P.M. This location can be most easily reached by car, but can also be reached by Bus Eireann. Check the schedule with the bus company or the Tourist Office. Not wheelchair accessible.

This is both a government-sponsored stud farm and a Japanese garden complex. Its private owner turned over the stud farm to the Irish government in 1943. There is an exhibit of the horse Arkle, who was Ireland's most favorite steeplechaser. There are many stalls for stallions, mares, and foals. Visitors are welcome to walk the grounds, look in the stalls at the horses, and watch them being exercised. There is also an hourly tour of the horse area. Many of Ireland's famous horses have been bred at this farm so you may be seeing a future winner. There is also an exhibit on racing, steeple chasing, hunting, and show jumping.

After seeing the stud farm and taking the tour, walk to the **Japanese gardens** located on the same grounds and included in the same entrance fee. These gardens are considered one of the most beautiful Japanese gardens in Europe. Built between 1906 and 1910 by a Japanese gardener named Eito, it shows the journey of the soul from the beginning (birth) to the end (death) and eternity. You start at number one and continue following the numbers until you reach the end, number twenty, of the self-walking tour. Each number also has a name, which tells what part of the soul or life you are at. Be sure to walk across the red Japanese Bridge and take a picture there. Also, be sure to walk inside the Monks Hut to see the under glass Waterford Glass exhibit, which is part of **St. Fiachra's Garden.** St. Fiachra's was a sixth-century Irish monk. While he was alive he encouraged his disciples to do manual labor, cultivate gardens, and distribute produce to the poor. He is the patron saint of Gardners, and his feast day is August 30. There is also Japanese-style gift shop and restaurant.

If you are lucky enough to be Irish, you are lucky enough.
♣ —IRISH PROVERB ♣

KILKENNY

Kilkenny is a medieval city founded in the sixth century by St. Canice and located approximately two hours southwest of Dublin by car, Bus Eireann, or Irish Rail. The Irish name of Kilkenny is *Cill Choinnigh,* which means "Canice's Church." Many of this walled city's thirteenth- and fourteenth-century churches, buildings, and narrow streets are well preserved and best seen on foot.

TOURIST OFFICE: Shee Alms House, Rose Inn Street; Phone: 56-51500. The Tourist Office conducts excellent daily walking tours throughout the year. Call ahead for a reservation.

Sights

KILKENNY CASTLE, The Parade, Open daily April and May 10:30 A.M.–5 P.M., June to September 10 A.M.–7 P.M., October to March, Tuesday to Saturday 10:30 A.M.–12:45 P.M. and 2 P.M.–5 P.M., Sunday 11 A.M.–12:45 P.M. and 2–5 P.M. Admission fee. Guided tour only.

You can't miss the castle with its towers, façade, and battlements next to the River Nore. The Norman leader Strongbow built it in 1192. It was eventually taken over by the Butler family who occupied it until 1935. In 1967 it was given to the Irish government as a national monument. You can tour the library, drawing room, bedrooms, and sitting rooms. The servants' quarters are now the Butler Art Gallery of Contemporary Art. The castle kitchen is now a tea-room.

KILKENNY DESIGN CENTER, Castle Yard, The Parade. Open daily April to December 9 A.M.–6 P.M., January to March, and Monday to Saturday 9 A.M.–5 P.M. You can watch workmen in their shops doing various types of crafts, and everything is for sale. There is also a self-service café on the second floor serving soups, salad, casseroles, and local food.

THE THOLSEL, Parliament Street, built in 1761 and now the Town Hall. Inside you can view Kilkenny's first book of records dating from 1230.

BUTTER SLIP, one of the city's medieval passageways built in 1616. The name derives from the story of a local woman who sold butter in the passageway.

ROTHE HOUSE, Parliament Street. Open July to August 9:30 A.M.–6 P.M., March to June and September to December Monday to Saturday 10:30 A.M.–5 P.M., Sunday 3 P.M.–5 P.M. Take the guided tour to see Kilkenny's oldest house built in 1594.

ST. CANICE'S CATHEDRAL, Coach Road, founded in the sixth century, but built mostly in the thirteenth century. It is Ireland's second-longest medieval church. The organ that is still in use dates from 1854.

THE BLACK ABBEY, Abbey Street. Open Monday to Saturday 8 A.M.–6 P.M., Sunday 9 A.M.–7 P.M. Founded in 1225 by William Marshall, Earl of Pembroke. It fell into disrepair, but in 1816 the local people started to use it as a church again and through the years have completely restored it.

Restaurants

CAFÉ SOL, William Street. Open Monday to Saturday 10 A.M.–5:30 P.M., Wednesday to Saturday 7 P.M.–10 P.M. Closed Wednesday off-season. Wheelchair access to ground floor only. **Moderate.** A good choice for lunch or dinner. Specialties range from Louisiana crab-cakes to rack of lamb, pasta, fish, chicken, and delicious desserts.

CAISLEAN UI CUAIN, The Castle Inn, Castle Street. Open daily except Sunday. This pub was built as a stagecoach inn in 1734. The food and atmosphere are wonderful.

KYTELER'S INN, St. Kieran Street. This tavern dates from 1324 and was the home of the witch, Dame Alice Kyteler. Serves hamburgers, steaks, and salads.

For a pint, stop into **Tynan's Bridge House,** 2 Horseleap Slip. No food is served.

It's the one place on earth that heaven has kissed
With melody, mirth and meadow and mist.

♣ —IRISH BLESSING ♣

WATERFORD

TOURIST OFFICE: 41 The Quay. Open all year.

Waterford is located one hundred miles southwest of Dublin on the south bank of the River Suir. It is easily reached by car, rail from Heuston Station, or bus. Trains and buses arrive at Waterford's Plunkett Station. The trip takes between two and three hours depending on traffic or the train.

Waterford crystal has been produced here since 1783, but Waterford is also the main seaport on southeast coast. The current Irish name of the city is Port Lairge, which means "Lairge's Landing Place." The Vikings founded Waterford in the tenth century and called it *Vadrefjord,* which means "weather haven."

Waterford can be seen on foot. The main sights are in a small area around the quays, the mall, and the nearby streets. There are local guides who conduct walking tours of the city departing from the lobby of the Granville Hotel.

Sights

WATERFORD CRYSTAL, Kilbarry, Cork Road; phone: 51-373311; fax: 51-378539. Open daily April to October. Tours 8:30 A.M.–4 P.M., showrooms 8:30 A.M.–6 P.M., November to March tours 9 A.M.–3:15 P.M., showroom 9 A.M.–5 P.M. Monday to Friday. Services at the center are a bank, tourist office, and restaurant. This self-guided tour consists of an audio-visual preview, then to see the master glass blowers, then the cutters, the engravers, and the gallery, and shop. Anything you buy can be shipped worldwide. Waterford Crystal is located two miles south of town and can be reached by car, a long walk, taxi or Bus #1 from the Clock Tower on the Quay. The bus says *Ballybeg*, but it stops at Waterford Crystal. You can buy Waterford Crystal at the **Visitor Center** in Waterford and every place in Ireland. The prices are the same in every shop so do not feel you have to go to the factory for a better price. Also at the Waterford Center you can buy Wedgwood China.

THE QUAY is about a half mile long with pubs and shops along the way.

THE CLOCK TOWER was built in 1861 and replaced in 1954. It is a Victorian Gothic local landmark.

THE CATHEDRAL OF THE MOST HOLY TRINITY, Barronstrand Street; phone: 53-874757. It dates back to 1793. The interior has a high vaulted roof, Corinthian pillars, a carved oak pulpit, and Waterford chandeliers donated by Waterford Crystal in 1979.

WATERFORD LIGHT OPERA FESTIVAL is held each September in the Theatre Royal. Check with the Tourist Office for the dates. It changes yearly. ·

REGINALD'S TOWER, the Quay; phone: 053-73501; admission charge. Open April, May, September, October, Monday to Friday 10 A.M.–5 P.M., Saturday and Sunday 10 A.M.–5 P.M. June, July and August daily from 8:30 A.M.–8:30 P.M. Built in 1003 by the Vikings, it has ten-foot-thick walls and a round roof. This is the oldest civic building in Ireland and maybe the oldest in Europe. It has provided many services to Waterford. First it was a fortress, then a prison, military depot, air raid shelter, and now a museum.

CHRIST CHURCH CATHEDRAL, phone: 53-874119. The cathedral was designed in 1714 and completed in 1779. A Viking church stood on this site from 1050.

WATERFORD HERITAGE MUSEUM, Greyfriars Street; phone: 53-871227. Open April, May, September, and October, Monday to Friday 10 A.M.–5 P.M., Saturday and Sunday 10 A.M.–5 P.M., June, July, and August daily from 8:30 A.M.–8:30 P.M. Admission charge. Located in a former church, this museum tells the story of Waterford's early days in medieval times and under Viking rule.

CITY HALL, the Mall; phone: 53-873501. Serves as the headquarters for the Waterford government. No admission charge. The **Theater Royal** built in 1876 is in the City Center building.

LADY LANE is a wonderful narrow medieval street.

BLACKFRIARS ABBEY The square tower is the only remains of this Dominican Abbey built in 1126 and used until the eighteenth century.

Did you ever wonder how some expressions become popular? Here is a good one:

By Hook or by Crooke
In 1170 the Anglo-Normans were battling for control of the southeast of Ireland. Strongbow, their leader said he would take Waterford "by Hook or by Crooke." What he really meant was he would capture the Tower of Hook and the Crooke Castle. He was successful and we had a new expression.

Restaurants

DWYERS OF MARY STREET, 8 Mary Street; phone: 051-877478; open daily for dinner only, closed Sunday. **Expensive.** An excellent restaurant featuring garlic prawns, quail, beef, lamb, and a good wine list.

WINE VAULT, High Street; phone: 051-853444; open daily except Sunday. **Moderate.** As the name indicates, this is a wine vault with almost four hundred varieties of wine to choose from plus a restaurant featuring seafood, pasta dishes, risotto, and vegetarian dishes.

WATERFORD CASTLE, The Island, Ballinakill, County Waterford; phone: 51-878203; fax: 51-879316. **Very Expensive.**

This is a major splurge if you come by car. Located only two miles from Waterford City, this seventeenth-century castle and golf course are located on an island in the River Suir and easily reached by car ferry. The restaurant serves a variety of delicious dishes and outstanding desserts.

It's a great thing to turn up laughing having been Turned down crying.

♣ —IRISH PROVERB ♣

WEXFORD TOWN

WEXFORD TOURIST OFFICE, Crescent Quay, Wexford; phone: 053-23111; fax: 053-41743. Open all year. The tourist office has free walking-tour maps and guided tours. **Gorey Tourist Office,** Town Center; phone: 055-21248. Gorey is fifty-five miles south of Dublin. **Rosslare Harbour Tourist Center,** Ferry Terminal, Rosslare Harbour; Phone: 053-33622; fax: 053-33421. All of these tourist offices are open year-round, but the Rosslare office is open daily when the ferries arrive.

WEXFORD TOWN is located eigthy-eight miles south of Dublin. It is an easy trip via car, train, or bus. Since Wexford is a small town with narrow streets there are no local buses. There is service to Rosslare and Gorey from Wexford on Bus Eireann. Take the excellent **Wexford Walking Tour** conducted by local guides. For information on walking tours stop at the Wexford Tourist Office, or plan ahead by calling 53-23111.

If you come by car, park, do your sightseeing in Wexford Town, and then drive to see the sights outside of town. As always, I like sightseeing by car especially in this area. So many of the major sights and villages are best and easiest seen by car. It is all possible by bus and train and taxi too. If you arrive by bus or train you can rent a car for the day to go further afield or take a taxi to a specific sight you want to see.

The Vikings called Wexford *Waesfjord,* which means the "harbor of the mud flats." The Irish name is Loch Garman, which means lake of the River Garma. Wexford is a busy seaport for shellfish and mussels, as well as a manufacturing center. Oscar Wilde's mother was born in Wexford.

Sights

JOHN BARRY MONUMENT, located on Crescent Quay. John Barry was born in Ballysampson in 1745, ten miles from Wexford Town. He left Wexford at age fifteen and fought in the American Revolution. He was one of America's first commissioned officers, and was appointed Commander-in-Chief of the U.S. Navy by George Washington. In 1956 the Americans gave this statue to Wexford as a gift.

CORNMARKET, off Upper George Street. The Wexford Arts Center dating from 1775 is located on this wide street, and it was once a marketplace.

THE IRISH NATIONAL HERITAGE PARK, Ferrycarrig; phone: 053-20733. Open March through October daily from 10 A.M.–7 P.M. Admission charge. There is a shop and café on the premises. Located beside the River Slaney three miles from Wexford Town, this is a thirty-acre outdoor museum depicting nine thousand years of Irish history. This should not be missed on a visit to Wexford, especially if you are traveling with children. The guided tour takes about an hour and a half and is well worth it. Beginning in the Mesolithic Period of 7000 B.C., the tour shows a stone circle from the Bronze age of 2000 B.C., a Viking longhouse, pre-Christian burial sites, a Christian farmstead, a tenth-century monastery and a tenth-century Norman Castle. Demonstrations of crafts from weaving to pottery complete the tour.

JOHN F. KENNEDY PARK AND ARBORETUM, Dunganstown, New Ross, County Wexford; phone: 51-388171. Admission charge. Open daily. Located twenty miles west of Wexford, this is a six-hundred-acre arboretum dedicated to President Kennedy. It overlooks the cottage in which JFK's great-grandfather was born. There are over 4,500 types of plants and trees from five continents that are grown here. Gorgeous panoramic views make this the perfect place to stroll and picnic.

WEXFORD WILDFOWL RESERVE, North Slob, Wexford Harbour; phone: 53-23129. Free admission. Open April to September daily 9 A.M.–6 P.M., October to April daily 10 A.M.–5 P.M. Located two miles from Wexford, this is an interesting sight for bird-watchers. There is an observation tower to watch the Greenland geese that spend the winters in Wexford, along with other wildlife such as Berwick's swans and wigeon.

BULL RING, dates from 1621 and is located on Quay Street, a market square in the center of Wexford. This was once where the town's butchers enjoyed the sport of "bullbaiting" to amuse the Norman nobility. Today the Bull Ring is used for the local weekly market.

THOMAS MOORE TAVERN The house where nineteenth-century poet Thomas Moore's mother was born.

TWO (TWIN) CHURCHES Church of the Immaculate Conception on Rowe Street and The Church of the Assumption on Bride Street are called the twin churches because they are identical, built by the same architect between 1851 and 1858. Their spires are both 230 feet high.

WEXFORD ARTS CENTER Art exhibitions and other events are held in the galleries.

WEXFORD EXPERIENCE Located in the Westgate Heritage Center the Wexford Experience is a continuous audio-visual history of Wexford.

WESTGATE HERITAGE CENTER, Westgate Street; phone: 53-46506. Open May to September, Monday to Saturday 10 A.M.–6 P.M., Sunday 2–6 P.M., October to April Monday to Saturday 11 A.M.–5 P.M. Admission charge. Here you can see parts of the original west gate and walls, which were part of the Viking, Norman town walls. There is also a restored thirteenth-century tower and displays of various artifacts.

ST. SELSKAR ABBEY The first treaty between the Normans and the Irish was signed here in 1169. Now this twelfth-century Abbey is mostly ruins.

MAIN STREET The main street of Wexford. Once a Viking market area, it is now a shopping street filled with restaurants, pubs, boutiques.

Wexford Festival Opera
The annual Wexford Festival Opera is eighteen days of opera and other musical events from the end of October to early November. Located in the **Theatre Royal** on High Street, which opened in 1832. For information and tickets call the Festival Office at: 53-22400.

Hotel

FERRYCARRIG HOTEL, First-class hotel; phone: 53-20999; fax: 53-20982; e-mail: *kilkerny@griffingroup.ie*; Web site: *www.grifingroup.ie.* Wheelchair accessible. Free-parking.

This is a ninety-room hotel overlooking the River Slaney and next to the Irish National Heritage Park, three miles from Wexford Town. Rooms are large with all amenities. A bistro by the water serves excellent food at reasonable prices. Also try the Tides Restaurant and the Dry Dock Bar.

Restaurants

LA RIVA, Henrietta Street; phone: 53-24330. Open for dinner only. **Moderate.** Located on the second floor, this restaurant/bistro overlooks the River Slaney and Wexford Harbour. The menu is varied including pasta, pizza, seafood, steak, grilled duck, and local fish.

OAK TAVERN AND RIVERSIDE RESTAURANT, located a mile from Wexford near the Irish Heritage Park. Phone: 53-20922. **Moderate.** Over 150 years old, the tavern overlooks the River Slaney and serves typical bar food and dinners like grilled steaks, local fish, seafood, and shepherd's pie. In nice weather enjoy dinner on the riverside patio.

BOHEMIAN GIRL, North Main and Monck Streets; phone: 53-23596. An inexpensive pub serving fresh seafood, soups, and sandwiches. Great atmosphere.

ROSSLARE

Located ten miles southwest of Wexford Town, Rosslare is a popular seaside resort with its six-mile-long pretty beach. There is also a championship golf course in Rosslare. The **ferry terminal** at the harbor is five miles south of the village and provides service to South Wales and northern France for both cars and passengers.

Hotel

KELLY'S RESORT HOTEL, phone: 53-32114; fax: 53-32222. Wheelchair accessible. This ninety-nine room, first-class hotel is located on a sandy beach next to the Saltee Island Bird Sanctuary. The hotel has been in the Kelly family since 1895. There is a restaurant, two bars, a cabaret, coffee shop, two swimming pools, tennis, squash, horseback riding, fishing, putting green, golf nearby, and free parking.

GOREY

Gorey dates from the thirteenth century and was originally a market town. The major sights are St. Michael's Roman Catholic parish church and the Loreto Convent.

I have included Gorey, even though it is a little out of the way when visiting Wexford Town, because of this wonderful resort hotel. It can be a base for sightseeing in the Wexford/Waterford area instead of a day trip.

Hotel

MARLFIELD HOUSE HOTEL, Deluxe Hotel, Gorey, County Wexford; phone: 55-21124; fax: 55 21572; toll-free in U.S.: 800-223-6510; e-mail: *marlf@iol.ie*

Open late January to mid-December. Wheelchair accessible. This small and beautiful deluxe nineteen-room hotel is located only sixty-three miles from the Dublin Airport, forty miles from Wexford Town, and ninety minutes from Waterford. Woodlands and gardens surround it. There is an excellent restaurant and three lounges. Golf, fishing, and riding are nearby and can be arranged by the hotel.

NORTHERN IRELAND

BELFAST

NORTHERN IRELAND TOURIST OFFICE, 551 Fifth Avenue, Suite 701, NY, NY, 10176; phone: 212-922-0101; toll-free: 800-326-0036; fax: 212-922-0099; e-mail: *infousa@nitb.com*; Web site: *www.ni-tourism.com*

NORTHERN IRELAND TOURIST BOARD, 16 Nassau Street, Dublin (opposite Trinity College). Open Monday to Friday 9 A.M.–5:30 P.M., Saturday 10 A.M.–5 P.M.

BELFAST TOURISM DEVELOPMENT OFFICE, Belfast City Council, 4–10 Linenhall Street, Belfast BT2 8BD; phone: 1-232-320202; fax: 1-232-270325. Open all year.

TOURIST INFORMATION CENTER, Wellington Place/Queen Street; phone: 28-9024-6609; fax: 28-9031-2424. Open daily all year.

For a copy of the **Belfast Visitor's Guide,** phone toll-free: 800-326-0036; e-mail: *info@belfastvisitor.com*; Web site: *www.gobelfast.com*

BELFAST, the capital of Northern Ireland, is an interesting and easy day trip from Dublin. A city since 1888, Belfast (*Beal Feirst* in Irish) means the "mouth of the sandy ford," and it is the center of the six counties that make up Northern Ireland, also erroneously called Ulster. (The Province of Ulster actually comprises nine counties, the six of Northern Ireland plus Cavan, Donegal, and Monaghan in the Republic). A newer city than Dublin, Belfast has a completely different feeling, being more Victorian and Edwardian as opposed to Dublin's Viking, Norman, and Georgian atmosphere.

It is true that Belfast had its "troubles" from the late 1960s to the late 1990s, but today the city is calm and anxious to welcome visitors. There are new hotels and restaurants in the city and the new Odyssey Center will incorporate a sports stadium, science complex and IMAX movie theater. If you like modern edifices, the new waterfront complex is already in operation, and is the pride of Belfast. If you stay for more than a day, explore the countryside and visit the pretty villages near the city.

GETTING TO BELFAST, Belfast is just one and a half hours or one hundred miles from Dublin. You can take the train from Dublin's Connolly Station; phone: 1-836-6222, located on Amiens Street, to Belfast's Central Station, phone: 01232-800411, located on East Bridge Street. There are six trains a day between these two cities (only four on Sundays). There is also a bus service between the two cities and it is an easy car trip.

CURRENCY, Northern Ireland's currency is the British pound, not the Republic of Ireland's Punt. The currencies are not interchangeable.

What to Do and See in Belfast

BELFAST CITYBUS TOURS, Donegall Square, phone: 1-232-246485. As always, our first suggestion in a new city is to get an overview tour to see the sights and get the lay of the land. Later, return to what interests you most. These tours depart from Castle Place, a block and a half from Donegall Square.

BLACK TAXI TOURS, Phone: 2890-642264; e-mail: *michael@belfasttour.-com*; Web site: *www.belfasttours.com*

The tours run from 10 A.M.–8 P.M. These ninety-minute tours take three or more passengers along Falls Road, which is Catholic, and Shankill Road, which is Protestant, both scenes of most of the serious fighting during the civil war. The tour also goes to Miltown Cemetery, the Peaceline, City Center, and more. It is not a good idea to walk in these areas on your own.

WALKING TOURS This is the best way to see this beautiful city. The Northern Irish Tourist Board has developed several short walking tours, with maps, averaging about one hour each through the safest areas of the city. The maps are free from the Tourist Office. Longer walks include St. Patrick's Way (five miles) and Hillsborough Forest (three miles). Tours depart from the Tourist Center on North Street, phone: 1232-238437. There are also shorter walking tours of the "Old Town," and Pub Tours of Belfast.

PARKING There is no parking in the city center. There are signs and double yellow lines all over the city. If you drive here from Dublin, reconcile yourself to parking near the city center, then walking everywhere. There are excellent car parks and "pay and display" areas just outside the center. Belfast has many pedestrian streets, no parking zones, control zones, and areas that are off-limits. It is easiest on a day trip not to have a car. If you do drive to Belfast, park your car at your hotel or a garage until you are ready to depart.

TRACING YOUR ROOTS: Public Record Office, 66 Balmoral Avenue, Belfast BT9 6NY; phone: 1232-251318; fax: 1232-255999. Open Monday to Friday 9:15 A.M.–4:15 P.M. You can do your own research here. **Ulster Historical Foundation,** Balmoral Buildings, 12 College Square East, Belfast BT1 6DD; phone: 28-9033-2288; fax: 28-9023-9855; e-mail: *enquiry@uhf.dnet.co.uk*; Web site: *www.uhf.org.uk* **General Register Office,** Oxford House, 49 Chichester Street, Belfast BT1 4HL; phone: 1232-252000. Records of all births and deaths since 1864, and all marriage registrations since 1922 in Northern Ireland are at this office. Records prior to 1922 are held in Dublin.

SHOPPING: Remember the **VAT** (value added tax). Belfast has pedestrian areas and covered arcades for shopping plus many independent shops. Stores are open from 9 A.M. to 5:30 P.M. except Thursday when they close at 9 P.M. Favorite purchases in Belfast are Irish linen, local crafts, books, beautiful Beleek, china and knitwear.

Sights

Most of the city's sights are within a few blocks of Donegall Square in the heart of downtown.

ALBERT MEMORIAL CLOCK TOWER, Victoria Square. The Tower, which is not open to the public, was named for Queen Victoria's husband, Prince Albert, and was built in 1867.

BELFAST CASTLE, Antrim Road; phone: 1232-776925; fax: 1232-370228. Open daily from 9 A.M.–6 P.M. Free parking and admission. Located two and a half miles from the center of Belfast. The third Marquis of Donegal built the castle in 1870. It was given to the city in 1934 and restored in the 1980s. It is now an excellent place to have dinner, do some shopping and enjoy walking, jogging, and picnicking. There is also a children's playground.

BELFAST ZOO, Antrim Road; phone: 1232-776277. Admission fee, seniors and children under four are free. Founded in 1920 and located on the slopes of Cave Hill overlooking the city, the zoo emphasizes education and conservation as well as breeding of rare species of birds and animals.

BELFAST BOTANIC GARDENS, Stranmills Road; phone: 1232-324902. Free admission. Open April through September, Monday through Friday 10 A.M.–5 P.M., Saturday and Sunday 1–5 P.M., October through March, Monday through Friday 10 A.M.–4 P.M., Saturday and Sunday 1–4 P.M., gardens 8 A.M.–sunset. The Botanic and Horticultural Society built these gardens in the early 1800s. The property contains rare plants and rose gardens, as well as a lovely Palm House, housing tropical plants, and quite similar to the greenhouse in Kew Gardens near London.

CITY HALL, Donegall Square; phone: 28-9032-0202.
   Wheelchair accessible. For a free guided tour call for an appointment, as a reservation is always required. City Hall dominates the main shopping area and resembles an American state capitol building (except for Queen Victoria's statue out in front). Built in 1906 in the

Renaissance style in white Portland stone, it has a copper dome that is 173 feet high. Don't miss the view from the top. Modeled after St. Paul's Cathedral in London, it was built after Queen Victoria granted Belfast the status of a city.

CROWN LIQUOR SALOON, 44 Great Victoria Street; phone 028-9027-990. Open daily 11:30 A.M.–midnight. This place was built in 1885 and the National Trust maintains it as a beautiful Victorian working pub. The interior is beautiful, with hand-painted tiles, carved doors, and gas lamps.

EUROPA HOTEL, Great Victoria Street at Glengall Street; phone: 1232-327000; fax: 1232-3278000. For thirty years, this had the reputation of being the most bombed hotel in Western Europe. It was refurbished each time it was damaged by the IRA. The hotel was completely renovated in 1995 after being damaged in the last bombing in 1993.

GRAND OPERA HOUSE, Great Victoria Street, located across from the Crown Liquor Saloon. Ticket Shop, 2–4 Great Victoria Street, is located opposite the theater. Phone: 1232-241919. Open for performances only. Built in 1896, the Opera House was restored in the 1970s with gorgeous gilt moldings and a beautiful ceiling fresco by the Irish artist Cherith McKinstry. This is the home of the Northern Ireland Opera Company. Ballet and concerts are also performed here.

LINEN HALL LIBRARY, 17 Donegall Square North (facing the City Hall); phone: 028-9032-1707. Open Monday, Tuesday, Wednesday, Friday 9:30 A.M.–5:30 P.M., Thursday 9:30 A.M.–8:30 P.M., Saturday 9:30 A.M.–4 P.M. Founded in 1788, this is the oldest library in Belfast. Housed in an old linen warehouse, its shelves have old and rare books about Ireland and its history, as well as recent releases.

QUEEN'S UNIVERSITY, University Road, phone: 028-9033-5252, is located in the southern section of the city. The original building was built in 1849 and was named for Queen Victoria, who visited Belfast the year the university was built. The annual arts festival is second only to the Edinburgh Festival in Britain and is known as the "Belfast Festival at Queen's" (every November). There is a new **Seamus Heaney Library** named after the 1997 Nobel Prize–winning author from Belfast.

ULSTER FOLK AND TRANSPORT MUSEUM, phone 1232-428428; fax 1232-428728

Located fifteen minutes from the city center, this is a living history museum of the life of Northern Ireland. Old farmhouses, town houses, and cottages have been reassembled. There is also a courthouse, police station, school, and church.

ULSTER MUSEUM, located in the Botanic Gardens on Stranmills Road; phone: 028-9038-3000; information line: 1232-383001.

Open weekdays 10 A.M.–5 P.M., Saturday 1–5 P.M., Sunday 2–5 P.M. Admission is free. This is an outstanding museum, filled with Irish art and antiquities from the Stone Age through the present day. Be sure to see the spinning wheels used in linen making, currency from the thirteenth century, and paintings of Belfast from its earliest days. There are also botany and zoology sections. There is a beautiful exhibit of gold and silver jewelry recovered by divers in 1968 from Spanish treasure ship *Girona*, sunk in 1588.

The Belfast poet William Drennan, born in 1754, is not well-known for his poetry, but he did coin a very famous saying. He named Ireland "The Emerald Isle."

Restaurants

Expensive

RESTAURANT AT DEANE'S, 36 Howard Street, phone: 28-9033-1134. Closed Sunday. This is one of the top restaurants in Belfast. There is a more moderate Brasserie downstairs. The chef (Mr. Deane), a Michelin-star cook, combines elements of Irish, British, Pacific Rim, and North American cooking in his unique dishes.

ROSCOFF, 7 Lesley House, Shaftesbury Square; phone: 1232-331532. Reservations required. Open Monday to Friday for lunch, Monday to Saturday for dinner. The most expensive restaurant in Belfast is worth the splurge for their delicious menu of beef, lamb, Irish salmon, sole, and shellfish.

Moderate

NICK'S WAREHOUSE, 35 Hill Street, phone: 28-9043-9690. Open daily except Sunday and Monday dinner. Reservations required for restaurant. The wine bar serves mostly salads and casseroles, while the restaurant serves meat and fish specials including duck with red cabbage.

Inexpensive
BEWLEY'S, Donegall Arcade, phone: 1232-34955. Open daily except Sunday. Located right in the middle of the shopping area, this restaurant is a branch of the Dublin Bewley's. They serve sandwiches, tea, coffee, and desserts.

CROWN LIQUOR SALOON, 44 Great Victoria Street, Belfast; phone: 011-44-28-902-79901. This is a Victorian style-pub serving typical Irish dishes such as Irish stew, Irish stouts, and Oysters.

Hotels

If you decide to stay overnight, here are a few suggestions. All hotel rates here include VAT (value added tax), but no breakfast unless otherwise noted.

CRESCENT TOWNHOUSE, 13 Lower Crescent, Belfast BT7 1NR; phone: 28-9032-3349; fax: 28-9032-0646; Web site *www.crescenttownhouse. co.uk.* The place is gorgeous, but not overdone, and in an excellent location. **Expensive.**

EUROPA HOTEL, *See* above.

WELLINGTON PARK HOTEL, 21 Malone Road, Belfast, phone: 28-9038-1111. A very comfortable place, this is in the university area and features a fine dining room, where a full Irish breakfast is extra. **Expensive.** Weekend rates are about half price.

TARA LODGE, 36 Cromwell Road, Botanic Avenue, Belfast BT7 1JW, phone; 28-9059-0900; fax: 28-9059-0901; e-mail *info@taralodge.com*; Web site *www.taralodge.com*
Halfway between the city center and the desirable university area, this is a cozy spot with eighteen rooms, each with private bath, TV, phone, and other amenities. Hotel facilities include dining room and lift for disabled visitors. **Moderate.**

JURY'S INN, Fisherwick Place, Great Victoria Street, Belfast BT2 7AP; phone: 28-9053-3500; fax: 28-9053-3511; e-mail: *Belfast_inn@jurysdoyle.com*
Located in the heart of the city, west of City Hall and south of the Castle Court Centre. Each of the 190 rooms has a private bath, data line, and tea/coffee tray. Facilities include a restaurant and pub. **Moderate.**

EXPRESS HOLIDAY INN, 106 University Street, Belfast BT7 1HP; phone: 28-9031-1909; fax: 28-9031-1910; Web site: *www.hiexpress.com/ belfast-univ*

Also located between downtown and the university, this modern hotel has 119 rooms, each with private bath, color satellite TV, and first-class amenities, including free continental breakfast. Hotel facilities include those for disabled guests, a bar and restaurant, and a beer garden in summer. **Moderate.**

OUTSIDE OF BELFAST

Contact the tourist offices, listed above, for packages (usually of three nights) including accomodations in charming bed and breakfasts in the villages within an hour or two of the city.

Among the prettiest villages are **Downpatrick,** site of the grave of St. Patrick and **Hillsborough,** whose delightful main street exudes

both power and charm. The former lies in the Hillsborough Castle, where the Secretary of State for Northern Ireland, Mr. Peter Mandelson, lives when he is not in London. Opposite the castle on the main street is a row of splendid Georgian buildings, many of them now pubs and restaurants. But be sure to turn down the alleys between the houses. Many of the back gardens contain antique and craft shops.

BY BUS FROM BELFAST, there are many **National Trust** beauty spots to visit that can be reached from Belfast by the **Citybus** in and hour or two. Among them are the following. (Many are open only during April to September, unless otherwise noted.)

Bus # 110: **Paterson's Spade Mill.** It may sound dull, but a spade is a spade, and this is the last surviving water-driven spade mill in Ireland. You can see spades being made the old-fashioned way (circa 1919) then buy one in the gift shop.

Bus # 61 or 67: **Ardress House.** Here is a seventeenth-century farmhouse, but elegantly added on to in the eighteenth-century. The farm boasts rare breeds, a house tour and nice walks in the woods and along the river.

Bus # 41 and change, or the train: **Derrymore House.** This late eighteenth-century thatched cottage was built by a member of the Irish House of Commons and is set in a pleasant estate laid out in the style of Capability Brown.

Bus # 15, then change. **Castle Ward,** open all year. In the middle of a 750-acre estate overlooking Strangford Lough sits a beautiful Georgian mansion. Highlights here include house tours, a water-driven corn mill, an old lead mine, horse trails, formal gardens, and a tea room, not to mention a large gift shop.

Bus # 9 or 10: **Mount Stewart,** open March to October. This is the grandest of them all. Here you will find a magnificent house and a splendid garden. Descendants of the owners, the lords of Londonderry, still live here, and you might see one of them on your tour. Lord Castlereagh, the hero of the Congress of Vienna, was a Londonderry, and artifacts from his life are on display.

Bus # 218 or train, change required. **North Derry Coast.** Portstewart Strand, a stretch of two-mile beach, is open all year. Downhill, a spectacular eighteenth-century estate set on a cliff is open from April to September. The Hezlett House, a seventeenth-century thatched cottage, is open from Easter through September. Bar Mouth, a bird watcher's paradise, is open all year.

Bus # 251, change required, and then a two-mile hike, open from February to September. **The Argory** is a nineteenth-century mansion with Edwardian furnishings

Bus # 210 plus a one-mile hike: **Springhill** is a seventeenth-century plantation house. Highlights include a marvelous costume collection, walled gardens and a tea-room.

Bus # 90: **Wellbrook Beetling Mill.** The beetling machines helped in the production of linen; this eighteenth-century water-powered beetling mill still works. After the demonstrations, amble through the wooded glen.

Index

226   INDEX

Bewley's Hotel at Newlands Cross, 45
Bewley's Oriental Café, 88
Bewley's Principal Hotel, 45–46
bicycle rentals and trips, 143–44
bird watching, 144–45, 213
Black Abbey, The, 209
Blackfriars Abbey, 211
Blackrock Market, 139
Black Taxi Tours, 218
Blarney Stone, 126
Blarney Woollen Mills, 138
Blazing Salads, 59
"Bloomsday" (June 16), 125
Blooms Hotel, 46
boating, 142–43
Bohemian Girl (pub), 215
Bon Appetit (restaurant), 195
Bona Spes (boat), 142–43
Book of Kells, 87, 98
book stores, 127–29
Books Upstairs, 127
Booterstown Marsh and Bird Sanctuary, 145
Bord Failte, 2–3
Bottom Drawer (department store), 133
Boyne River Valley, 199–200
Boyne Valley Hotel and Country Club, 201–2
Brasserie na Mara, 183
Bray, 179–81
Brazen Head, The (pub), 68
Break for the Border (restaurant), 59
Brian Boru commemoration, 78
bridges, 103–4
British Embassy, 3
Brownes Brasserie, 59
Brownes Townhouse (guest house), 49
Brown Thomas (department store), 133
Bruno's (restaurant), 59
Buddhist worship, 17
Bull Island Interpretative Center, 145
Bull Ring (sight), 214
Burlington Hotel, 40, 84
Bus Eireann (tours), 145–46, 187–88, 200
buskers, 79
bus service, 25
    tours, 145–47, 187–88, 199–200, 217
Buswells Hotel, 42
Butler Antiques, 134

Butlers Town House (guest house), 49–50
Butterfield and Robinson (tours), 144, 168
Buttergate (restaurant), 201
Butter Slip, 208

Café en Seine, 60, 68
Café Sol, 209
Caislean ui Cuain (restaurant), 209
Camac Valley Tourist Caravan and Camping Park, 51
camping, 33, 51, 148
Canadian Embassy, 4
canals, 104–5
Captain Americas (restaurant), 60
car rentals, 18, 28, 29
Carr Golf Travel (tours), 154
carriage tours, 148
Carrickmines Equestrian Centre, 161
car travel, 27–30
Casa Pasta, 60
Castletown House, 205–6
Cathach Books, 127
Cathedral of the Most Holy Trinity, 210
Catholic churches, 17, 120, 121–23
Caviston's (restaurant), 184
cell phones, 11, 29
Cellular World Rental Phone, 11
Central Hotel, 46
Central Library, 177
CEOL—Irish Traditional Music Centre, 83
Chaddagh rings and necklaces, 135
Chapter One (restaurant), 60
C. Harding (bicycle rentals), 144
Chase Manhattan Bank, 6–7
Chester Beatty Library and Gallery of Oriental Art, The, 90
Chief O'Neill's Hotel, 46
Children of Lir, 102, 107, 127
children's activities, 173–78
Chimney at Smithfield Village, The, 103
china, 134–35
Christ Church Cathedral (Dublin), 17, 88, 120
Christ Church Cathedral (Waterford), 211
Christmas Eve carols service, 122
churches, 17, 120–23

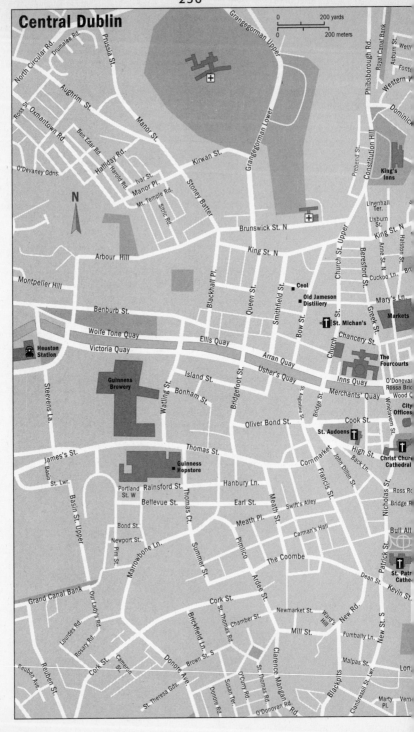

Central Dublin

0 ___ 200 yards
0 ___ 200 meters

North Circular Rd.
Drumalee Rd.
Prussia St.
Ross St.
Oxmantown Rd.
Aughrim St.
Ben Edar Rd.
Halliday Rd.
O'Devaney Gdns.
Harold Rd.
Ivar St.
Manor Pl.
Mt. Temple Rd.
Stric Rd.
Manor St.
Kirwan St.
Stoney Batter

Grangegorman Upper
Grangegorman Lower
Prebend St.
Constitution Hill

Phibsborough Rd.
Royal Canal Bank
Auburn St.
Wellt
Western V
Fonte
Dominick

King's Inns
Linenhall Ter.
Lisburn St.
King St. N
Anne St. N
Halston St.
Bri

Cuckoo Ln.

Brunswick St. N
King St. N
Arbour Hill
Montpelier Hill
Blackhall Pl.

Queen St.
Smithfield
Bow St.

Ceol
Old Jameson Distillery

Mary's Ln.
Greek St.
Markets

St. Michan's
Chancery St.
Church

Benburb St.
Wolfe Tone Quay
Victoria Quay
Ellis Quay
Arran Quay
Usher's Quay

The Fourcourts
Inns Quay
O'Donovan
Rossa Brid
Wood C

Heuston Station
Guinness Brewery
Steevens La.
Watling St.
Island St.
Bonham St.
Bridgefoot St.
St. Augustine St.
Merchants' Quay
Bridge St.

City Offices
Winetavern St.

Oliver Bond St.
Cook St.
St. Audoens
High St.
Back Ln.
Christ Chur Cathedral

Thomas St.
Cornmarket
John Dillon St.
Francis St.

James's St.
Basin St. Lwr.
Guinness Hopstore

Portland St. W
Rainsford St.
Bellevue St.
Thomas Ct.
Hanbury Ln.
Earl St.
Swift's Alley
Meath St.
Ross Ro
Nicholas St.
Bridge R

Bond St.
Newport St.
Pim St.
Marrowbone Ln.
Summer St.
Meath Pl.
Pimlico
Carman's Hall
The Coombe
Bull All

St. Patr Cathe

Basin St. Upper
Grand Canal Bank
Lourdes Rd.
Our Lady's Rd.
Rosary Rd.
Ardee St.
Cork St.
St. Thomas Rd.
Chamber St.
Newmarket St.
Ward's Hill
Mill St.
New Rd.
Dean St.
Patrick St.
Kevin St.
New St. S.
Fumbally Ln.

Reuben Ave.
Reuben St.
Cameron St.
Cork St.
Brickfield Ln. S
Brown St. S
Donore Ave.
St. Theresa Gds.
St. Thomas Rd.
Donore Rd.
Susan Ter.
O'Curry Rd.
Clarence Mangan Rd.
O'Donovan Rd.
Mill St.
Malpas St.
Blackpits
Clanbrassil St. Lwr.
Lon
Marty Pl.
Verne